IMAGES
*of America*

# THE PULLMAN PORTERS AND WEST OAKLAND

**On the Cover:** Oakland was a transportation hub as the western terminus of the railroad. This is a scene of passengers waiting on the train station platform when African Americans were allowed to travel by Pullman Sleeper Cars. (Courtesy of the African American Museum and Library at Oakland curator, Rick Moss.)

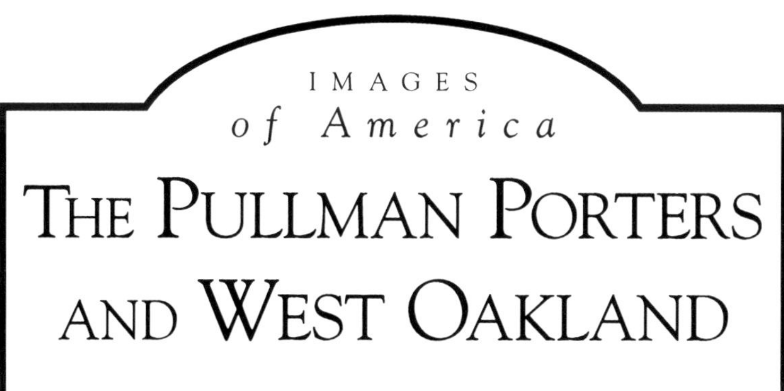


Thomas and Wilma Tramble

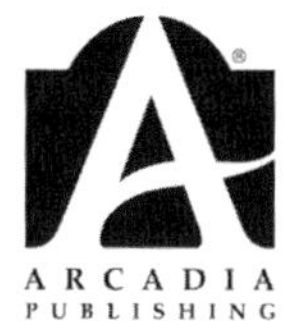

ISBN 978-0-7385-4789-3

Published by Arcadia Publishing
Charleston SC, Chicago IL, Portsmouth NH, San Francisco CA

Printed in the United States of America

Library of Congress Catalog Card Number: 2007924986

For all general information contact Arcadia Publishing at:
Telephone 843-853-2070
Fax 843-853-0044
E-mail sales@arcadiapublishing.com
For customer service and orders:
Toll-Free 1-888-313-2665

Visit us on the Internet at www.arcadiapublishing.com

*Dedicated to Gabriel Thomas Tramble, Ryan Christopher Tramble, and Ezra Sidney Tramble: the grandsons who provided the emotional inspiration for completing this project.*

# Contents

# ACKNOWLEDGMENTS

Located on an Oakland downtown corner stands a two-story Carnegie Library, restored and renamed the African American Library and Museum at Oakland. Inside, a magnificent, three-paneled mural surrounds the top eight feet of the stairwell connecting the first and second floors. This mural, "The Journey of Promise," ignited our desire to publish the story of the west side of Oakland, California. Stimulated by this mural, we developed an invaluable network with other Oakland historians. Annalee Allen, an *Oakland Tribune* columnist and Oakland Tours Coordinator, Office of the City Administrator, heard our story and introduced us to the person who provided the opportunity to publish it: Hannah Clayborn, an Arcadia Publishing editor. Annalee also introduced us to Paul Cobb, editor of the *Post* newspaper, who expressed his great interest in our topic, and he quickly offered and graciously placed our story on the front page of the *Post*. To get a feel for the task ahead, historian Don Hausler welcomed our inquiry and he along with news reporter Chauncey Bailey of the *Post* offered their services. The photographs were found in the archives of the African American Museum and Library at Oakland (AAMLO); unless otherwise noted, images are courtesy of this institution. We extend a special thanks to Rick Moss and his staff for their expert assistance. Many inspired persons assisted in this research, including reference librarian Veronica Lee, museum project coordinator Vida Silva, and archives librarian assistant Shannon McQueen. It seems that we spent hundreds of hours in research in the archives and Shannon was always available with needed assistance. Noveline Simmons provided historical images of her Pullman Porter husband, the now deceased Herman Simmons. Their collections of railroad photographs and family scrapbook photographs assisted in portraying the family activities duplicated in the lives of many African American family's vacations, outdoor outings, and memorable moments.

# INTRODUCTION

This is a story of a people, having found themselves freed of a horrid slavery system in 1865, who by the late 1800s had created a social enclave in West Oakland from which blossomed an African American dreamscape. Black West Oaklanders found a non-extinguishable and stable source of income to build their life in California as Pullman Company employees.

West Oakland offered the long-denied opportunity to establish the family unit consisting of a father with a steady job. No longer was he in danger of being sold "down the river." The nurturing mother could legally be woman to her man, an academic protector of her children, and no longer the property of a master. Together West Oaklanders families built their American dreamscape.

George Pullman, creator of an American dynamic—the opulent railway sleeping car—inadvertently created fertile ground for the rich and integrated community of West Oakland. He recruited black men to serve as porters because they were experienced at working for no wages and were trained from birth in the rules of a societal caste etiquette that created a social distance between blacks and whites.

## TWO STORIES BEGIN IN 1869 AND END IN 1969

One dynamic story is of the African American Pullman porters influence in establishing a sense of husbandry and fatherhood for a family structure ripped and distorted by an inhuman slavery system. The second story is of the seemly intuitive and carefully created concept of community that nurturing African American women built within the city of West Oakland in support of their Pullman Porter men.

The SagaSeekers' research reveals how the two stories meld into a third, very moving painting of an African American dreamscape. This work presents how African American men and women molded their environment of family values and dreams into a community that included all the tangibles—a sense of self-appreciation, a safe haven in which to raise families, an opportunity for property ownership, desire to enter various occupations, business ownership, and leadership roles in community building.

# *One*

# THE PULLMAN COMPANY CONCEPT

The American railroad story touches many things good and bad about commercial control of the distribution of wealth in this country. Most significant was the completion of the great transcontinental railroad. With this achievement came increased communication; travel; business; and a new style of life for men, who only four years earlier had been slaves in a degrading agricultural setting in the South. Men, who had only four years earlier spent their intellectual pursuits creating new ways to resist the slavery system and relocate their families in lands free of oppression, were suddenly qualified for a job offered by a railroad system. African American slaves worked from sunup to sundown for meager clothing allowances for their families.

On the basis of having served as slaves, they were qualified for a job offered by the Pullman Palace Sleeping Car Company. The sleeper cars were railway carriages with marble bathtubs, gold-filled plumbing, cedar wardrobes, jewelry safes, swimming pools, and brass-railed observation platforms.

George Pullman had found the perfect match for his company. This also marked the beginning of the struggle for the average African American family to achieve the "American dream." He decided to lease the cars complete with operating personnel and maintenance responsibility. Pullman cars could be seen in many of the various train companies.

The story is one about struggle, lost battles, and finally victory led by A. Phillip Randolph and Oaklander C. L. Dellums in unionizing wars. The story is about the Pullman Strike in 1894, led by Eugene Debs. The story is about the formation of fraternal groups, combating the African American spies of the Pullman Company, African American Women clubs, social orders, and church organizations.

The story is about great Oakland women: Hettie Blonde Tilghman, Mrs. Willie Henry, Frances Mary Albrier, Delilah Beasley, Melba Stafford, Mrs. Fred Williams, and Ida Louise Jackson. The story is of the heroic C. L. Dellums, Oakland's great civil rights warrior.

The story includes little known facts about African American occupations in Oakland, including personal servants for wealthy households, hotel waiters, railroad porters, messengers, cooks, and janitors. African Americans were entrepreneurs who operated barbershops, restaurants, and boardinghouses. Oakland men and women organized fraternal organizations, social clubs, newspapers, and literary societies and were coachmen, butlers, and cooks.

The story is of African American men and women building a community at the railroad terminus called West Oakland. The Pullman porters influence provided a springboard for men from a slavery heritage to hold elite positions as doctors, lawyers, newspaper editors, civil servants, ministers, and schoolteachers.

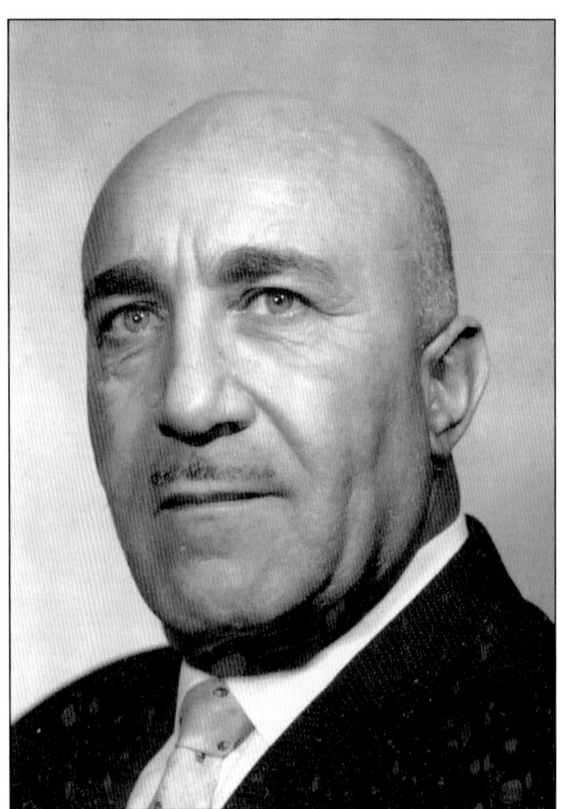

C. L. Dellums left his birthplace of Corsican, Texas, because "I don't plan to wear these overalls for the rest of my life." He became vice president of the Brotherhood of Sleeping Car Porters Union, in charge of the West Coast activities.

Oakland was a transportation hub as the western terminus of the transcontinental railroad. The Porters found Oakland's climate, and its social and economic opportunities, attractive to raising healthy families.

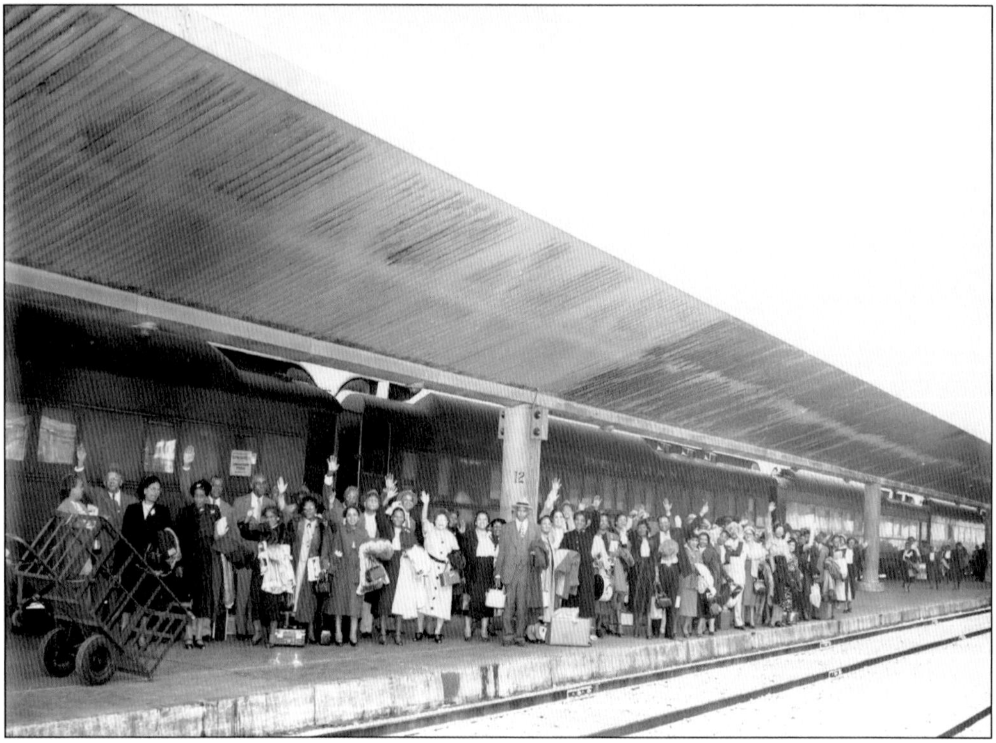

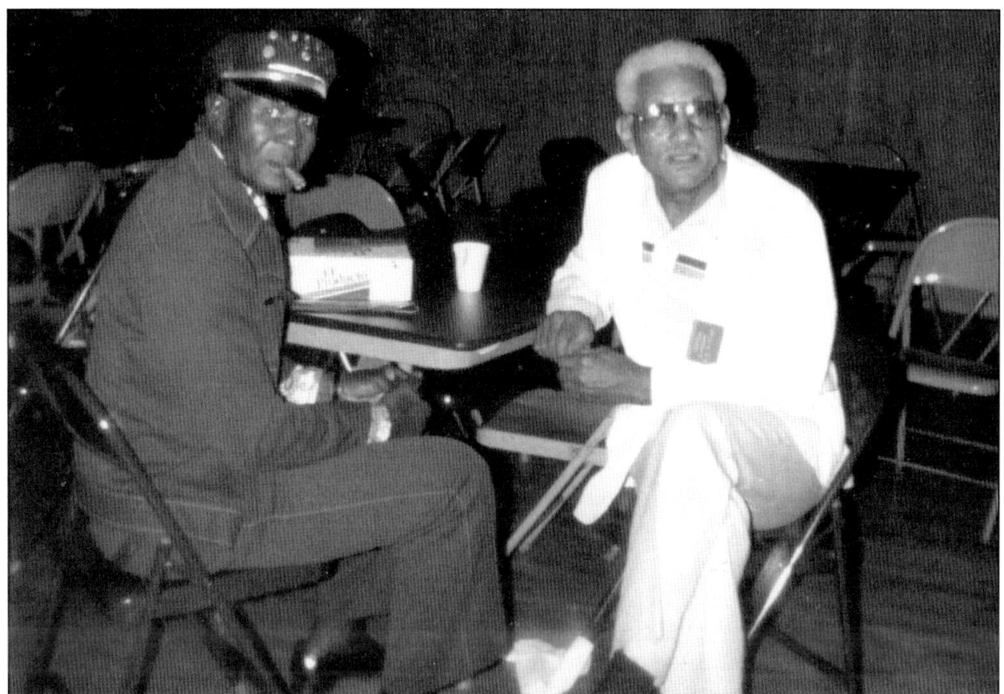

The Pullman Company leased their cars and porters to railroad companies throughout the United States and Canada. (Simmons Collection.)

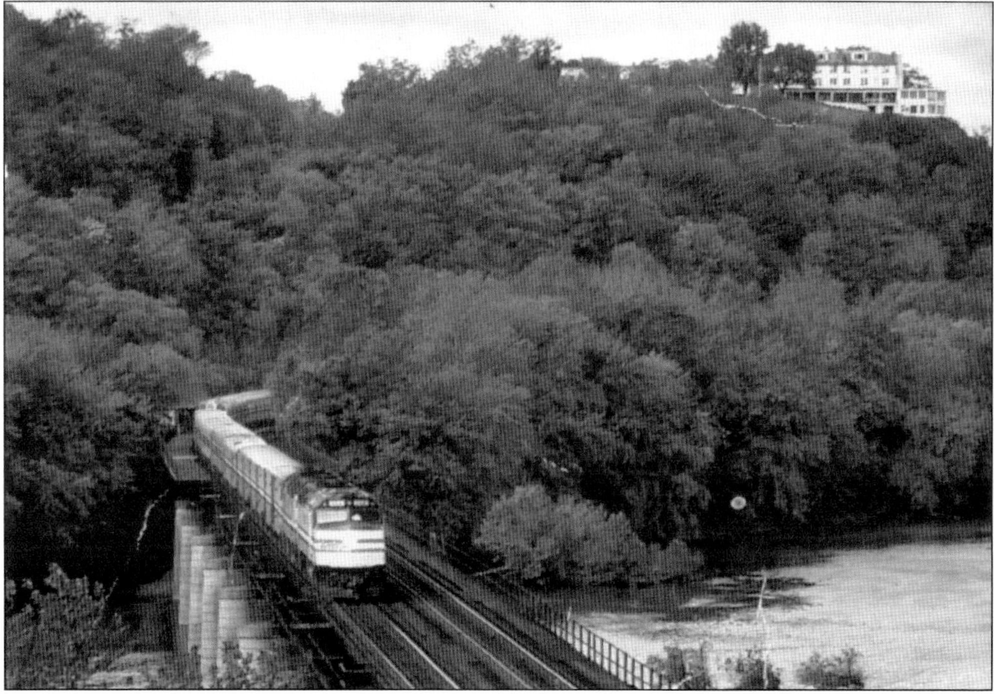

The Pullman Company operated the largest hotel outfit in the United States, accommodating up to 100,000 sleeping travelers each night. Pictured is a postcard of the "Capitol Limited" crossing the Potomac River. (Simmons Collection.)

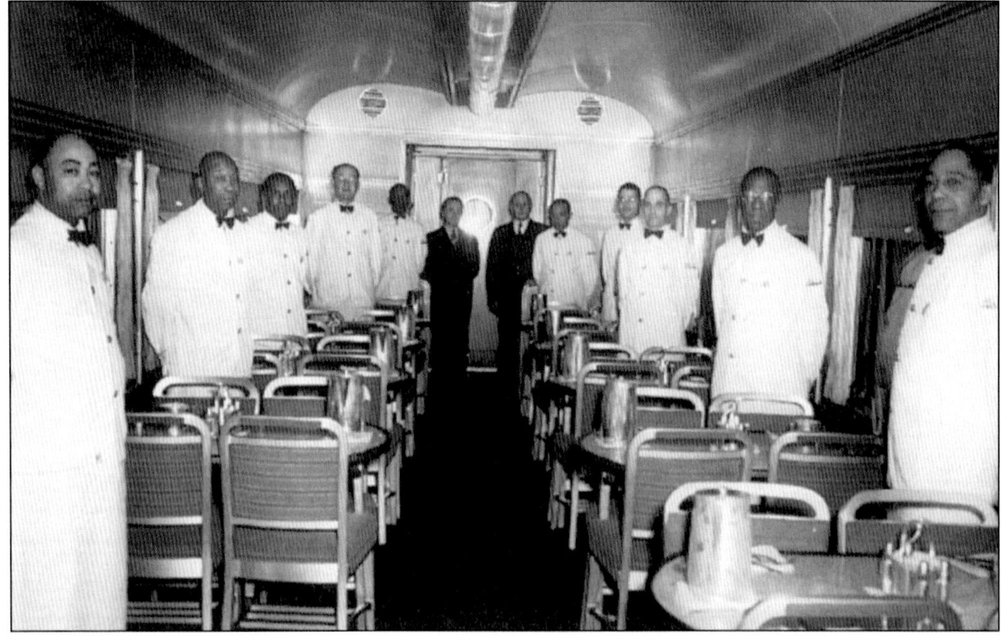

Here a group of porters stand at attention in the dining car before patrons arrive. All porters completed three days of unpaid training in the "Art of Portering," a rigorous course designed to instill the highest standards of cleanliness and personal service.

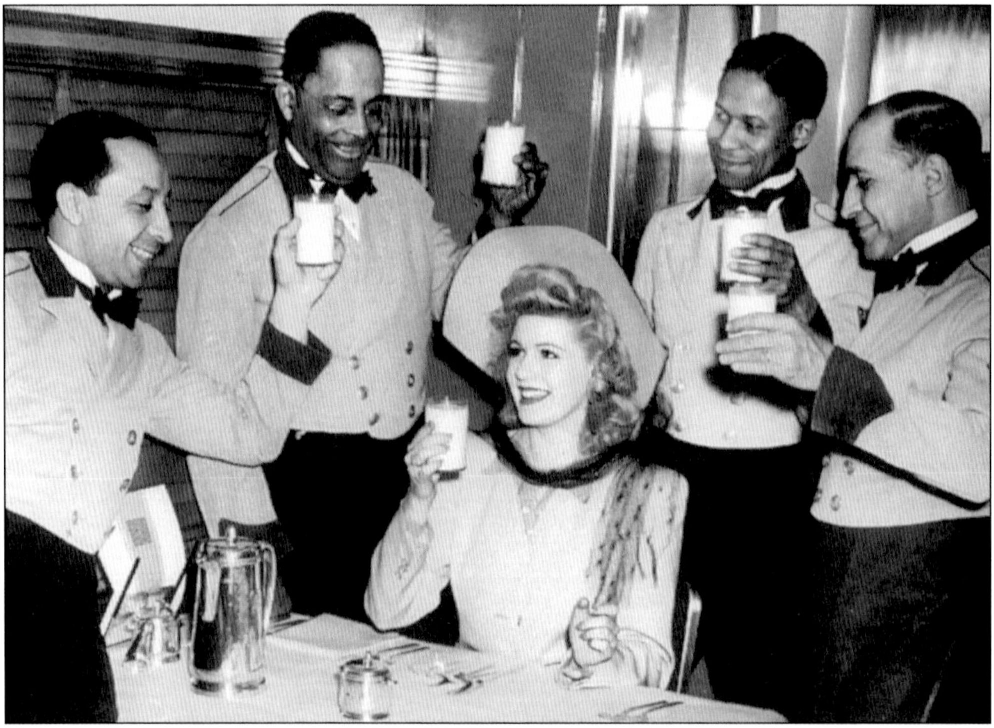

Porters are seen here sharing a toast with a passenger, ever careful of spies and "spotters." Spotters were special agents who reported shortcomings such as dirty bathrooms, missing towels, dust on the sill, unanswered call bells, knocking down fares, or failing to write up food orders.

Pictured here is a cook removing a well-prepared turkey from an oven on the train.

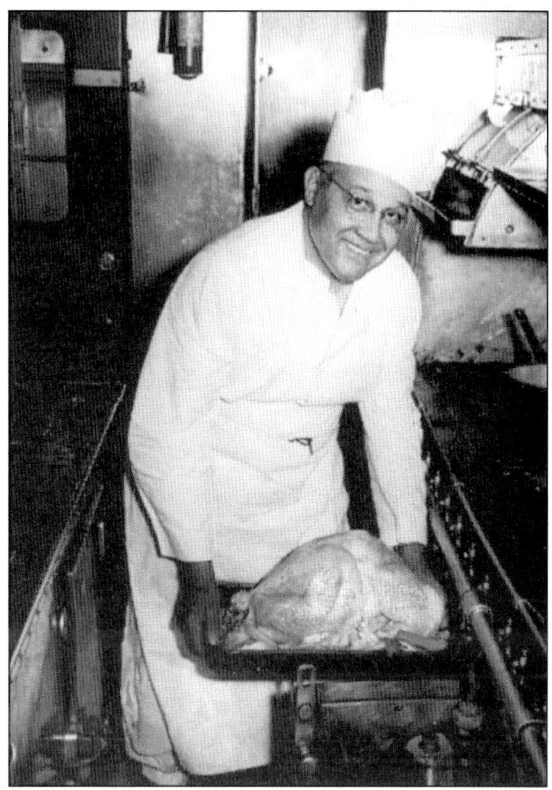

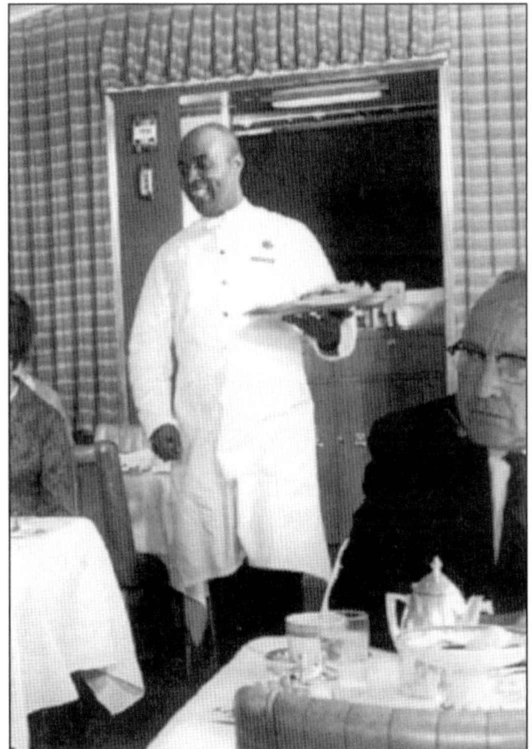

The Pullman Company hired blacks as porters because they could be paid less than whites. It is believed that passengers preferred being waited on by friendly blacks.

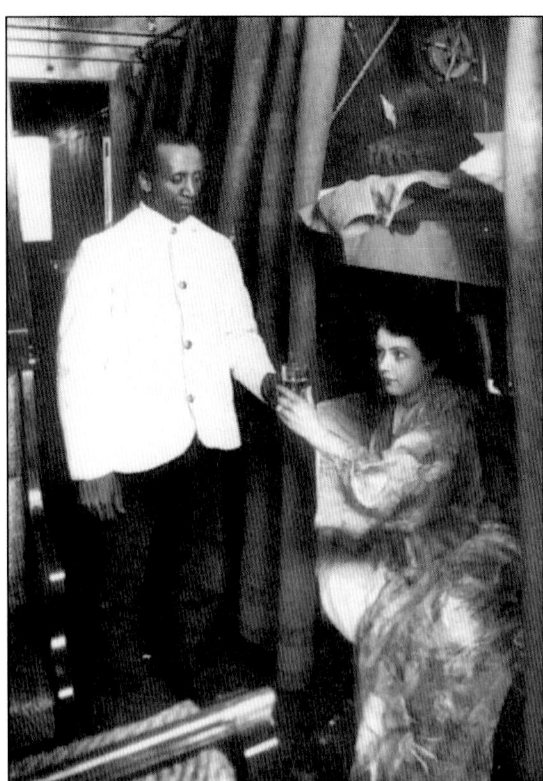

Always helpful and attentive, here a porter serves a drink to a female passenger in her bottom bunk.

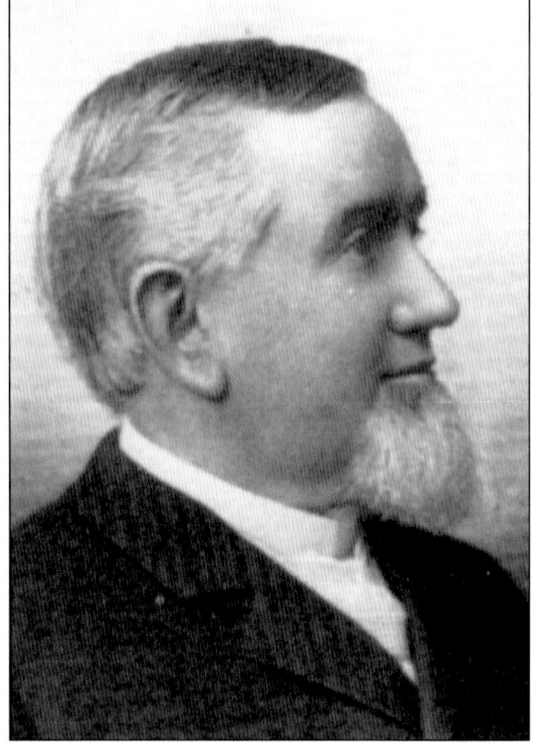

George Pullman, creator of the Pullman Palace Car Company, solicited black porters because they were a source of cheap labor and understood the societal distinction between blacks and whites, which created a social distance between passengers and servants.

In 1925, the porters approached A. Phillip Randolph, who had been fired by the railroad for talking about unionization in 1917, to be the leader of the Brotherhood of Sleeping Car Porters Union. Other unions refused to accept black members.

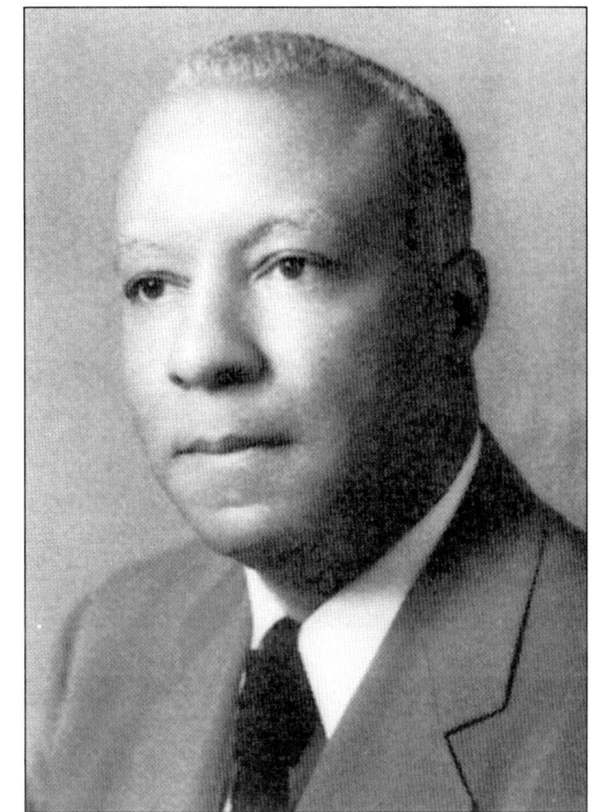

"Fight or be slaves" was the credo of C. L. Dellums, seen here third from the right inspecting conditions at a Richmond pier. He was described as being impeccably dressed, wearing a Homburg hat and polished shoes. His voice carried the certainty of a college professor.

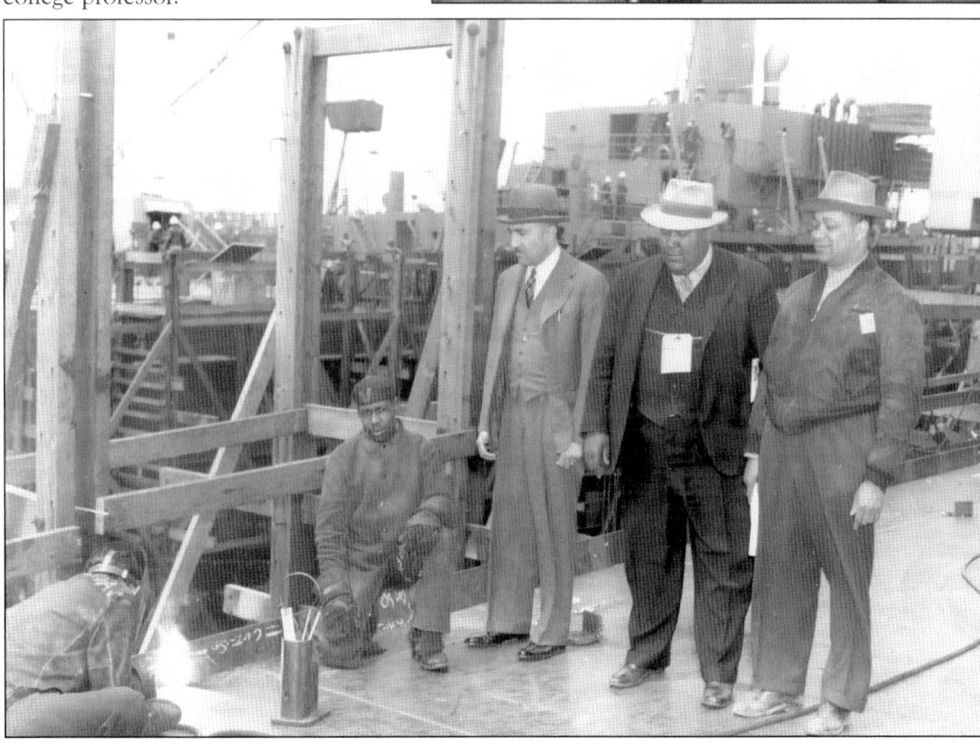

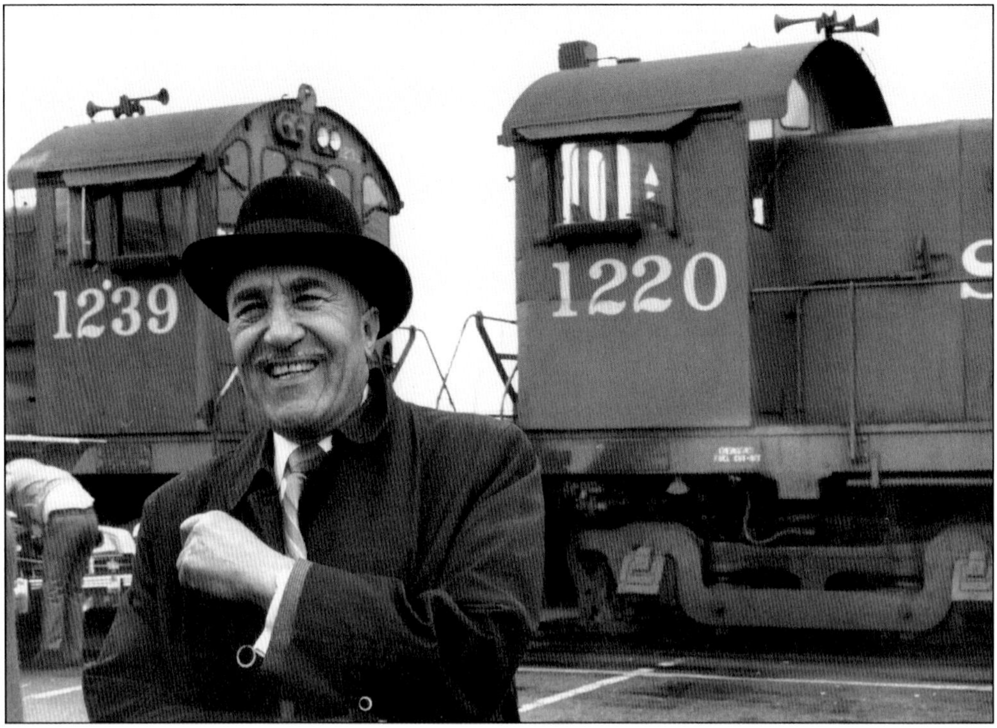

Here is Dellums in front of some locomotives. After 12 years, in August 1937, the Brotherhood of Sleeping Car Porters Union won a contract with the Pullman Company. It was the first agreement ever signed between African Americans and a corporation.

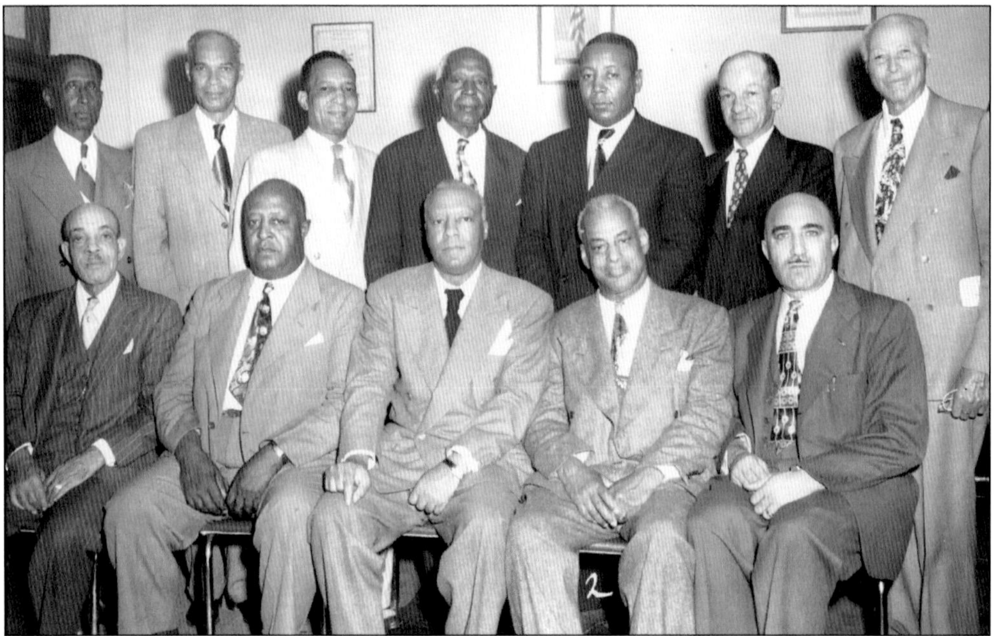

The executive board accepted nothing less than a standard workweek, pay equal to that of other unionized workers, a full range of fringe benefits, and the right to bargain collectively with their employers on any vital matter.

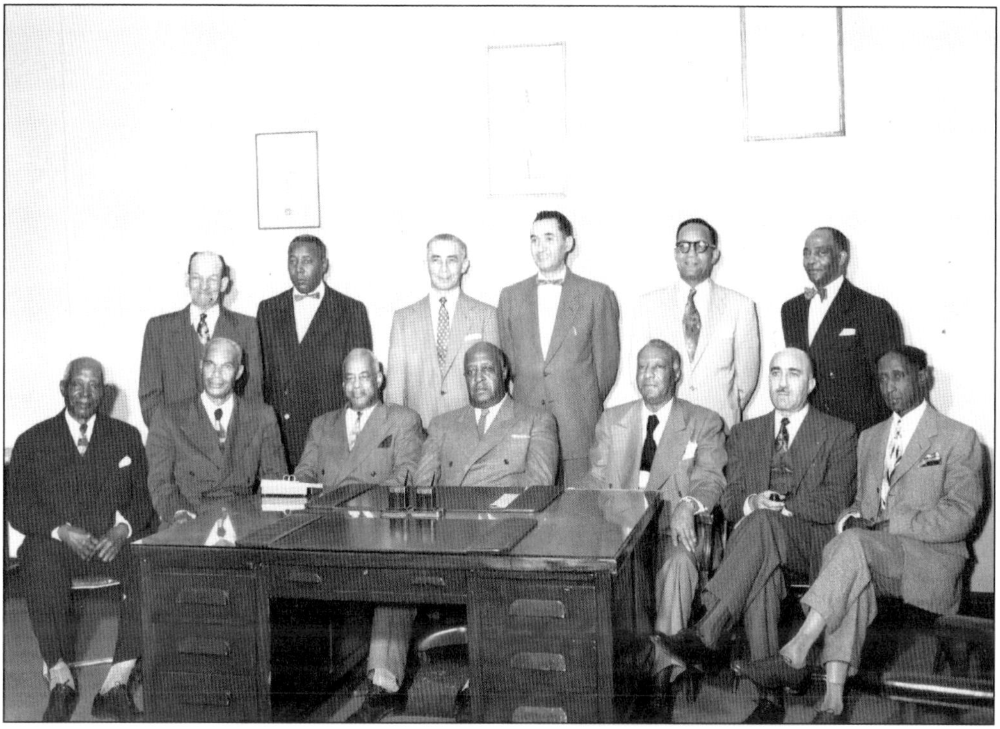

Here the International Board of the Brotherhood of Sleeping Car Porter's Union poses for a group photograph. Third from the right is the tireless union president A. Phillip Randolph. Seated second from the right is the West Coast vice president C. L. Dellums.

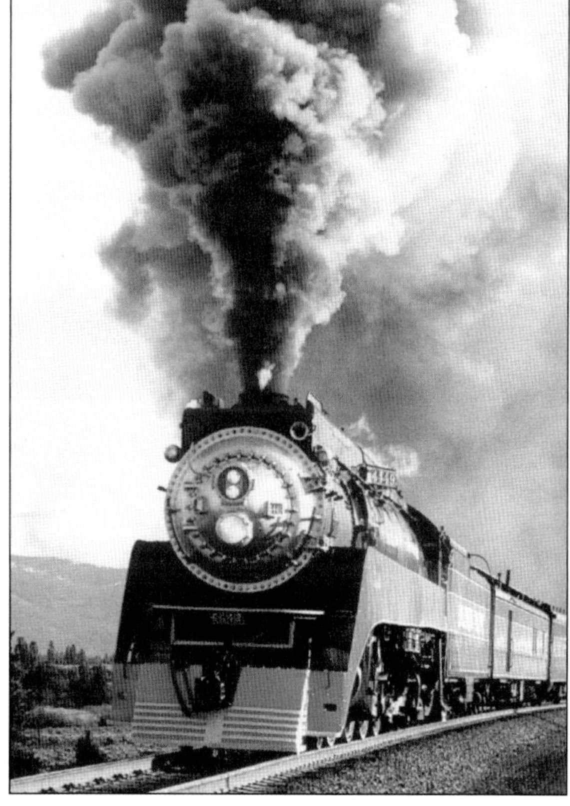

When the destination was 400 miles away or more, overnight passengers began the journey with dinner or ended it with breakfast. Pictured here is a postcard of "Daylight." (Simmons Collection.)

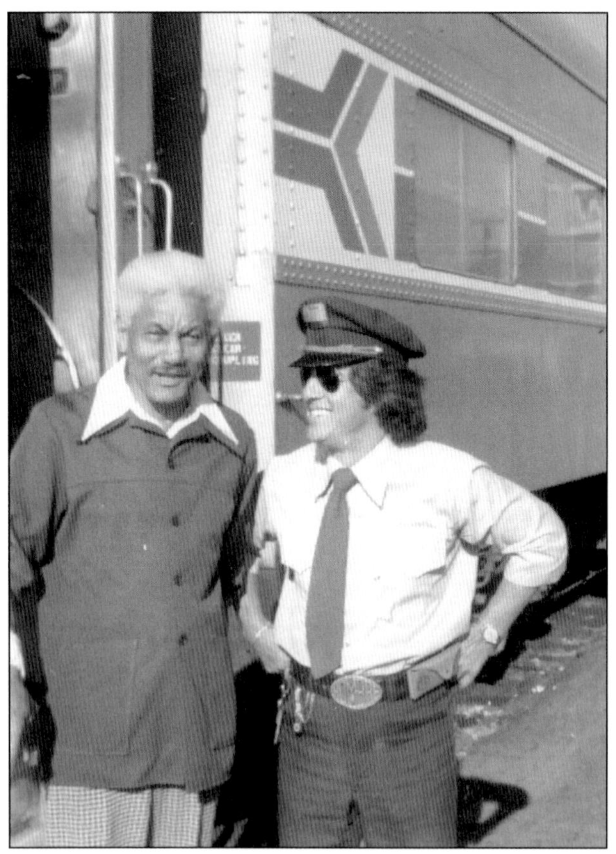

Pictured here is the retired Herman Simmons with an Amtrak employee. From the 1870s to the 1960s, tens of thousands of African Americans worked for the Pullman Company as sleeping car porters. In 1920s, the Pullman Company was the largest single employer of black men. (Simmons Collection.)

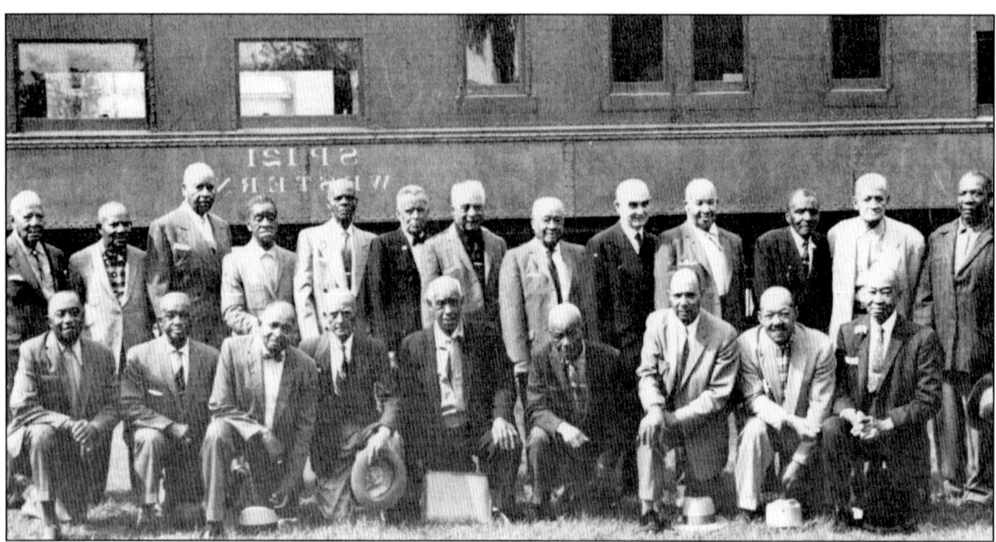

Members of the Retired Railroad Men's Club, pictured here, commemorate their many achievements. A. Randolph led 100,000 black men to march on Washington, and Pres. F. D. Roosevelt signed Executive Order 8802, which bared discrimination in employment in the defense industries.

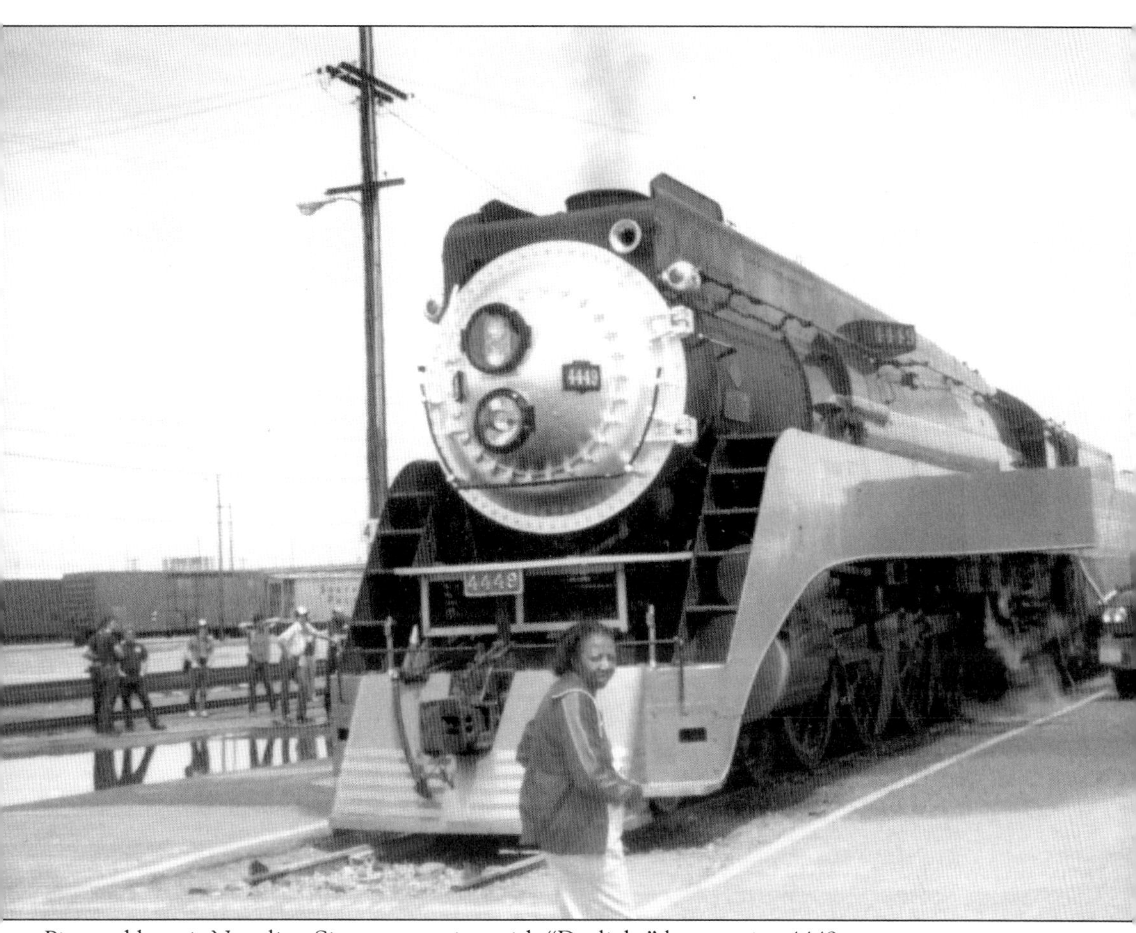


Pictured here is Noveline Simmons posing with "Daylight" locomotive 4449.

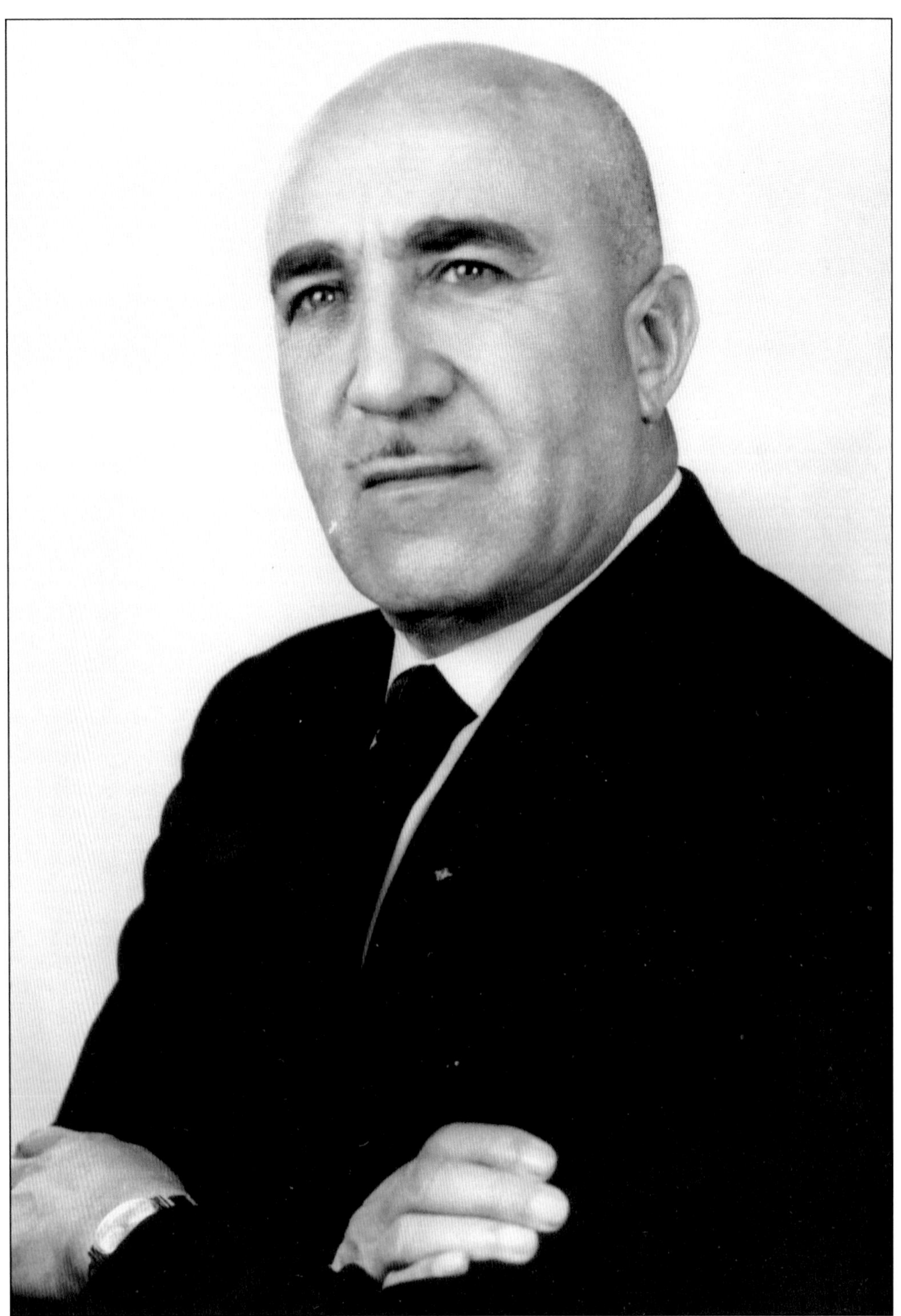

C. L. Dellums became a major figure in Oakland's African American community, heading its NAACP and supporting the 1946 Oakland General Strike. In 1968, he replaced Randolph as president of the Brotherhood of Sleeping Car Porters Union.

# *Two*

# The Soul of a Pullman Porter

The abolition of the slavery system in the United States revived the essence of the African American man. The qualities of manhood recorded in the history of great African kings, princes, leaders, and wise men, stifled within the slavery system, was abruptly released with the passage of the 13th, 14th, and 15th constitutional amendments. The Pullman Palace Car Company's policy that porters were only to be black men provided them the means to partake in the American dream—the ability to acquire wealth to purchase real property.

But much preparation was to take place as the revived essence resulted in leadership roles in the family structure and the community at large. While the accepted measure of a man was in his ability to earn a comfortable living and contribute to his community, the porters' specific job duties lacked the prestige held by African American community leaders. The porters set up the cars before departure, settled people into their rooms, and cared for them while they were aboard.

The porters greeted and cared for passengers, making beds and changing linens, cleaning rooms, cleaning bathrooms, shining shoes, pressing suits, and mailing letters. The porters were expected to answer passenger calls at any hour. All Pullman porters were called "George," and the porters worked an average full-time duty of 400 hours per month. Although the wages were comparatively low to white males, the work was steady and conditions were better than other vocations. Their working conditions were much superior to those of southern sharecroppers or northern domestics.

Despite the work conditions, the home community revered the Pullman porters as pillars in their communities. The porters dressed as white-collar workers, wearing neckties, white shirts, and shinned shoes. They were well educated and their substance was pride and self-respect.

The unanticipated outcome was that the essence of the porter was the building block of a black community in West Oakland, California. A stable foundation of men and their women and the influence of the Pullman porter remained an important anchor in the West Oakland community until 1969 and beyond.

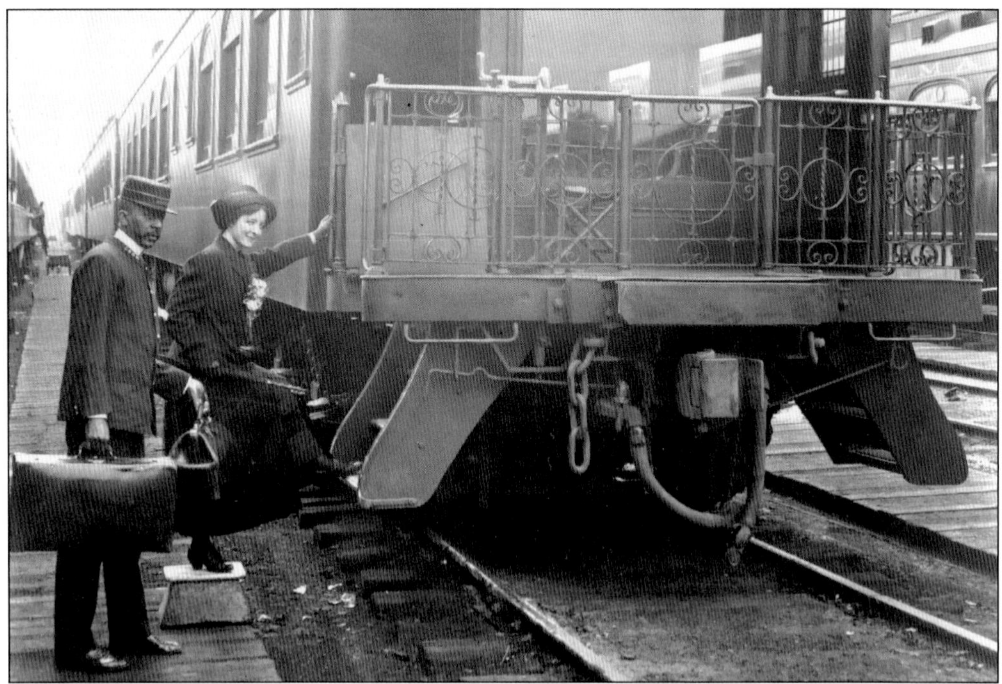

Pictured here is the exterior of an observation car at the platform, with a porter helping a lady board a Los Angeles Limited car in the 1900s. Railroad workers were required to live west of Adeline Street in order to be on call for unscheduled duty.

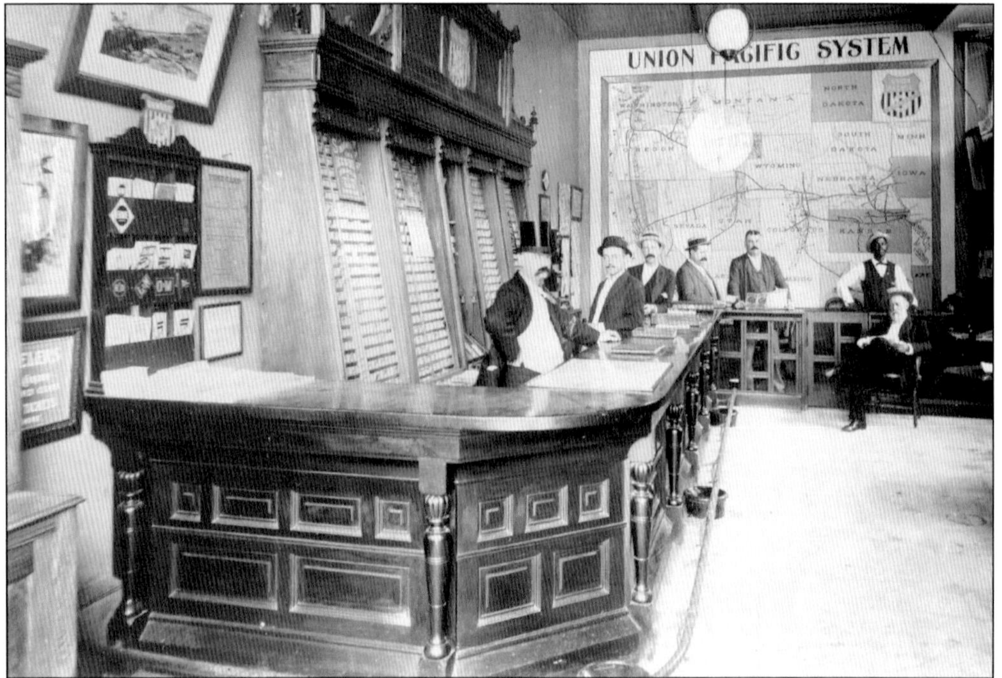


Pictured here is the Union Pacific Railroad ticket office. Many children of Pullman porters pursued professional careers such as scientists, college professors, politicians, and jazz artists. Ronald Dellums, Thurgood Marshall, Tom Bradley, and Willie Brown were all children of Pullman porters.

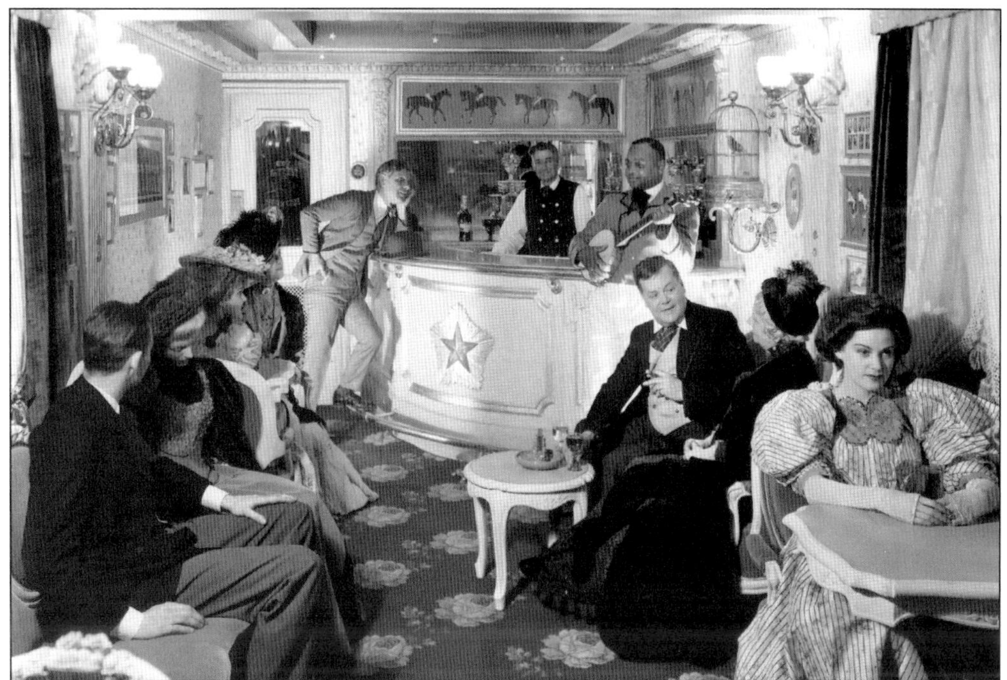

Pictured here is a porter playing a banjo for passengers in a lounge car. The "art of soliciting" generous tips allowed porters to become both servants and psychologists. Porters realized that passengers would tip liberally for the impression of being catered to and entertained.

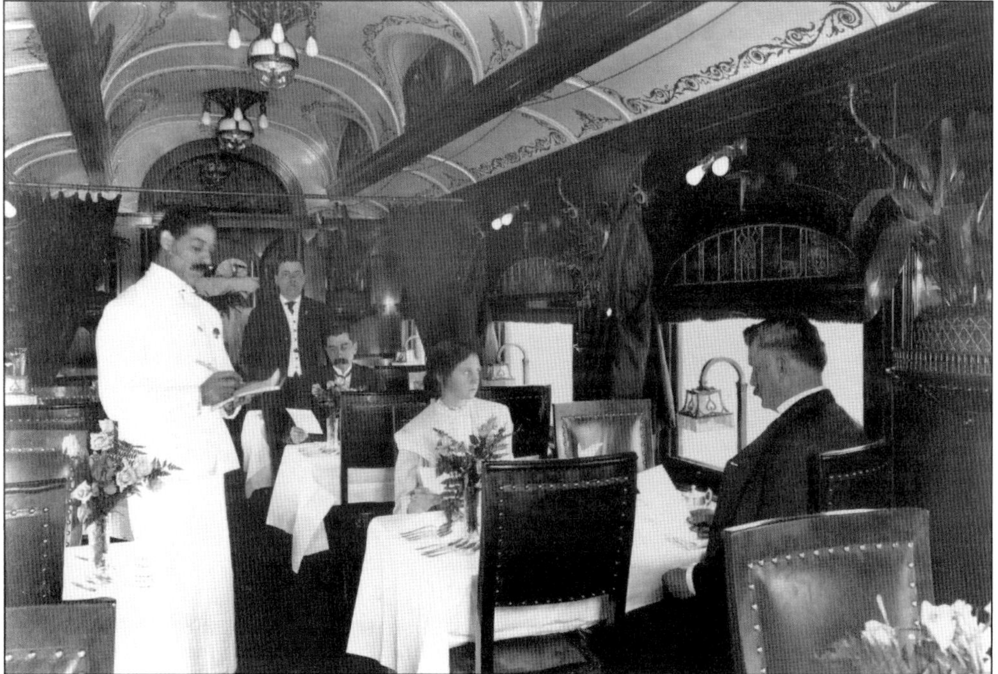

The dining car had ornate ceilings and hanging chandeliers, and each area was separated by floor-length curtains. Leather chairs sat at tables set with linen, crystal glass, porcelain dishes, cut flowers, and heavy silverware place settings.

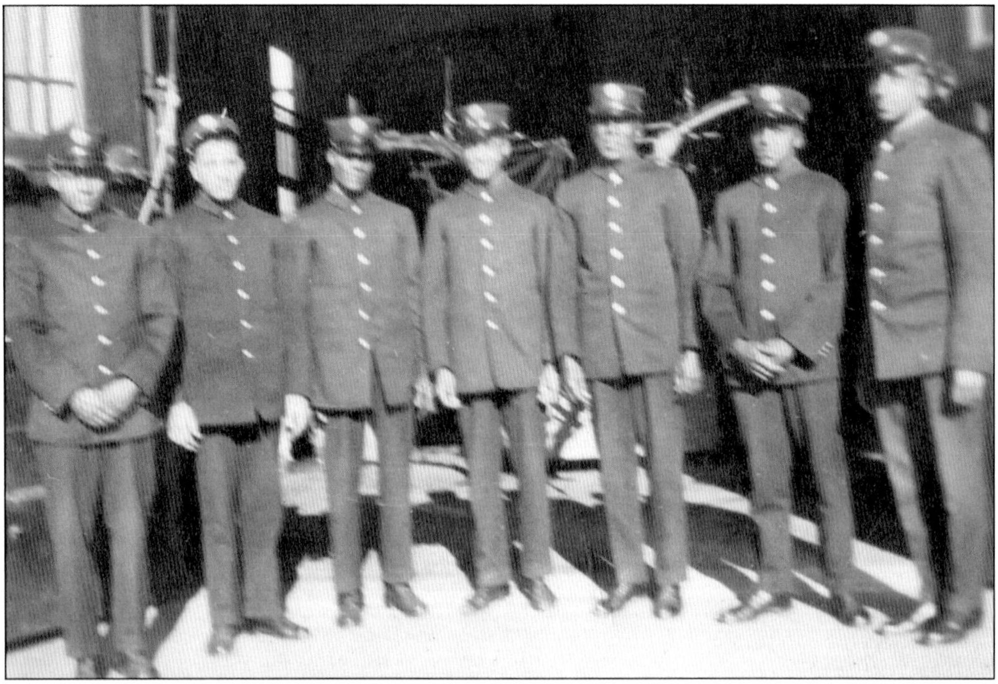

Porters were expected to answer a passenger call at any hour. His job was to make up the berth, shine shoes at night, nurse passengers with hangovers, change the bed sheets, awaken sleeping passengers at their stop, and perform other tasks that earned tips—all with a smiling face.

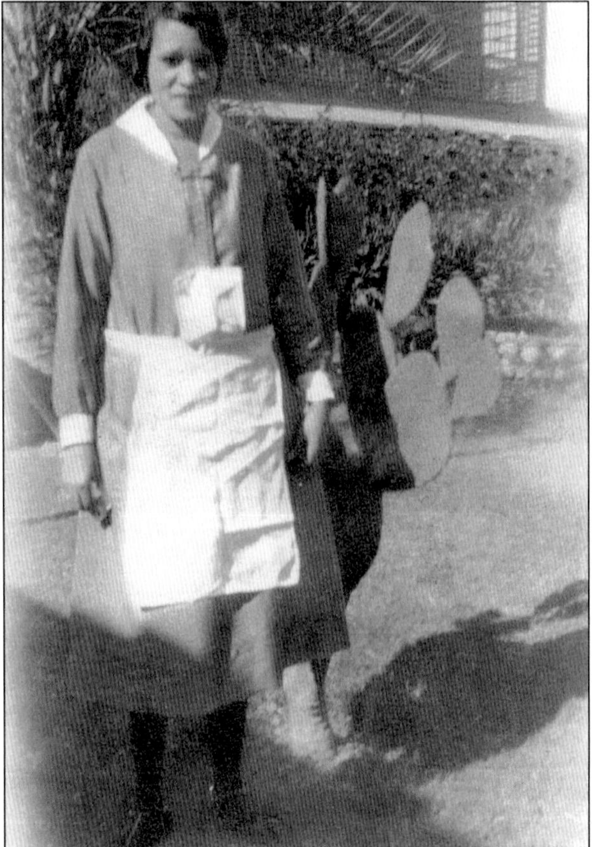

Frances Albrier, pictured in a Pullman maid's uniform, was required to be and was a certified nurse; unfortunately, she couldn't become a registered nurse due to racism. By 1926, there were 200 Pullman maids. They wore all gray dresses with starched white collars, cuffs, and aprons. Their wages and tips were low, and they were prohibited from socializing with the porters.

The porters were relatively well educated, and their constant travel was an important avenue for spreading information about better opportunities and living conditions for blacks in various parts of the country.

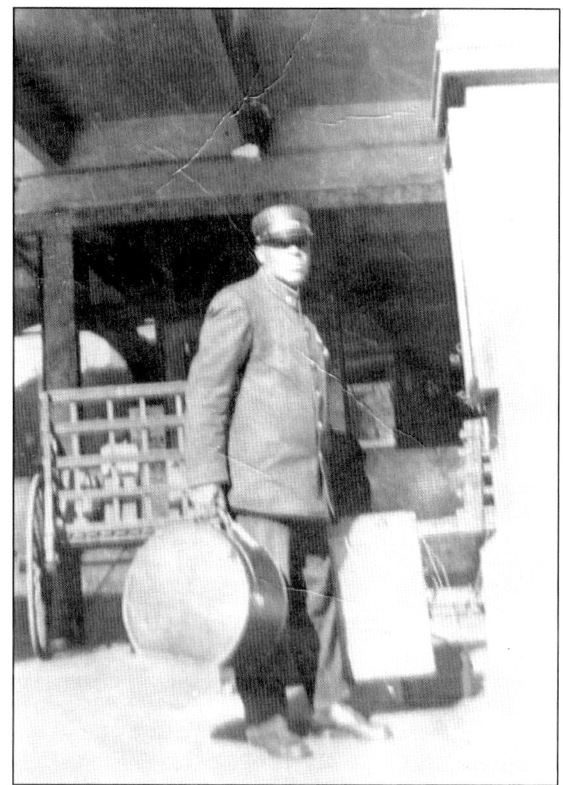

This drawing shows a waiter serving in a dining car. Most waiters wanted to become porters. Porters dressed differently, earned tips, and interacted with the wealthy "high-class people" riding in the sleeper cars.

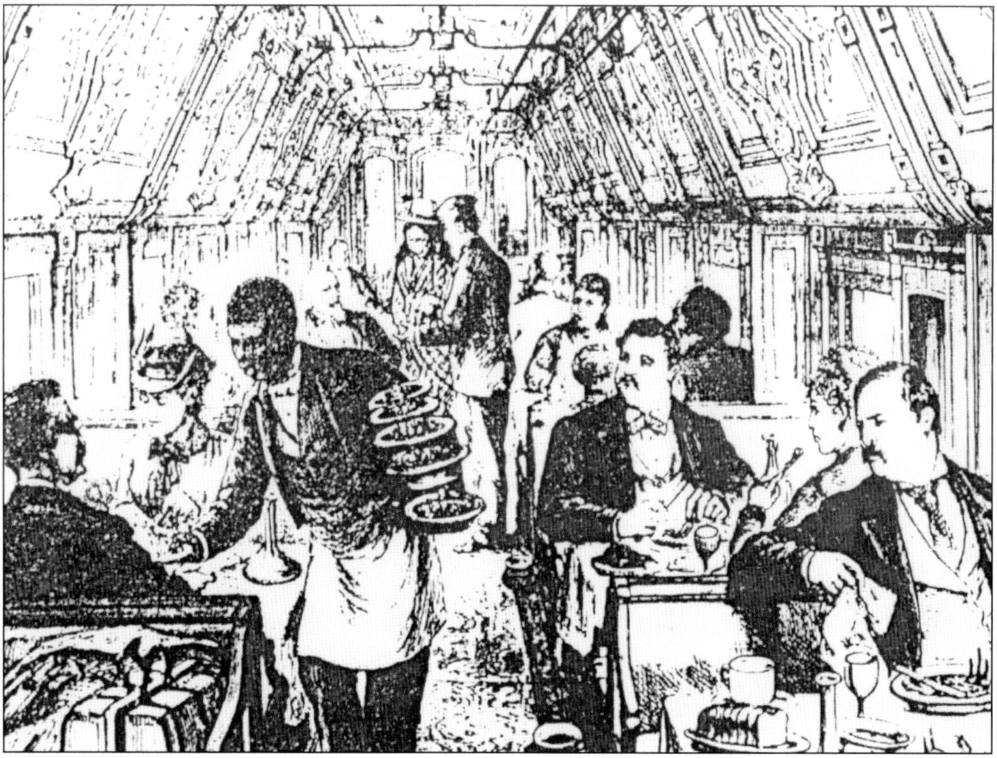

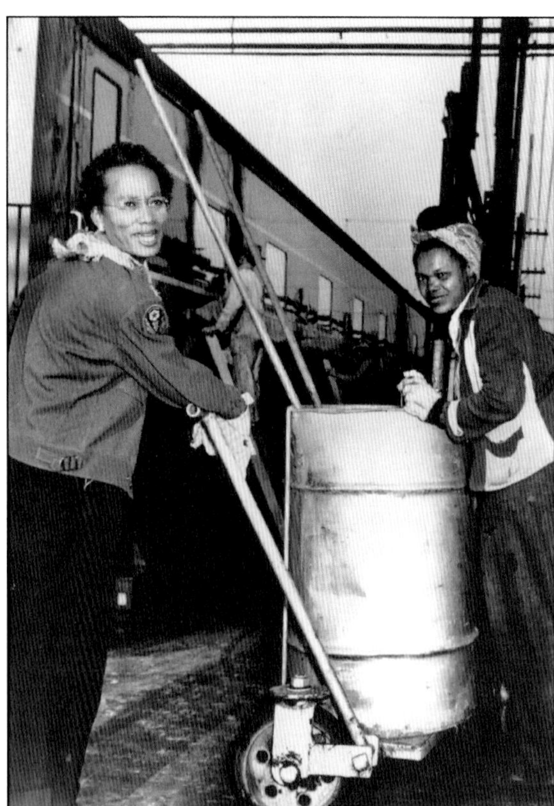

Here two unidentified women, with a barrel working around a train, do scheduled maintenance. Women took jobs maintaining the exterior of trains.

A porter learned to depend on using good judgment in a wide variety of circumstances. No matter how taxing the work, a sense of humor and the ability to read passengers personalities were critical skills. They could never forget that the job of a porter was easier than work as a field slave.

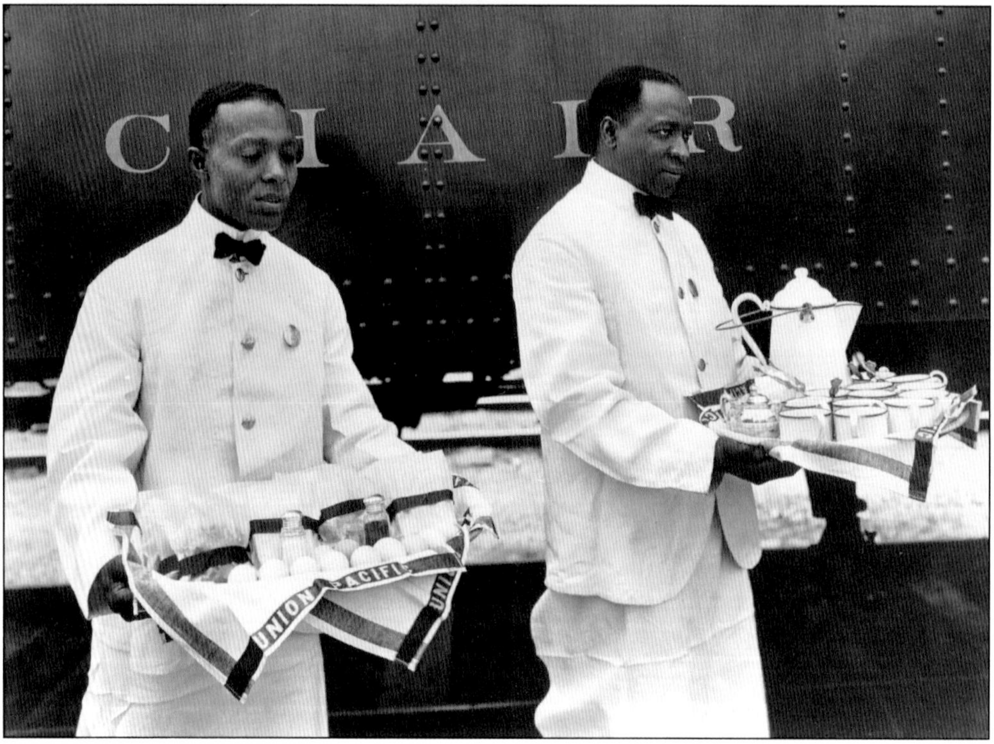

Pictured here in a dark suit is porter Cleaton L. Jones. Many porters lived in company-owned rooming houses, others boarded with black homeowners in the area, and some bought their own homes. Eventually the black community in the East Bay took shape as an African American dreamscape.

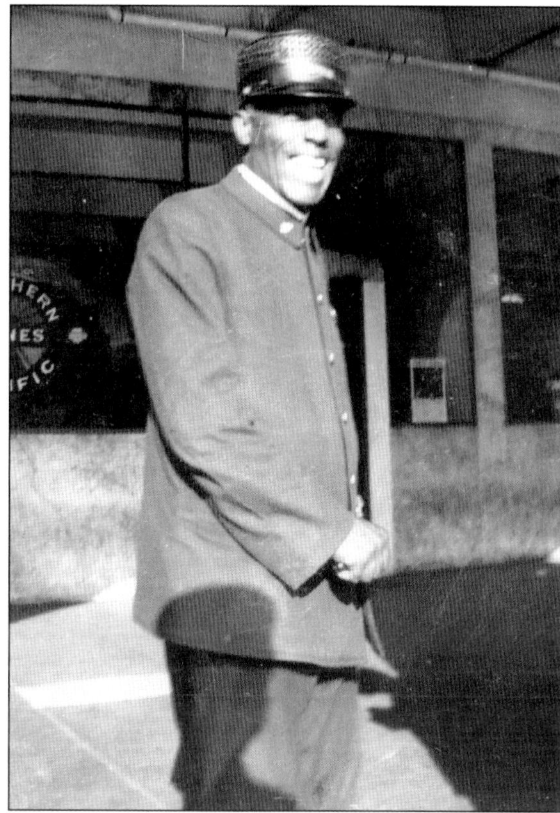

Pictured here are Pullman porters J. Simms, Richard Sox, and C. L. Jones. The porters learned to lean on one another. The porters, waiters, and maids created their own code of terms, which they used to communicate among themselves. Most of the expressions came from the black community.

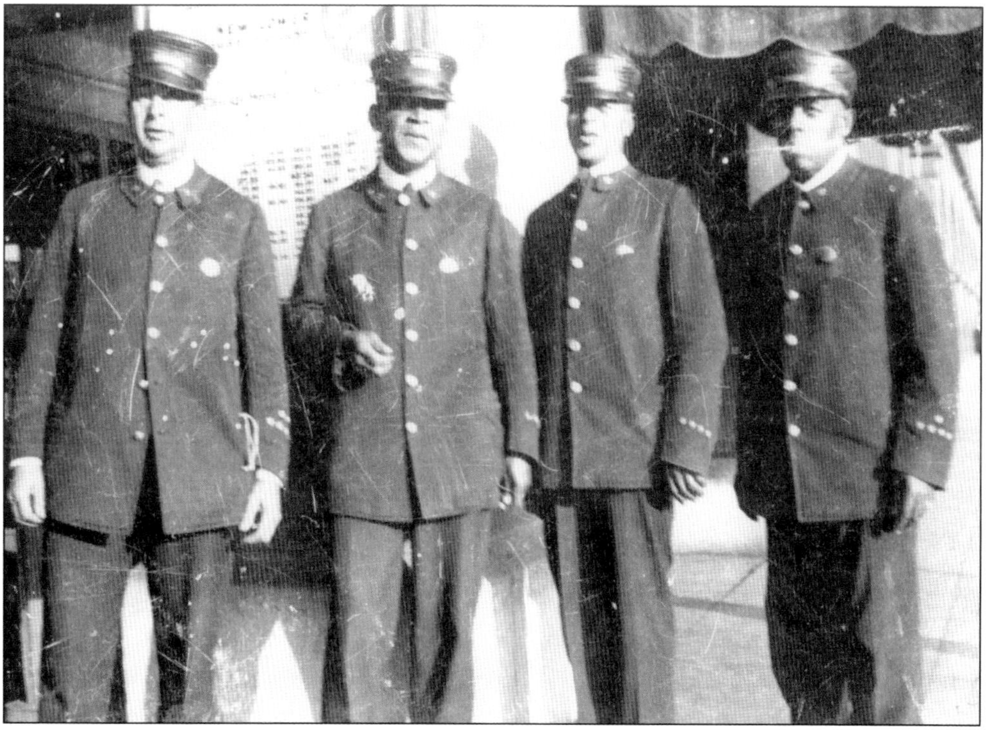

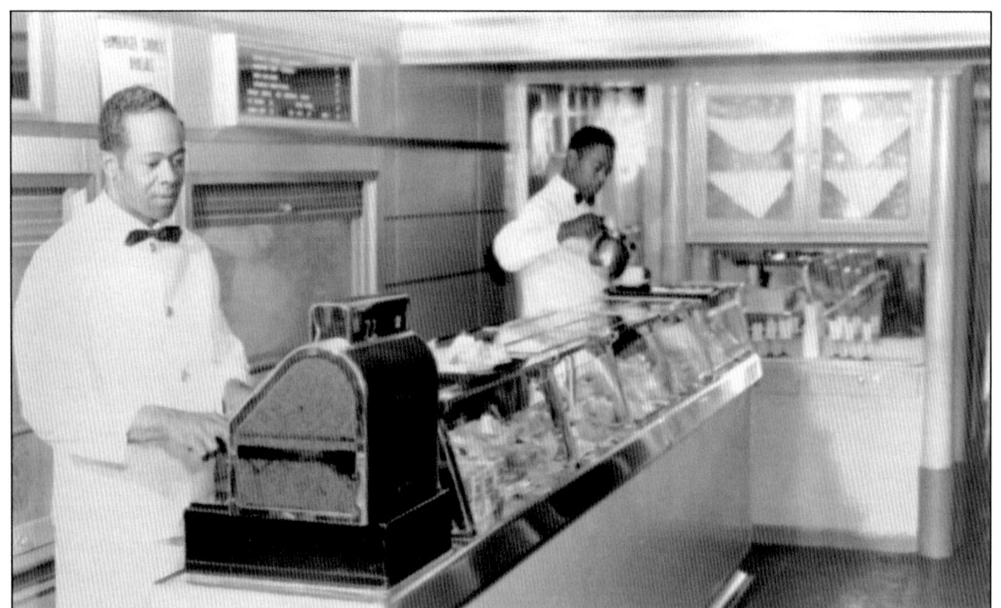

Porters were seen as moving up in the world. They picked up newspapers, books, stock tips, and lessons of how to mold a black American dream. By watching and listening to the wealthy passengers, they realized how much education and saving money equaled a chance for advancement for their children.

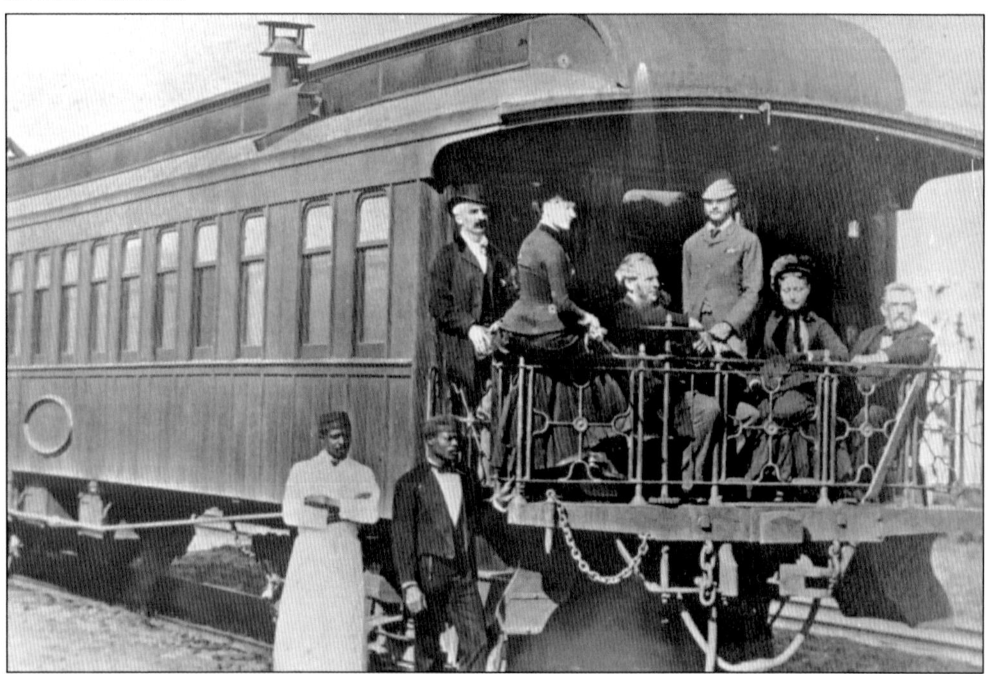

Two porters are keeping a watchful eye on passengers on the rear deck of a train car. Porters were official greeters, helped passengers climb on board, and carried their baggage. They were also chambermaids, using mops and brooms to clean dirty washrooms, passageways, and platforms. The porters polished spittoons, mailed letters, wired telegrams, set up card tables, and loaded wood for the engine.

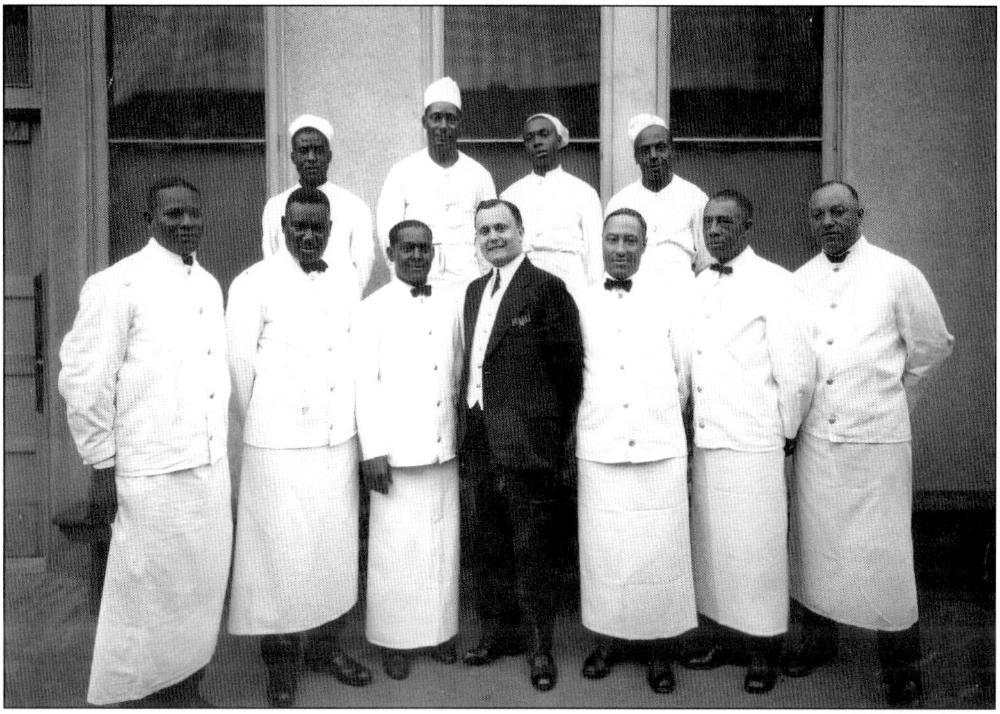

These men aspired to set a standard of excellence in the performance of their duties. They took a job that was considered menial at the time and molded it into something of substance.

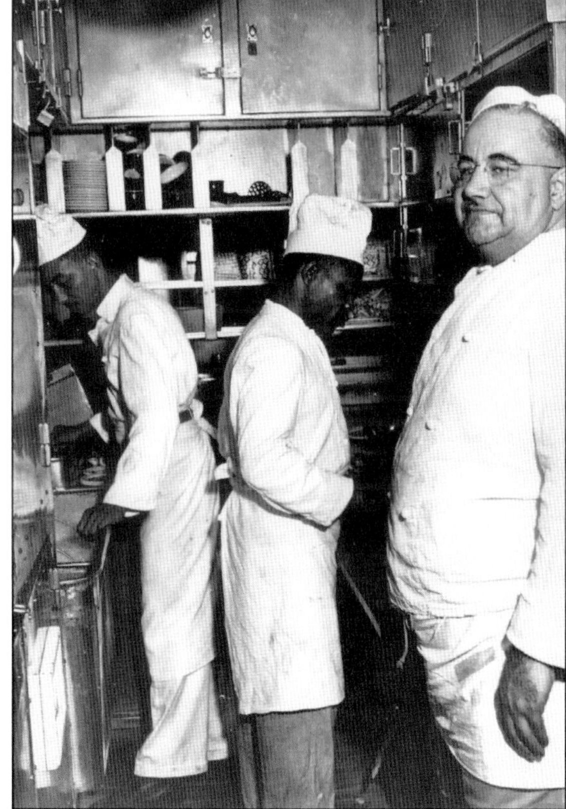

Here an unidentified chef poses with second cooks in the galley. Among other things, the porters were expected to be health inspectors. Fingernails had to be clean, no sideburns or mustaches were allowed, and no torn or soiled jackets were permitted.

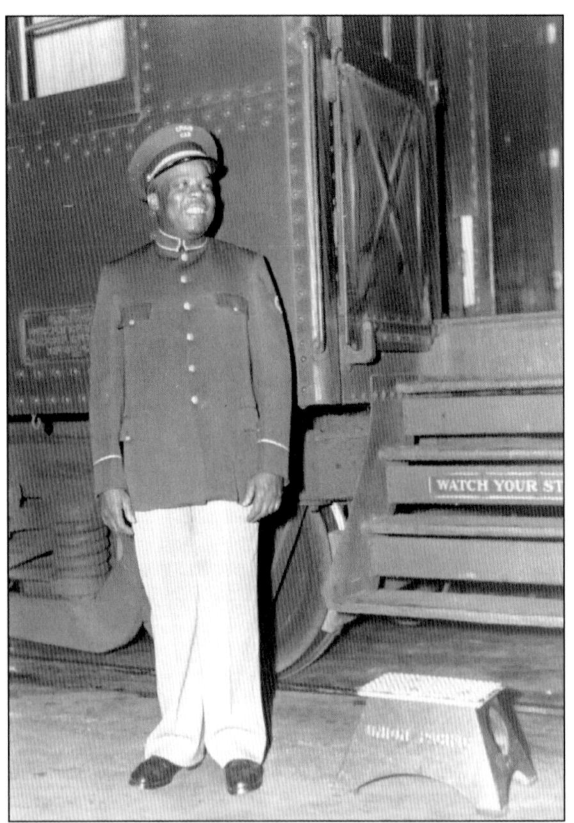


This porter is standing outside a car with step stool. Helping passengers often meant stoking their heaters, recovering misplaced items, selling them cigarettes and candy, and playing cards. They also tended to the sick and invalid, warmed bottles for newborns, and played midwife to premature moms.

Herman Simmons is seen here standing on the sidewalk at his home. "I left New Orleans to work for the Pullman Company in Oakland because they needed men. I didn't have a place for my family." (Simmons Collection.)

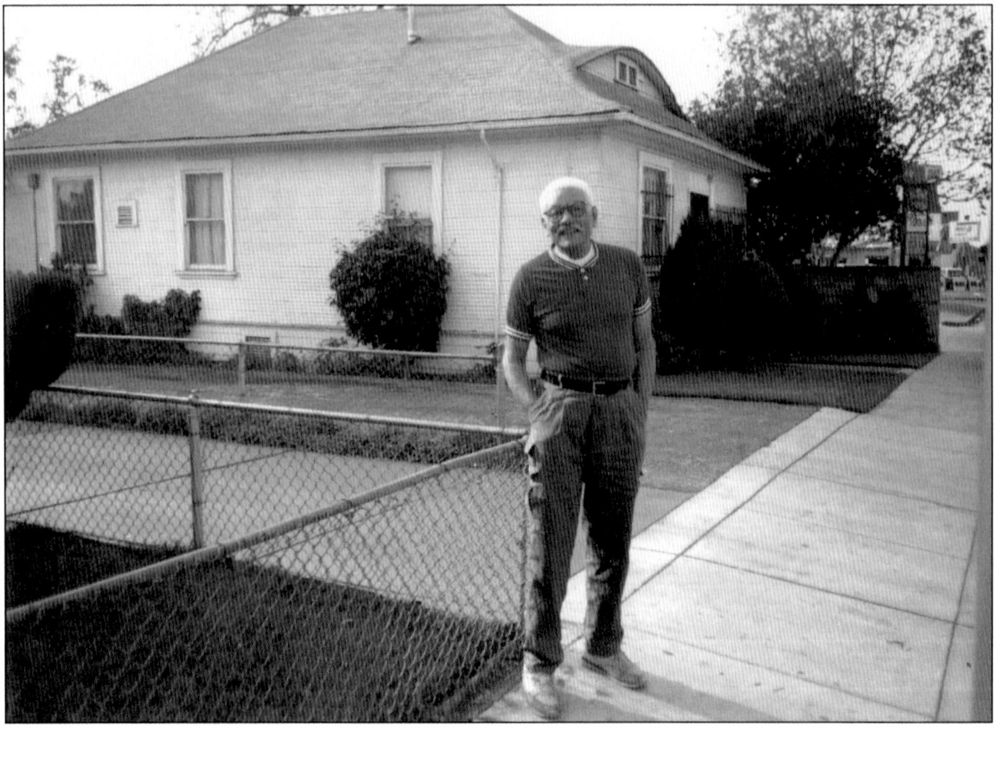

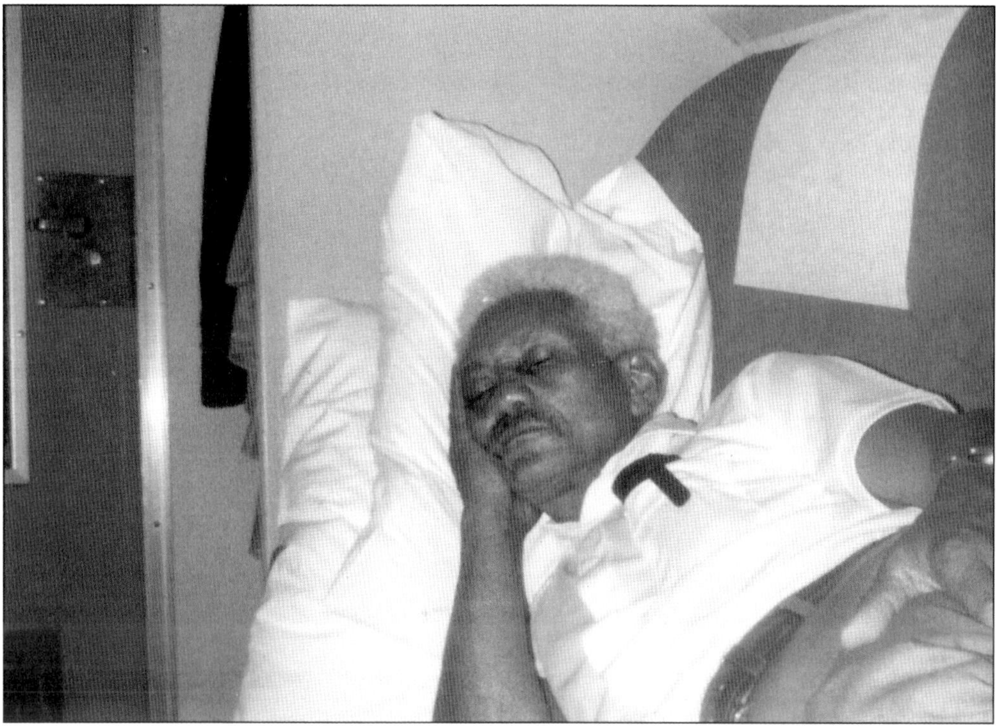

Before 1937, porters received $67.50 per month for 300 to 400 hours of work, allowing less than three hours of sleep between shifts. After 1937, the working hours were reduced from 400 to 240, with increased time for undisturbed sleep. (Simmons Collection.)

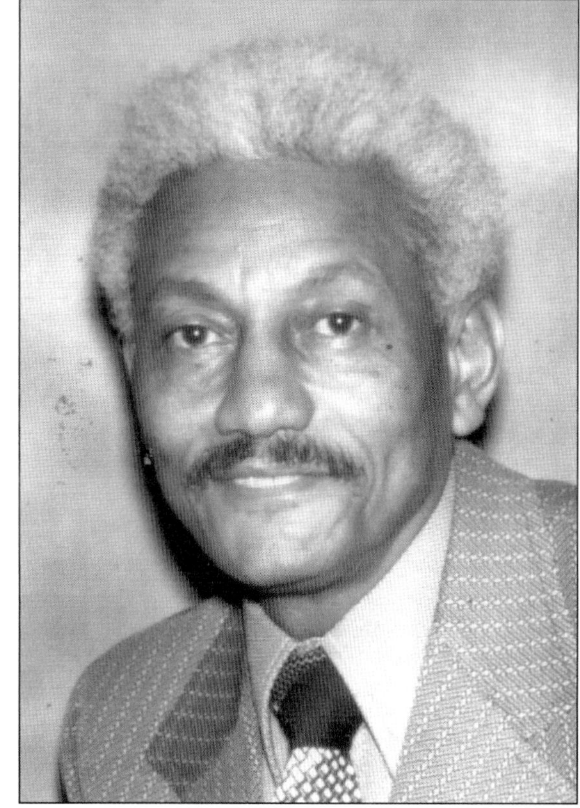

Herman Simmons said, "It wasn't the best of jobs, but it was a good job. We got a chance to travel. We got a chance to raise our family and send our kids to college. It was a black pride thing." (Simmons Collection.)

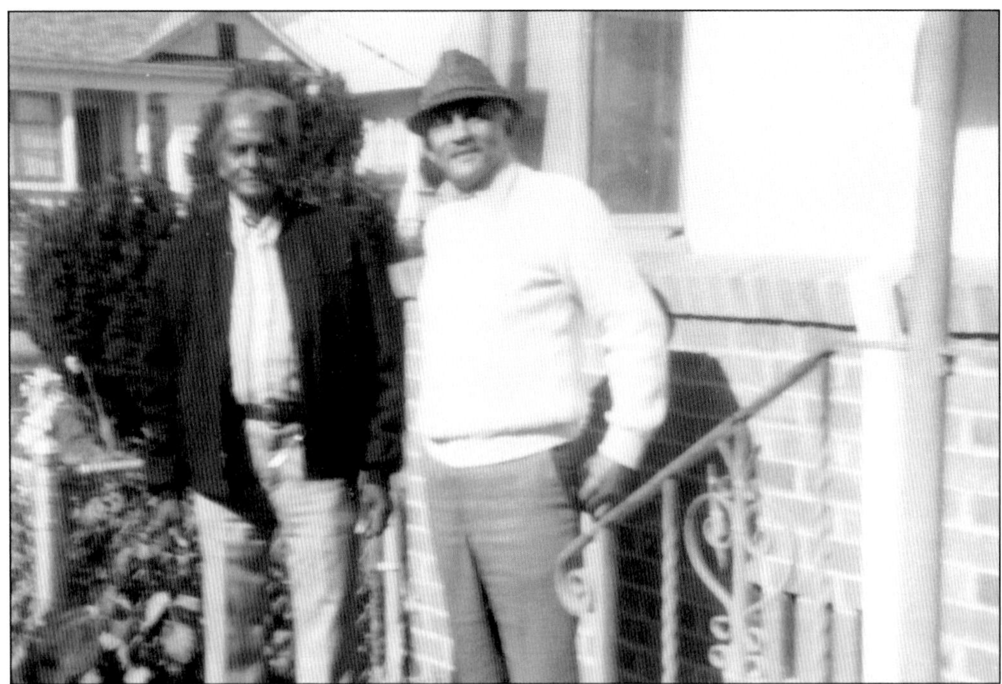

Herman Simmons is pictured here standing on the steps to his home with a friend. He said, "The Pullman Company had headquarters for the porters, but not for our families." In 1954, Simmons purchased a home in East Oakland. (Simmons Collection.)

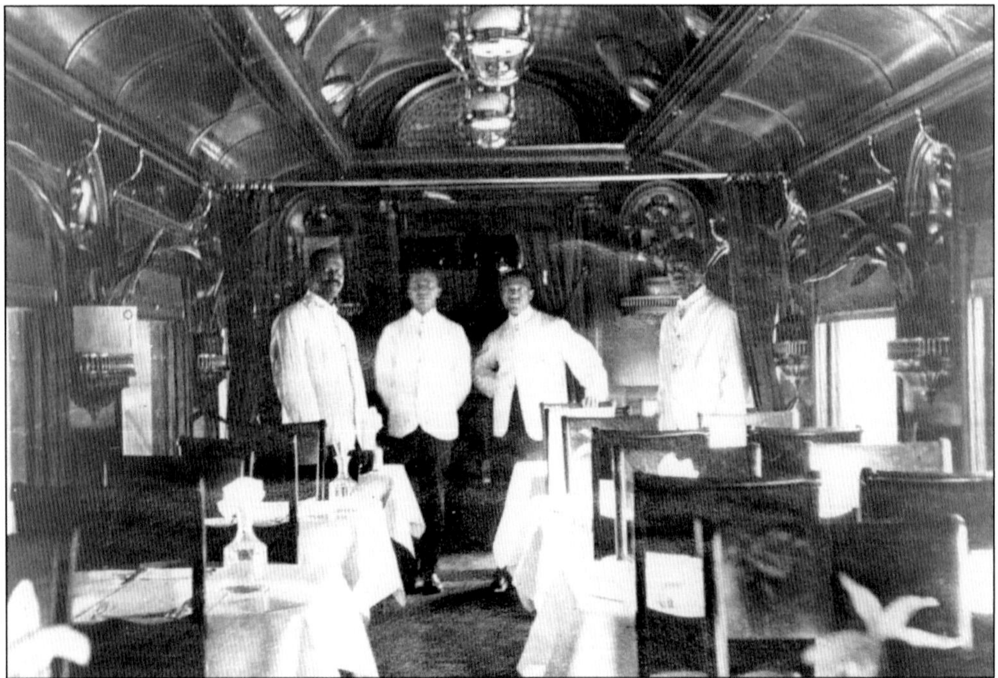

The porters' salary of $67.50 per month in 1925 was far greater than the salaries paid to black schoolteachers. Porters assigned to the "extra board" (waiting to be assigned a route) were at the complete mercy of the sign-out man.

# *Three*

# West Oakland
## A Haven for Black Families

No longer were men, women, and children working collectively in the fields and returning to slave quarters each night. Porters had the means to be responsible for their own families. In West Oakland, the porters had found a place to call their own, a place to paint their own American dreamscape.

As the railroad generated rapid expansion in the East Bay economy, Oakland became home base for a growing number of Pullman porters and their families. A terminus for the First Transcontinental Railroad, West Oakland established a community of Portuguese, Germans, Irish, Chinese, Japanese, Europeans, and African Americans. The 1910 census showed over 3,000 black residents living in West Oakland.

At the beginning of the 20th century, the Pullman porters, changed by what they saw of the white American dream, began to lay the groundwork in a West Oakland black community dreamscape, different from the vision that white passengers enjoyed. The Pullman porters laid the groundwork for a solid middle class of people with black skin, even when their modest wages seemed to belie it.

When the West Coast office of the Brotherhood of Sleeping Car Porters was established under the direction of C. L. Dellums, West Oakland was truly a richly diverse, well-rounded community of all ethnic groups and economic levels of people. Blacks chose West Oakland, with its pleasant climate, as their home when not traveling, especially in light of its relative social freedom. Also, West Oakland was near the railroad yard.

They wanted the American dream as much as the passengers they saw living it every day. Some Pullman porters owned homes and cars and seemed like men of wealth. Some had choice routes, with tips considerably higher than the average porter. Some had higher salaries earned through years on the job. Others lived beyond their means or looked wealthier in pre-union years. A number of porters relied on extra income from other jobs, or their wives found employment. When the porters' salary is assessed, not in context of general society but in context of the black community where wages were universally low, porters tended to look rich by comparison.

The African American dreamscape materialized as African Americans mastered investing and saving money as well as making higher-education plans for their children. As a result, the porters and others wage earners in the community became owners of real property.

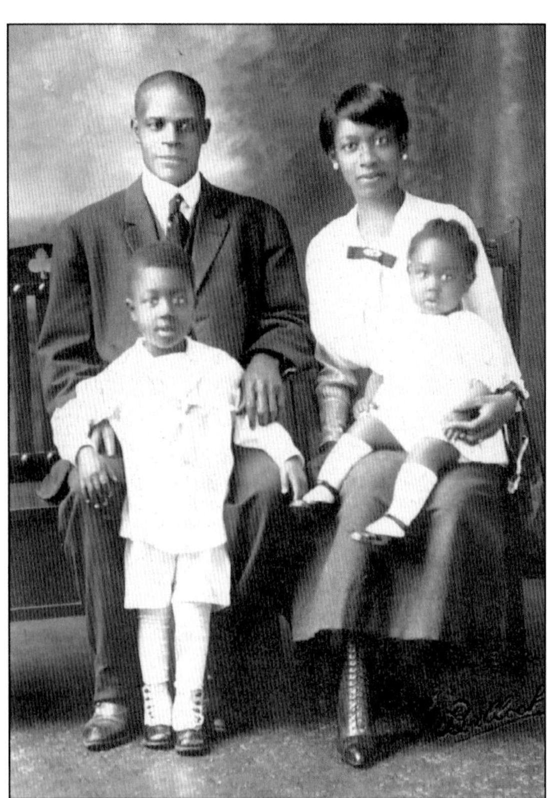

Pictured here in this 1919 family portrait are, from left to right, father John G. Wiggins, Walter Wiggins, mother Elvira Davis Wiggins, and Carlton Wiggins (sitting on mother's lap).

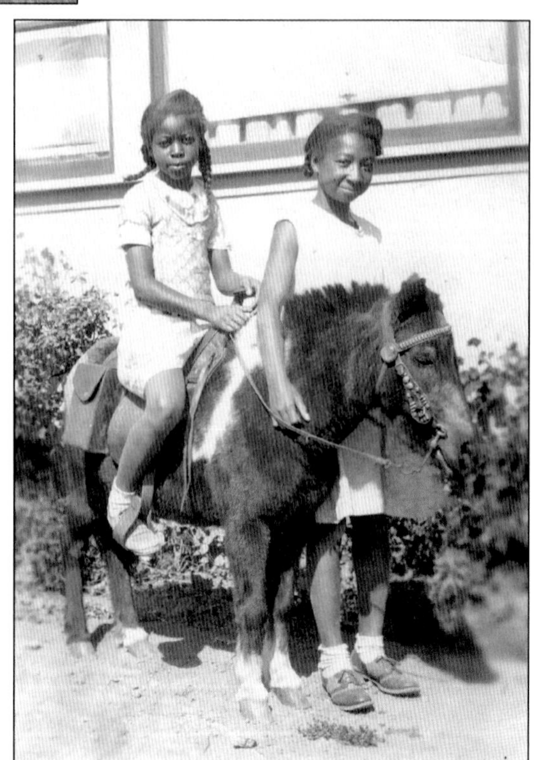

Pictured here in 1932 are first cousins Delores Cooper and Elvira Wiggins at 1235 Sixty-second Avenue, both at the age of 10. Elvira Wiggins is the daughter of John Wiggins and Elvira Davis Wiggins.

Here is a man dressed in the fashion (a suit) of the period.

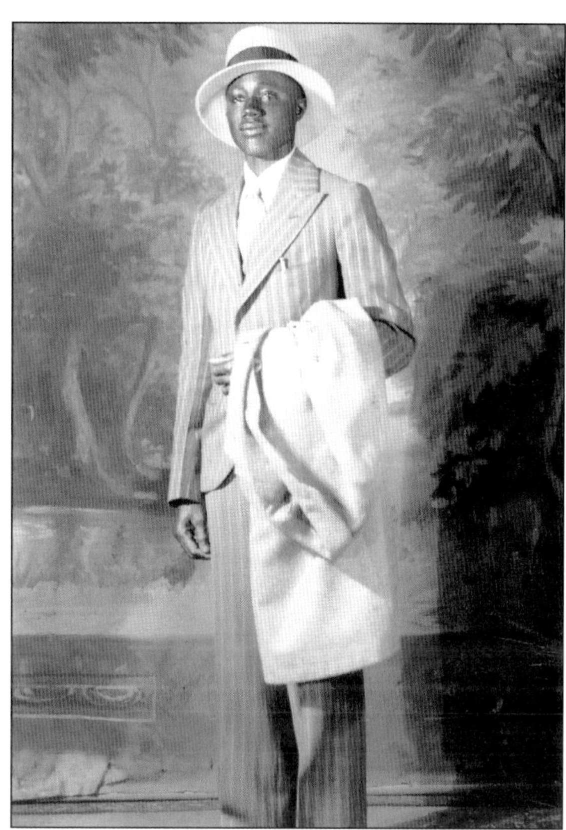

This unidentified group, posing proudly and smiling brightly, is typical of many West Oakland families.

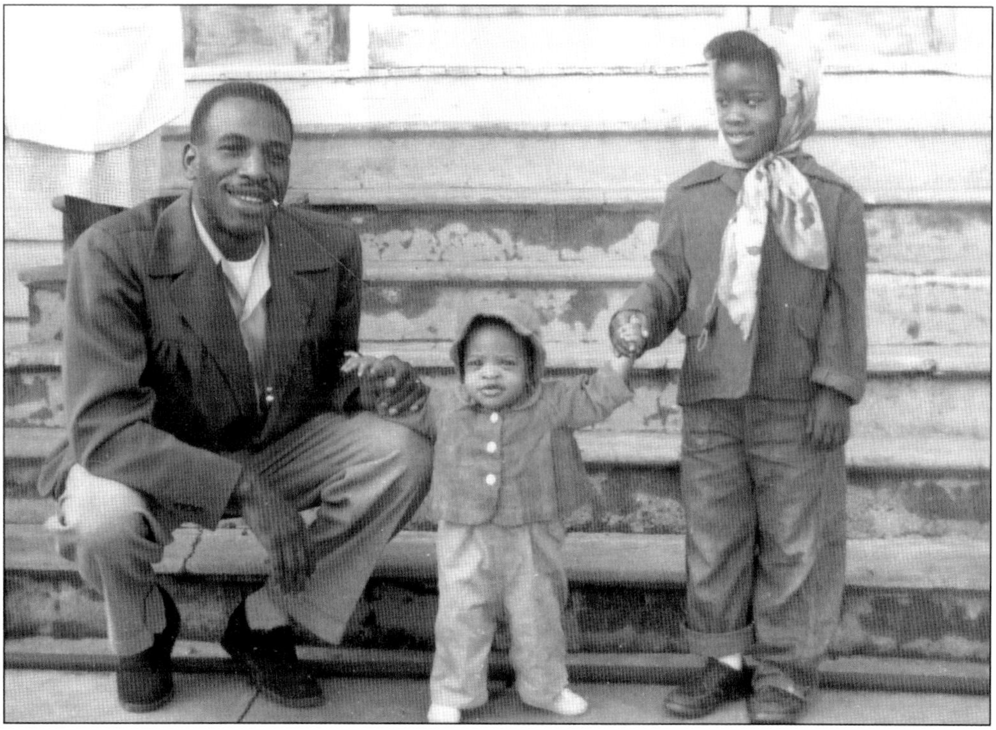

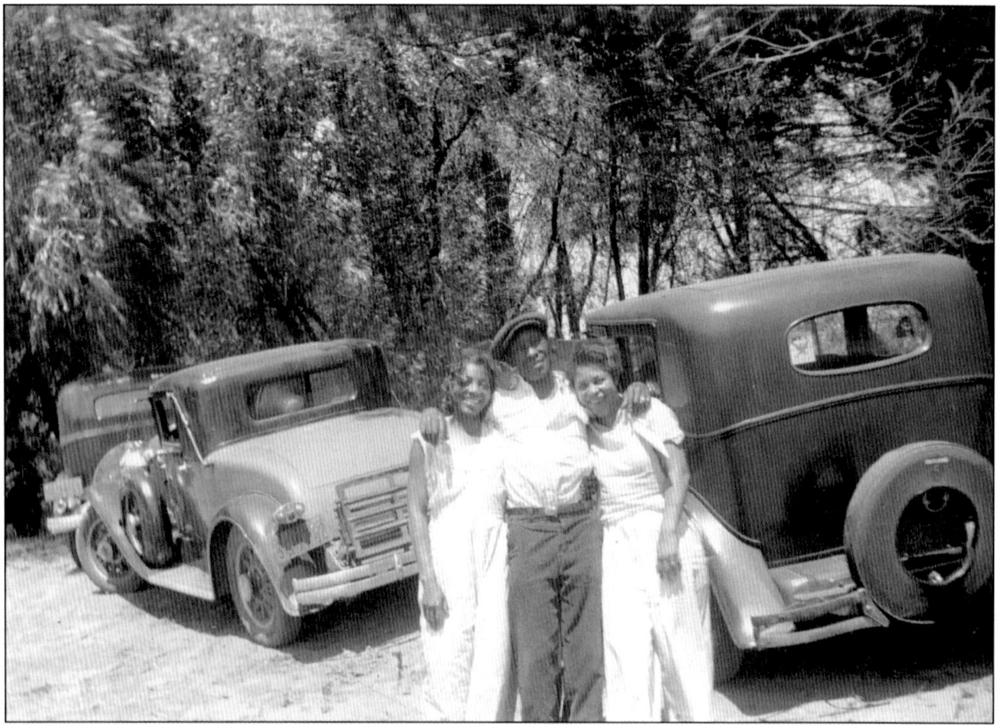

Posing in this 1934 photograph are unidentified family members out on an excursion.

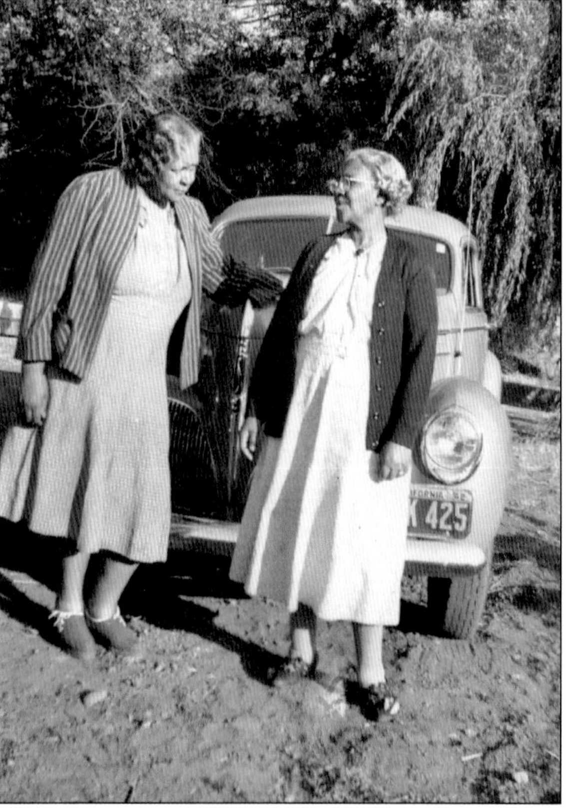


Pictured here are two women posing in front of their car.

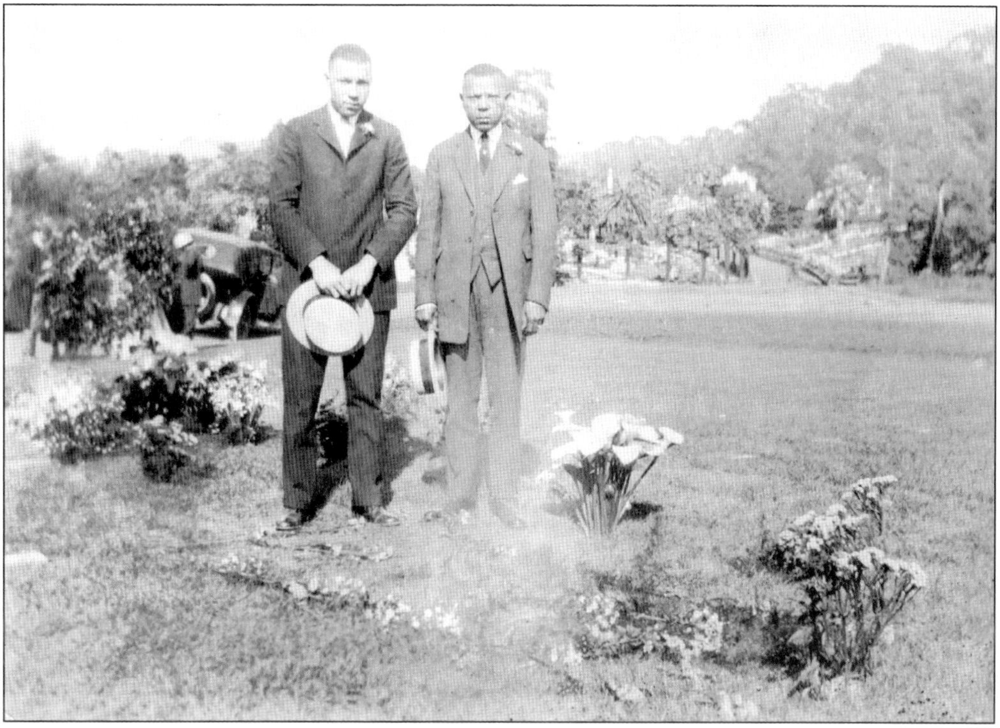

This photograph is of two unidentified well-dressed young men visiting a cemetery. Note the automobile in the background.

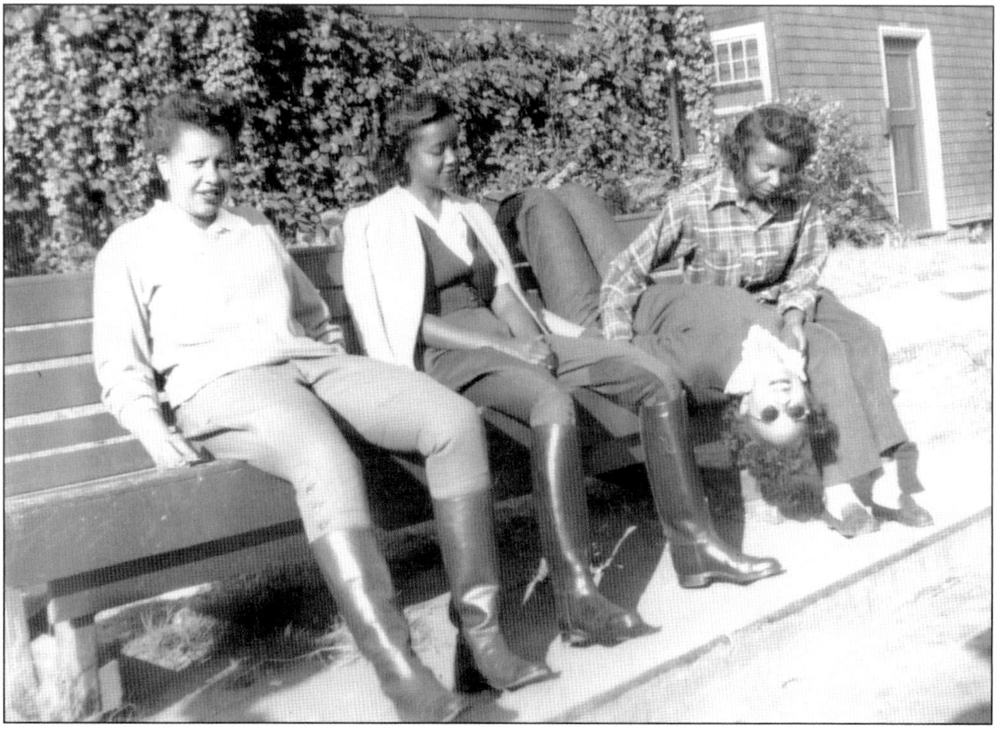

Here a group of four girls pass the time as they wait for the bus.

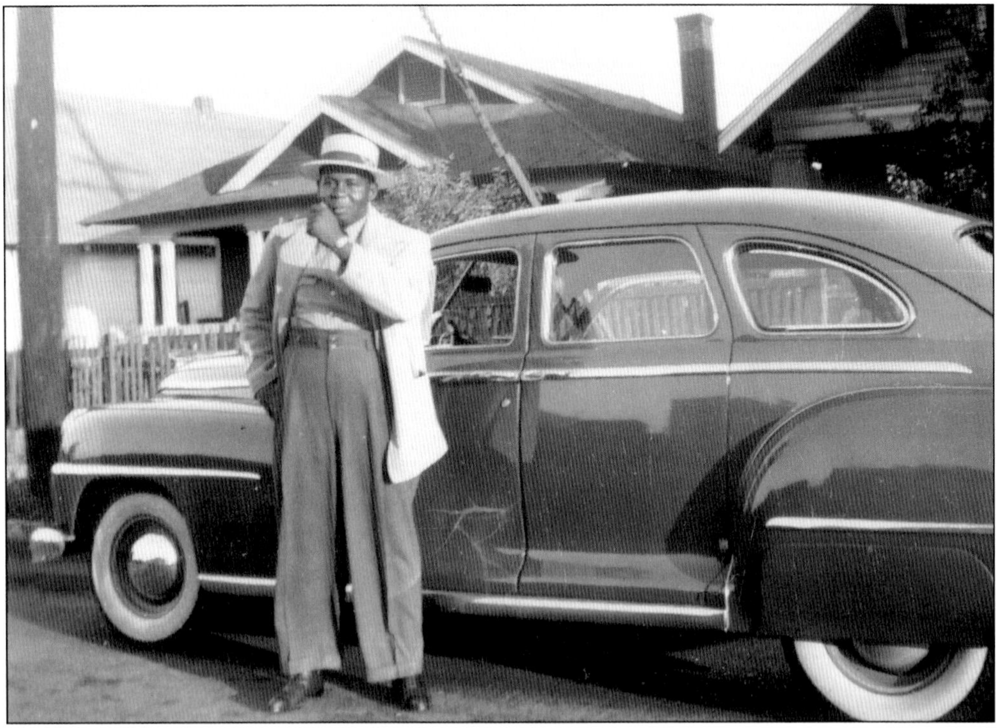

With automobiles being symbolic of diligence and hard work, this image shows just how proud of that car he is.

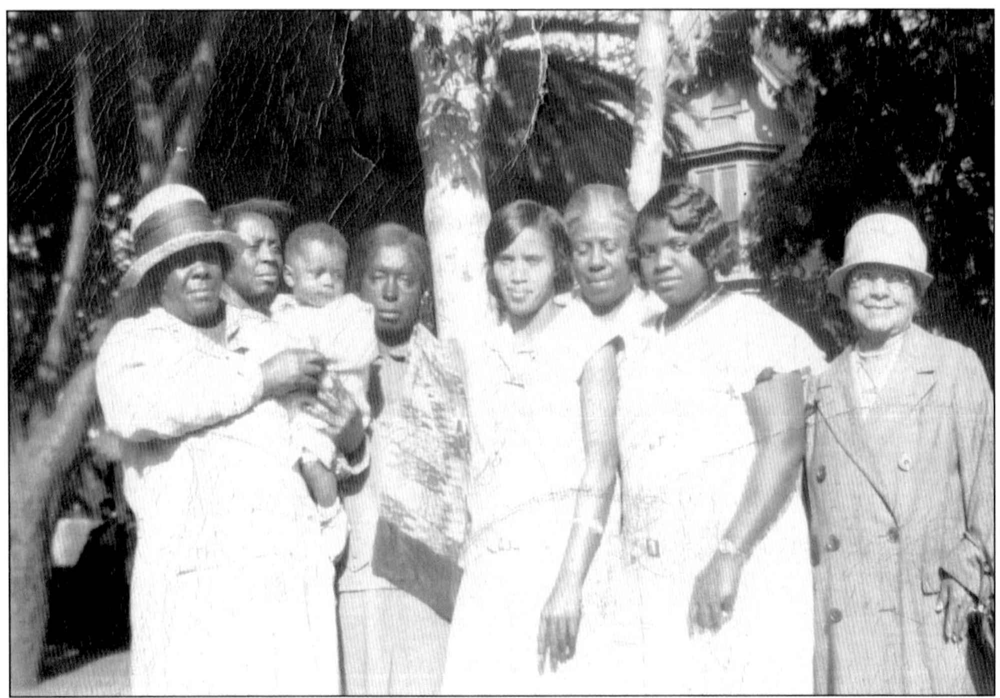

Here is another group of women posing for the camera and depicting the styles of the day in fine fashion.

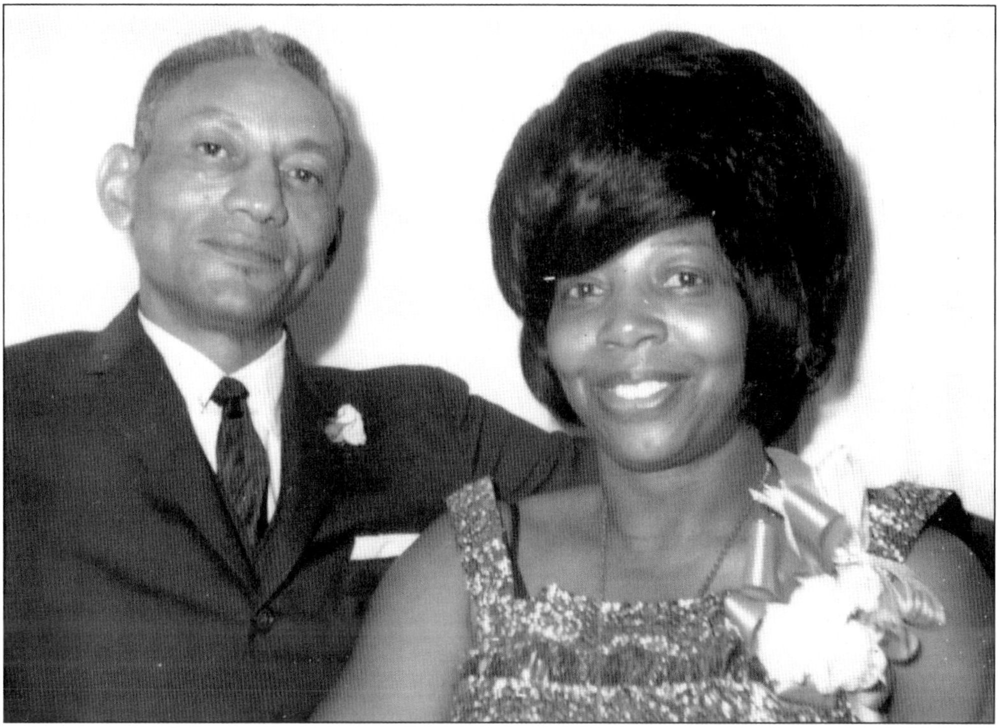

This couple models their "Sunday best." The dark suit and the corsage are a sign that this sitting was on a special day, possibly Mother's Day. (Simmons Collection.)

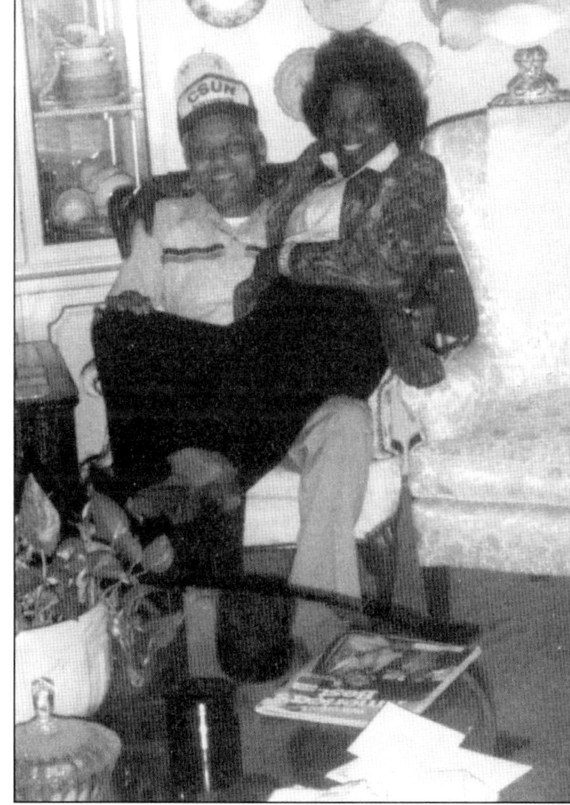


Oakland Pullman porter Herman Simmons and his wife, Noveline, are pictured sitting together in their home. The furniture and other items in the photograph are a statement of the above-average incomes of the porters. (Simmons Collection.)

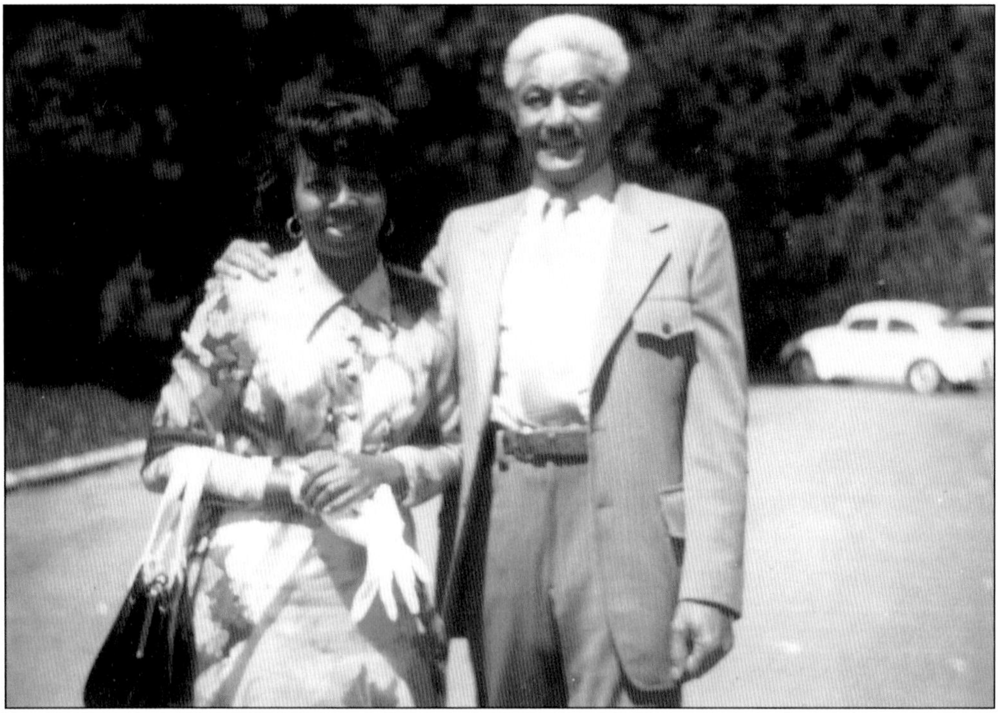

The Simmons's dress and demeanor shows a state of satisfaction with their station in life. (Simmons Collection.)

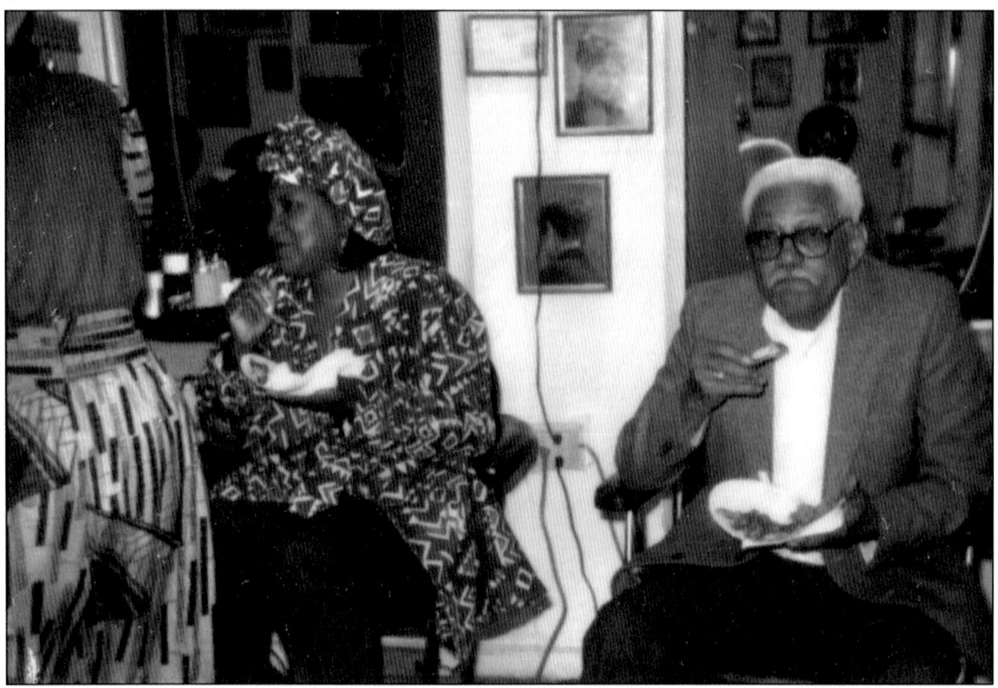

Here a man and woman enjoy a chicken dinner. When Sunday dinner was potluck and included an extremely large crowd, it was customary for everyone to sit in individual chairs, without the benefit of a table, to eat their meals. (Simmons Collection.)

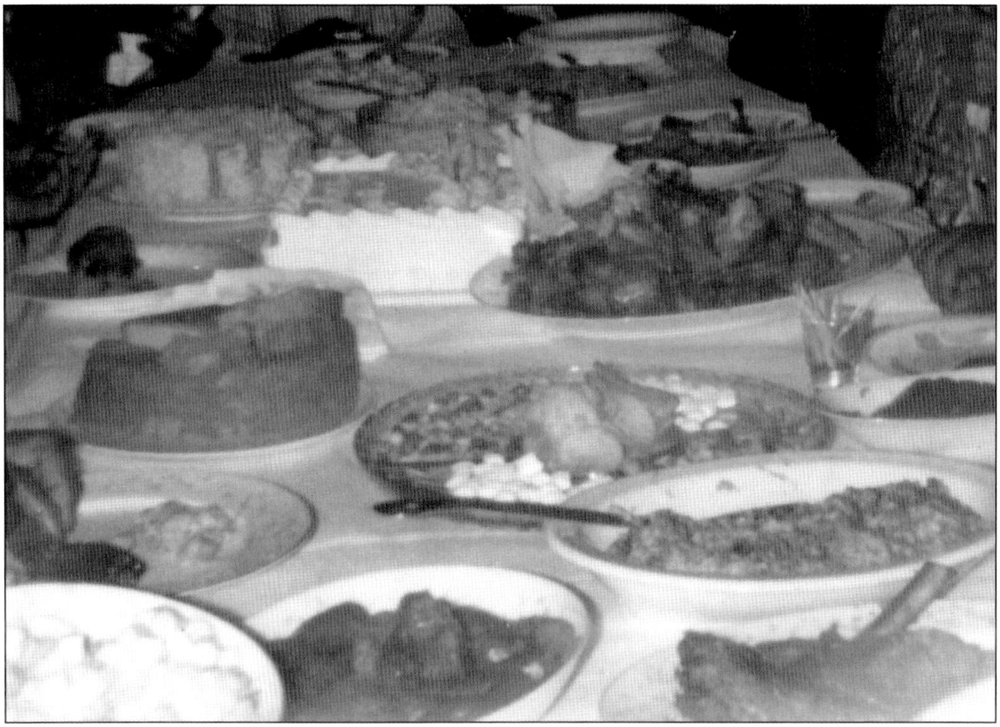

This dining table, filled with a potluck-type dinner, was a symbol of economic success for the host family, and they felt proud to invite everyone to their home. This table display boasts the cooks' best dishes. (Simmons Collection.)

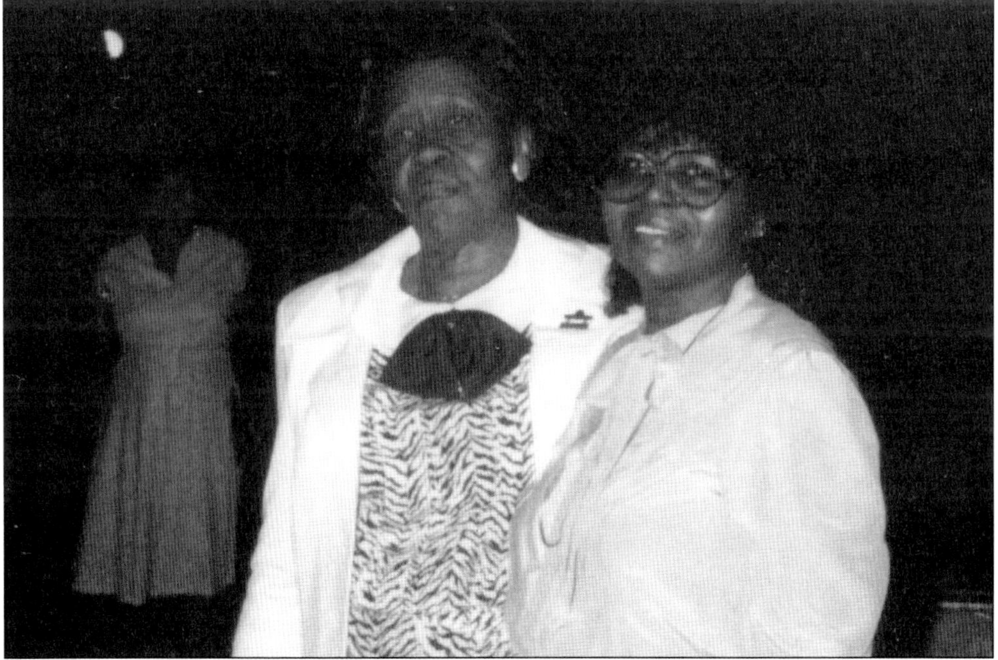

These women enjoy a night event. One woman in this photograph is wearing eyeglasses, an often-unaffordable luxury. (Simmons Collection.)

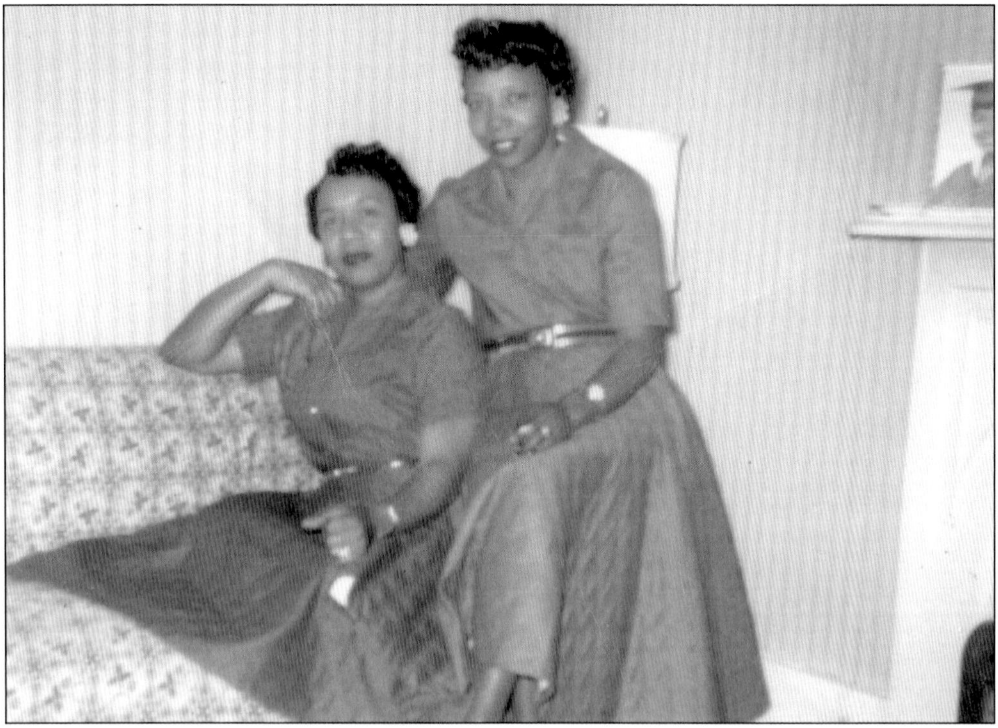

Two ladies are showing off their hoop skirts. Wearing the latest fashion was a sure sign of relative affluence among the Oakland citizens. (Simmons Collection.)

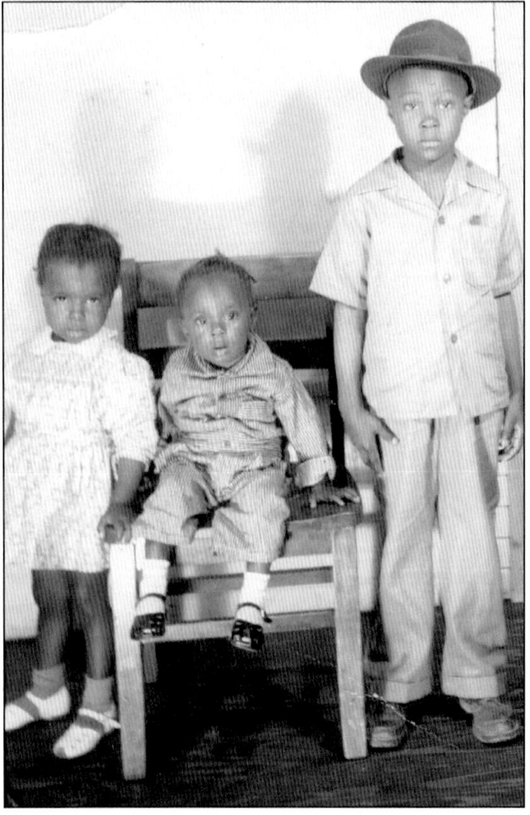

Often children were dressed for photographs to reflect the parents' aspirations for them. These three youngsters well represent their parents as adults. (Simmons Collection.)

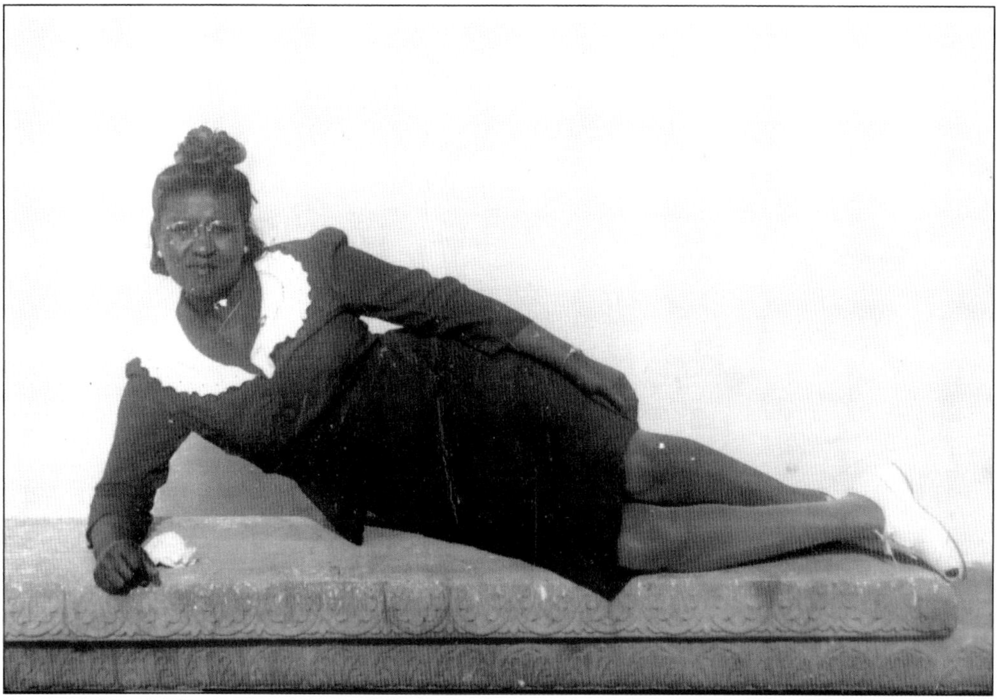

This unidentified woman is dressed to impress. (Simmons Collection.)

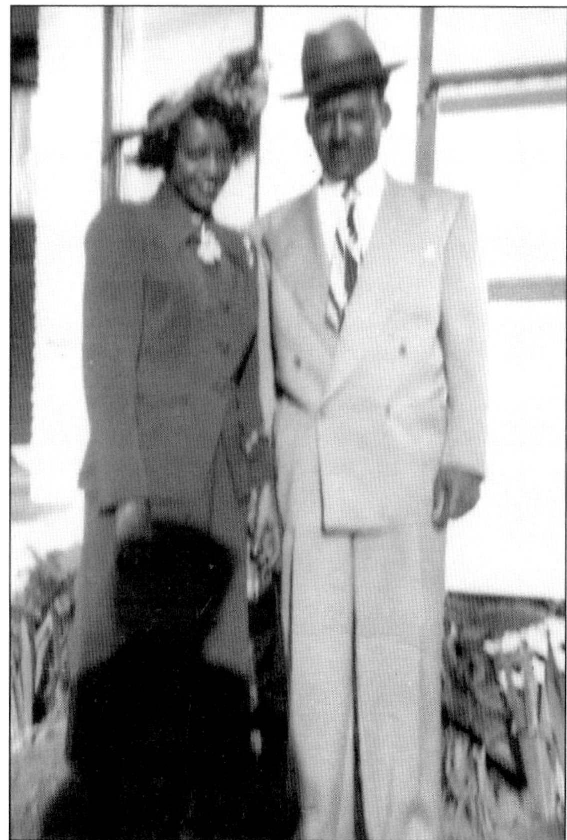

Pictured here is an unidentified couple in typical Sunday dress or for a formal evening out. (Simmons Collection.)

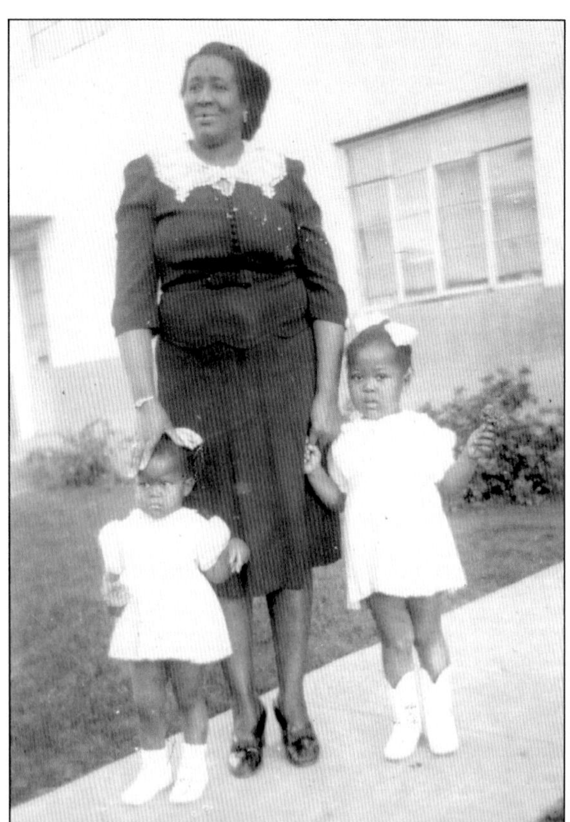

Here an adult woman poses with two little girls. Small children close in age were often dressed alike, in this case indicating that they were sisters. (Simmons Collection.)

Here two young ladies sit on a new Cadillac car, the ultimate announcement of the owner's wealth. Those who could afford such a car were careful to park it so that it could be seen, and it was invariably pictured in every family shot. (Simmons Collection.)

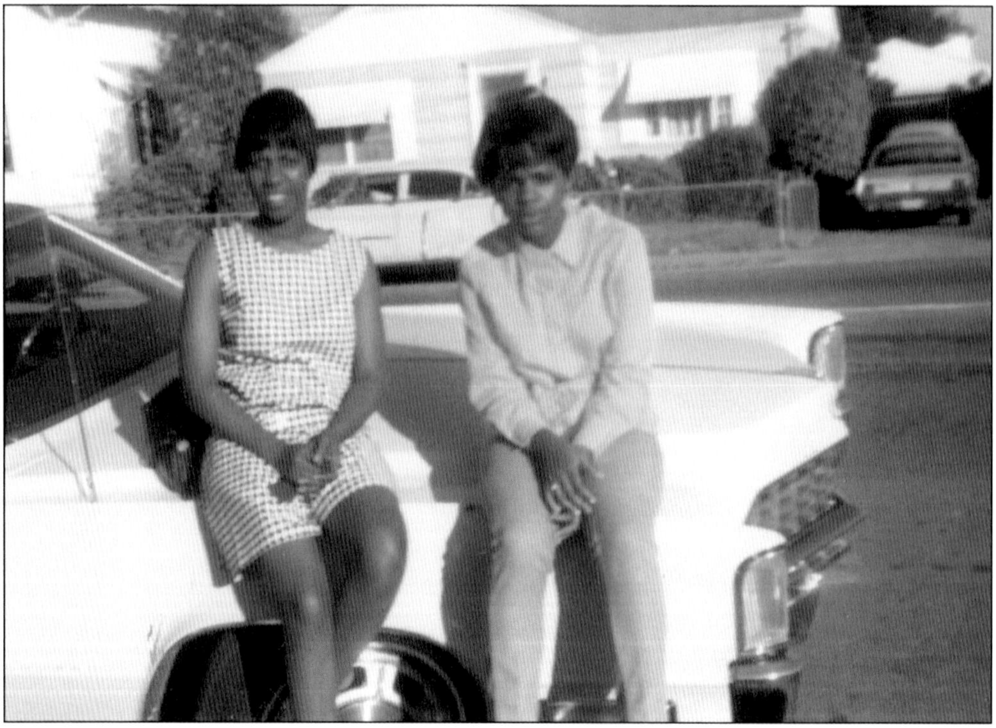

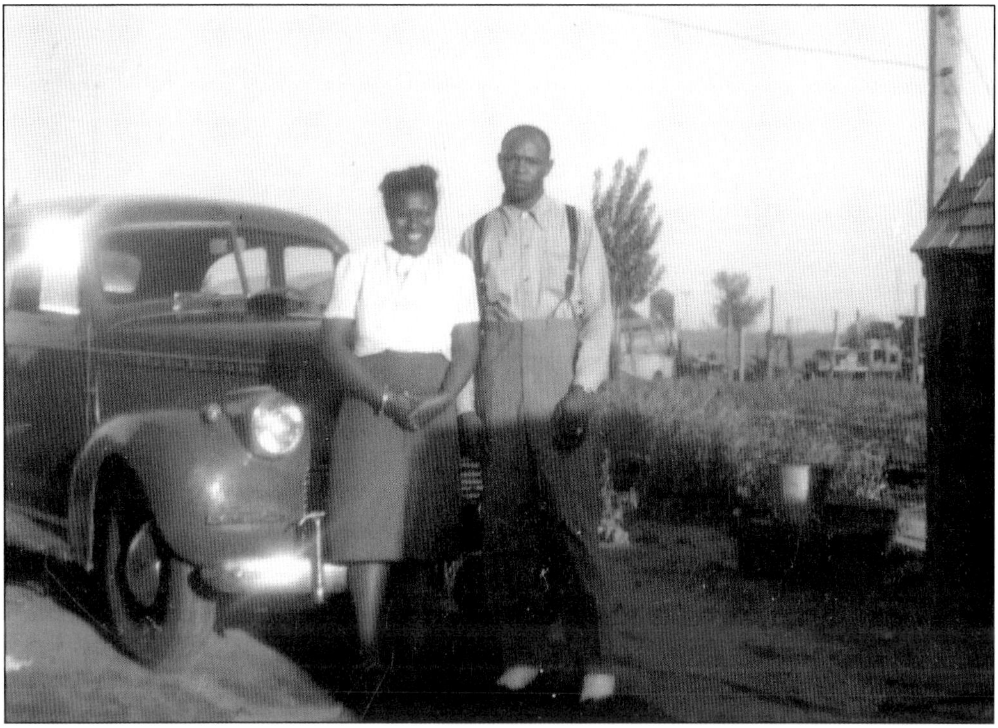

These unidentified people tell a typical story. Well dressed, they are proud of their real estate and their car. (Simmons Collection.)

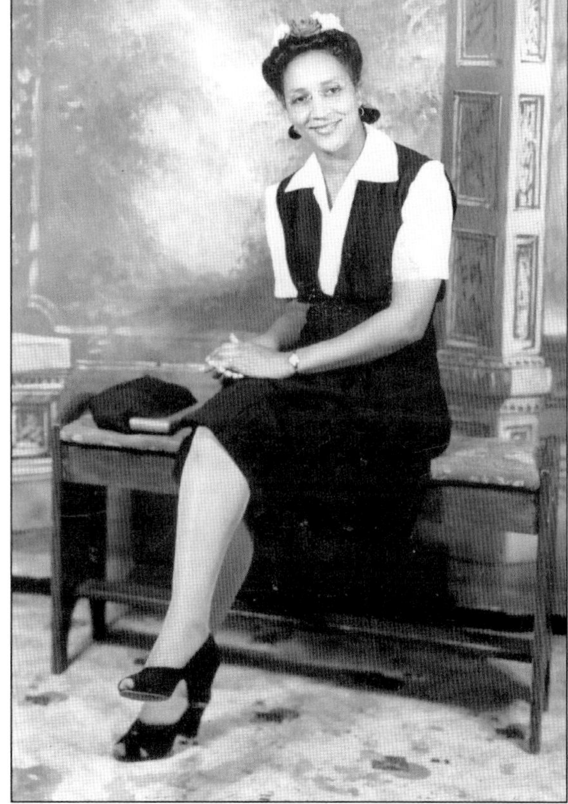

This photograph could have been a sitting for the fine paintings often on exhibit in museums, giving a glimpse of the aristocrats of the era. This well-dressed, well-posed woman illustrates the African American dreamscape. (Simmons Collection.)

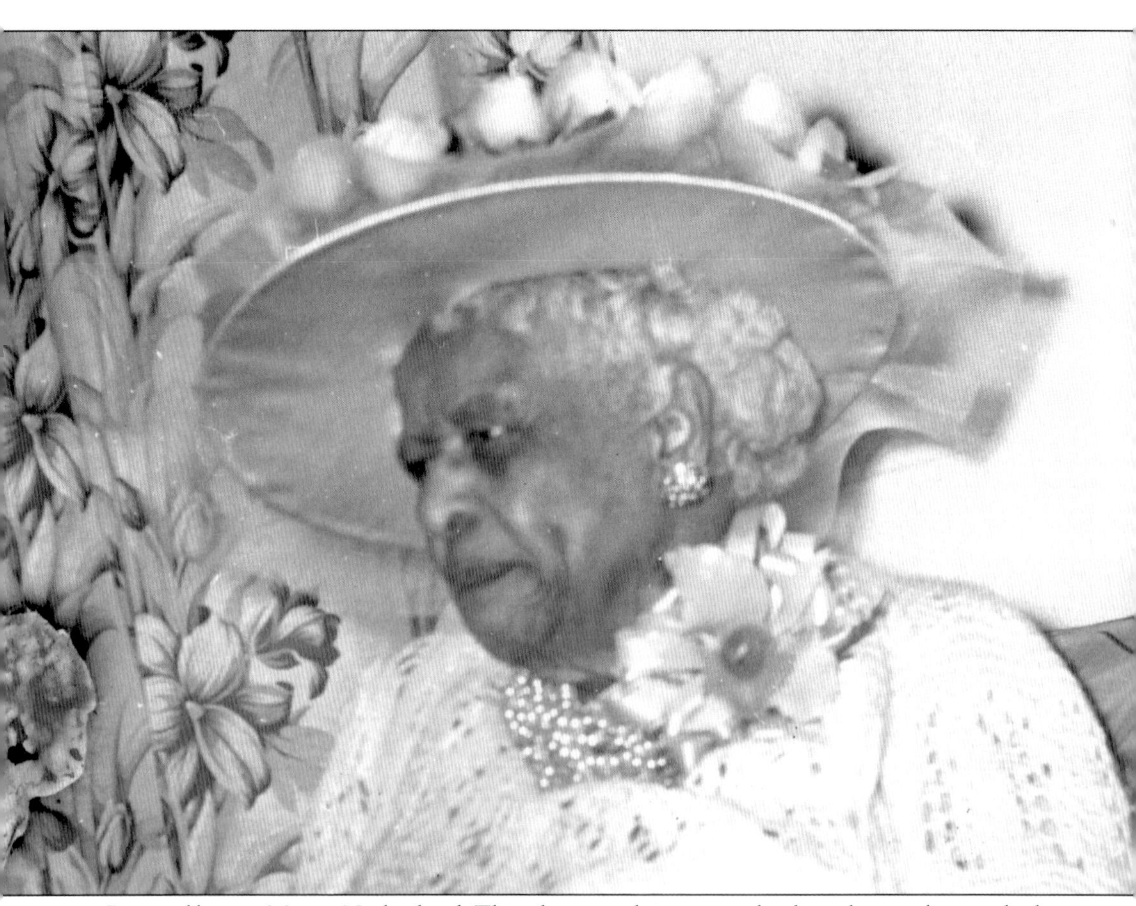

Pictured here is Mamie Netherland. This photograph is reported to have been taken in the house of her birth, located at 714 Pine Street in Oakland.

# Four

# TIME FOR COMMUNITY BUILDING

The modern technological conveniences of the 1940s were not available to everyone. Horse-drawn buggies traveled down Broadway, complete with gas streetlights. The few automobiles were toys of the rich, and a drive outside of town meant encountering rutted dirt roads and no gasoline stations. The average consumer lacked access to the radio, the television, and the movie theater. Running water was a luxury; only prosperous city homes had bathtubs and toilets.

The Pullman porter's job environment exposed them to the ways of the white world. While serving on the trains, they observed what worked and from that created their own community. They observed the different lifestyles of people throughout the country. The porters picked up stock tips and listened to conversations—not meant for them—about how to invest in the stock market. They picked up newspapers and books that passengers left behind. Though working for low wages they learned lessons of how whites became successful. Most important, they realized the value of combining the principles of acquiring education and saving money.

While the Pullman porters led the way as principle heads of the household, the women began to identify the necessary components of a community and to put those components in place. With the opportunity for reliable, full-time employment came a place to raise a family and a way to defend the rights of that family.

The people in the community bought real estate, took new jobs, and opened businesses, defying old denials and built an African American enclave in the West Oakland community. The community grew as word spread to relatives "back home" in the southern states that California was sunny and the jobs were plentiful.

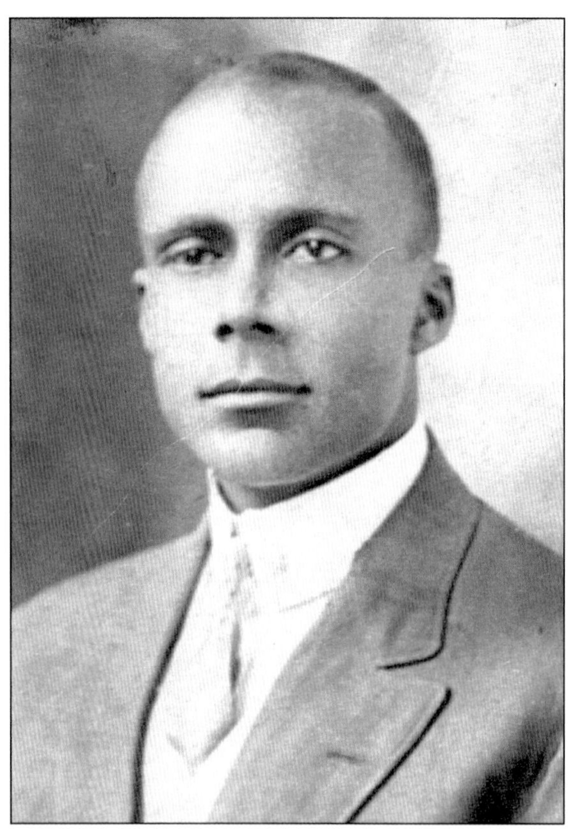

Dr. William. M. Watts is pictured here in the mid-1920s. In 1926, Watts opened a new for-profit, 22-bed hospital facility "with all the latest equipment." The hospital provided in-patient care for Oakland's black citizens who were unwelcome at other health care facilities. The facility also offered a training program for black nurses. Unfortunately the hospital was financially unsuccessful and closed.

William Watts is seen here in California posing with his automobile, the typical symbol of financial success in the 1920s.

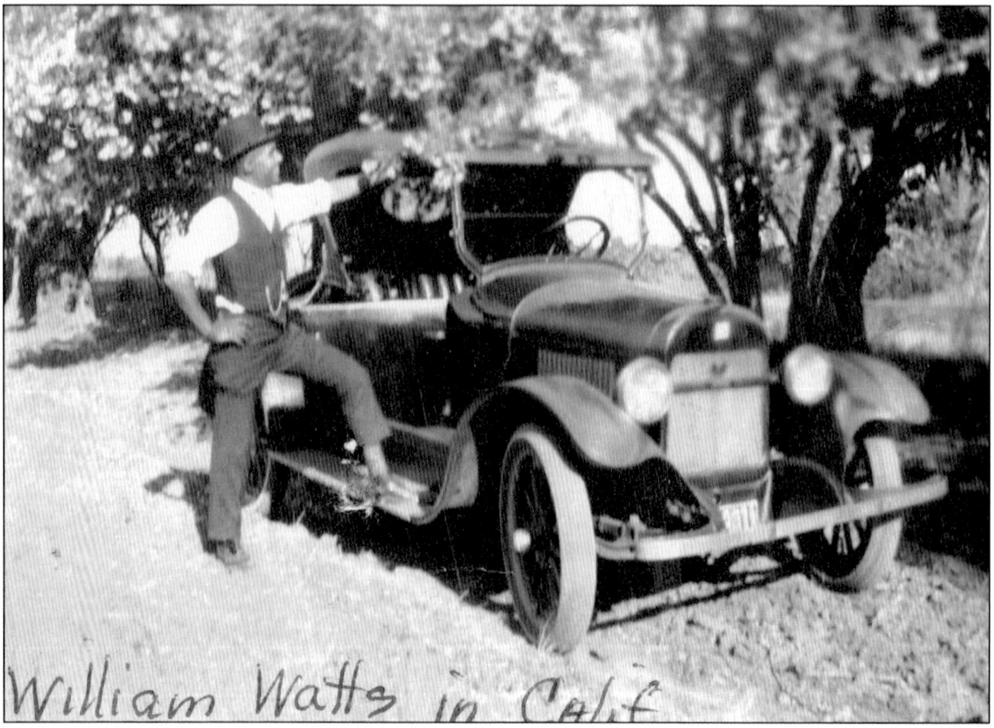

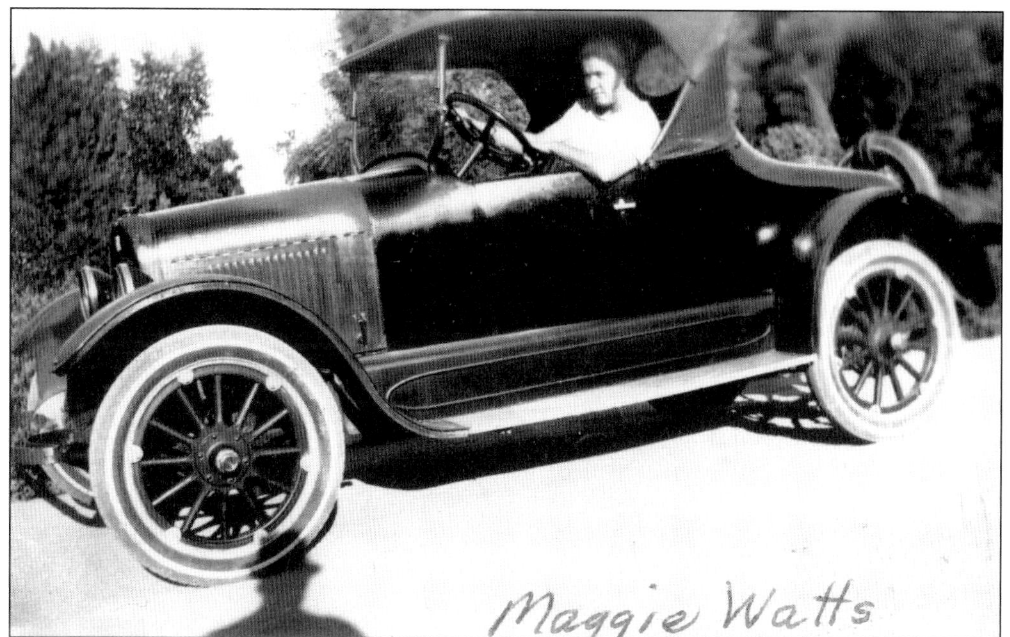


Maggie Watts, William's wife, enjoyed the car and had time to contribute to community organizational activities.

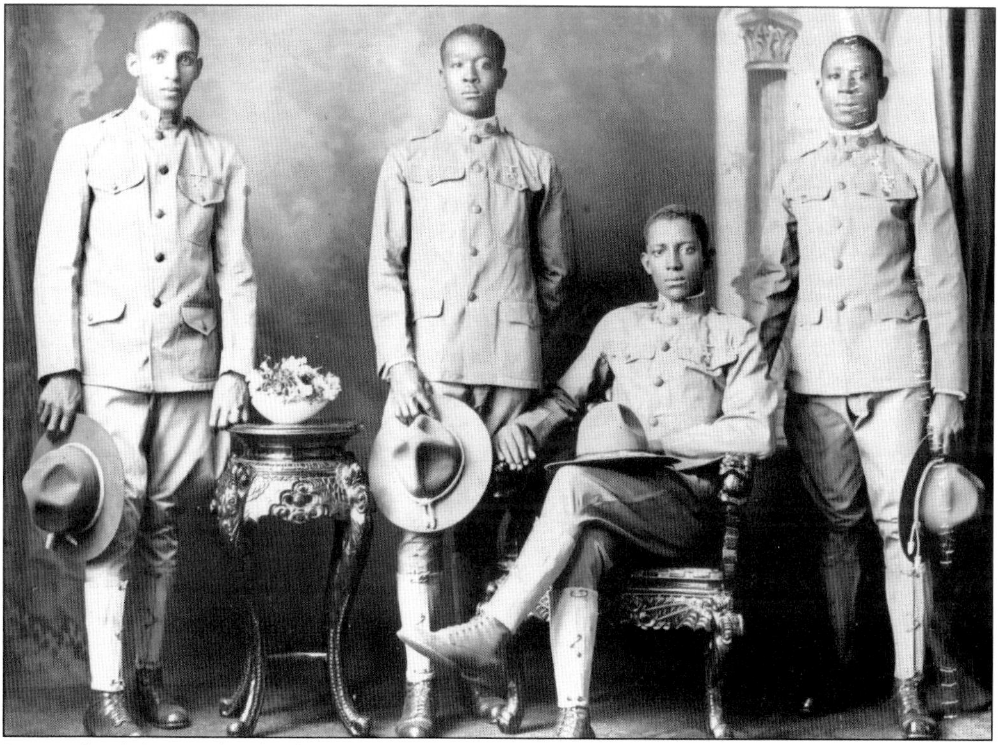

Pictured at left is Hadwick Thompson's uncle, Edwin Thompson, who was serving in the military in France in 1918. The other unidentified soldiers are members of Edwin's unit. Close family ties were a mainstay in Oakland police officer Hadwick Thompson's life.

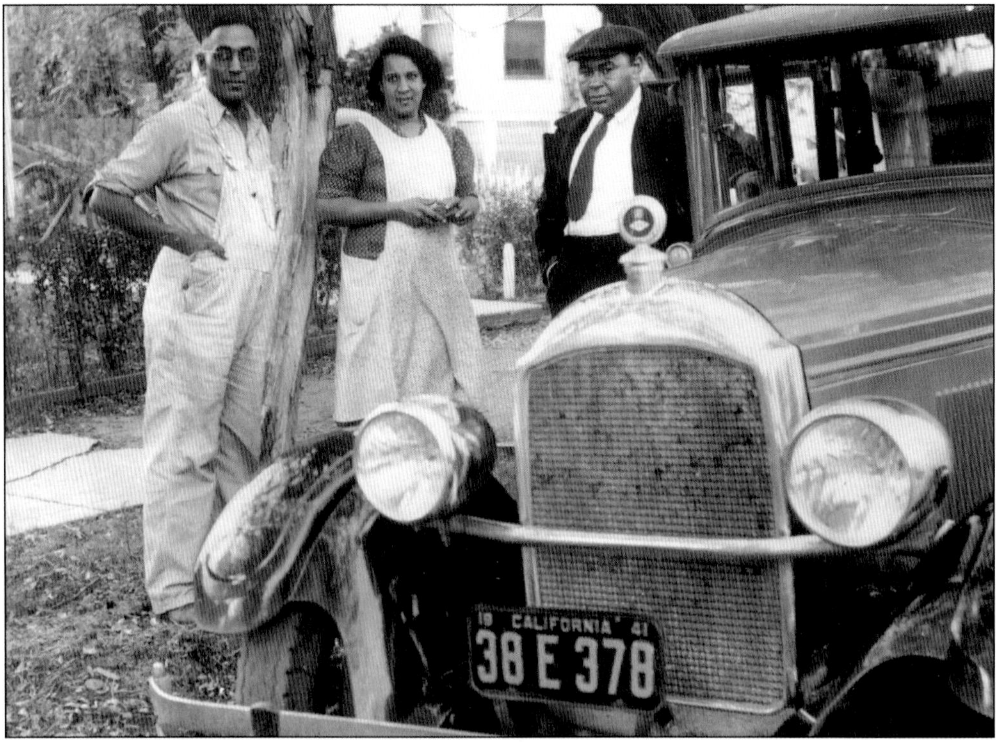

Pictured in 1941 are, from left to right, Hadwick Thompson's parents, Hadwick William and Edna Ora, with an unidentified family friend. The Thompsons contributed to Oakland's community, raising a son who became a police officer.

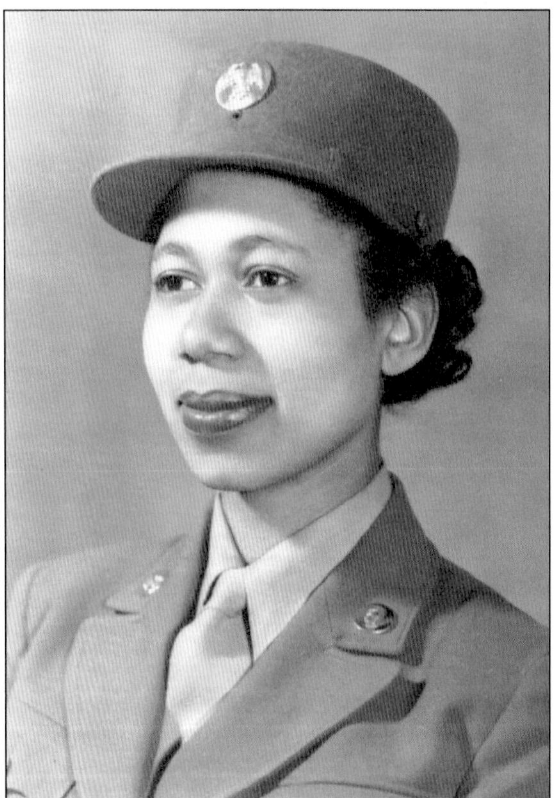

Pictured here in March 1943 is Faracita Hall Wyatt of Oakland, a member of the World War II Women's Army Corps Auxiliary. In 1948, Public Law 625 gave women permanent status in the army, navy, air force, and marines. The Women's Army Corps 688th Battalion was a World War II unit composed of approximately 850 black women. Wyatt acquired important career skills in this unit, which she used upon her return to Oakland.

This navy officer is a worthy representative of America's most revered branch of the military. Although the navy admitted relatively few blacks and restricted job assignments, the pride of this position, and the ability of him to act as a community builder through it, is evident in this officer.

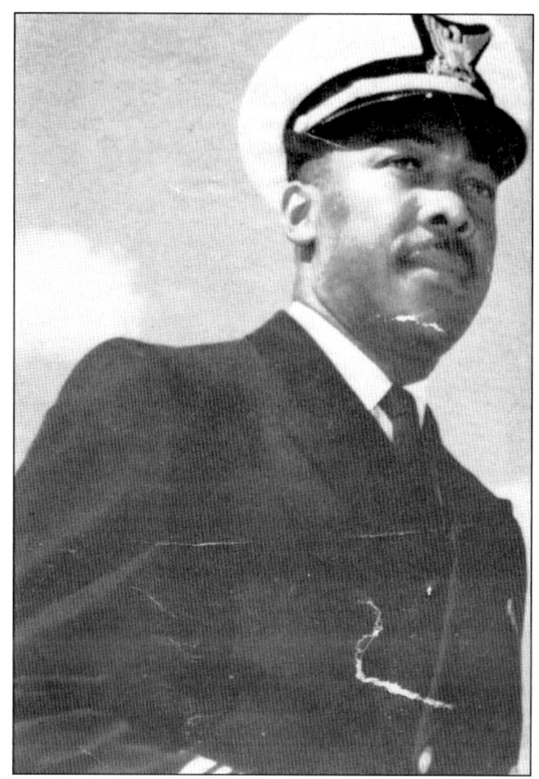

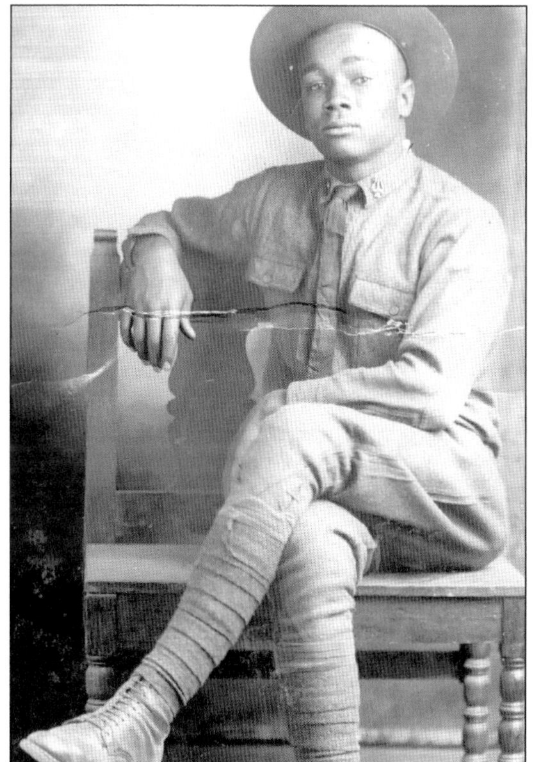

Pictured here is a World War I soldier. At the outbreak of war, young African American men quickly rushed to enlist; a desire to serve and protect the home front was a natural extension to the value of community building. However, the War Department issued an order to halt the recruitment of "colored volunteers."

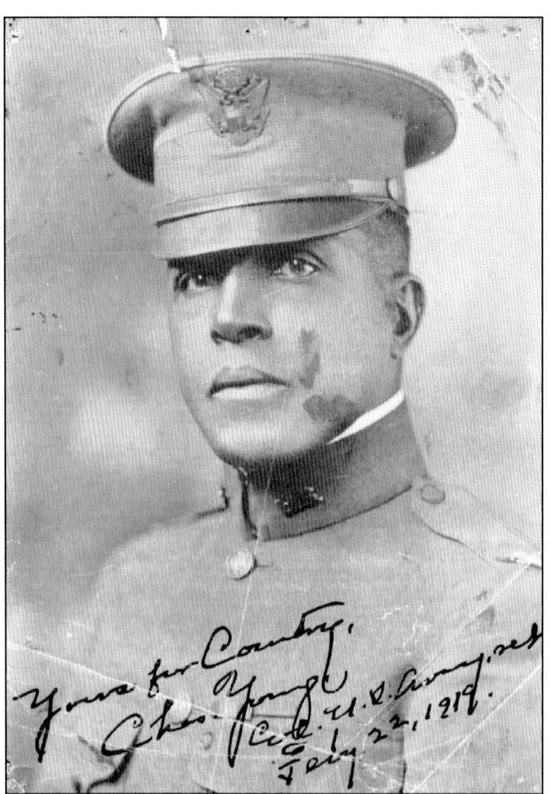

Charles Young, pictured here on July 22, 1919, was colonel of a Buffalo Soldier unit, building community pride while serving as acting superintendent of the Sequoia National Park. He named a giant redwood tree the Booker T. Washington Tree. Later the National Forest Service named a tree in honor of Colonel Young, and a street in Allensworth, California, bears his name.

Here is a group of shipfitters on the swing shift at Yard No. 3 at the Kaiser Company Inc. Because of the consistent work of advocates such as Francis Albrier and C. L. Dellums and their organizations, war industries were forced to open jobs for qualified workers. In the early 1940s, African American migration to Oakland caused the population to jump to four times what it had been in the 1930s.

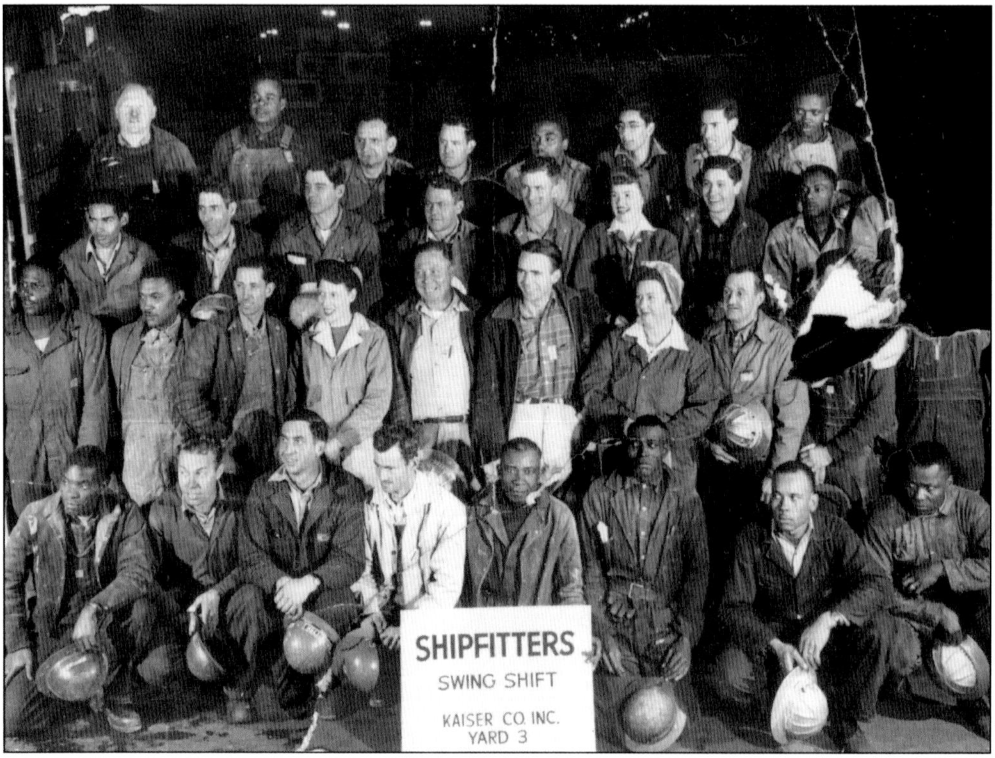

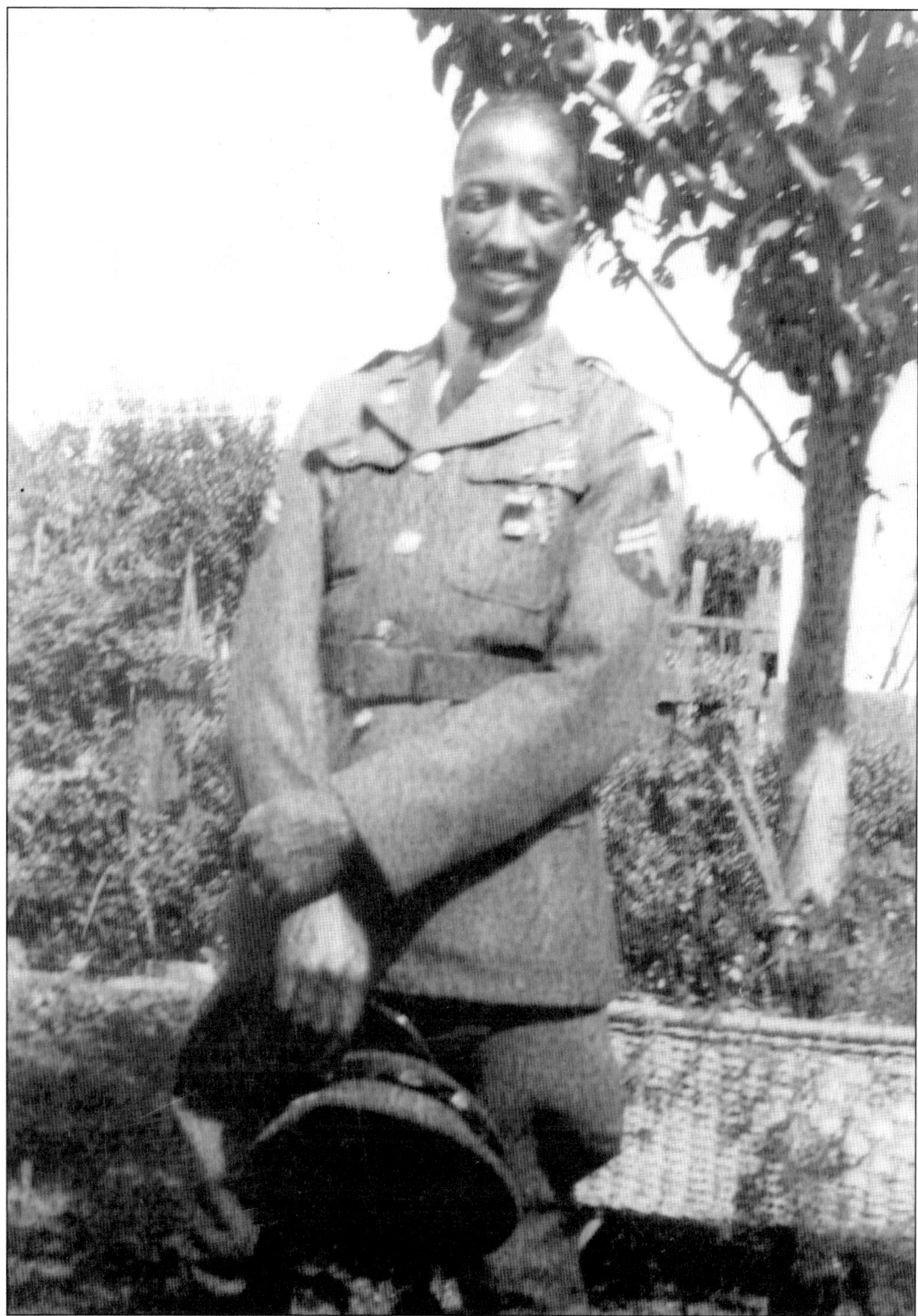

Beverly Ward, an Oakland resident during World War II, benefitted from Executive Order 8802, which granted legal support to African Americans' right of equal access to government jobs.

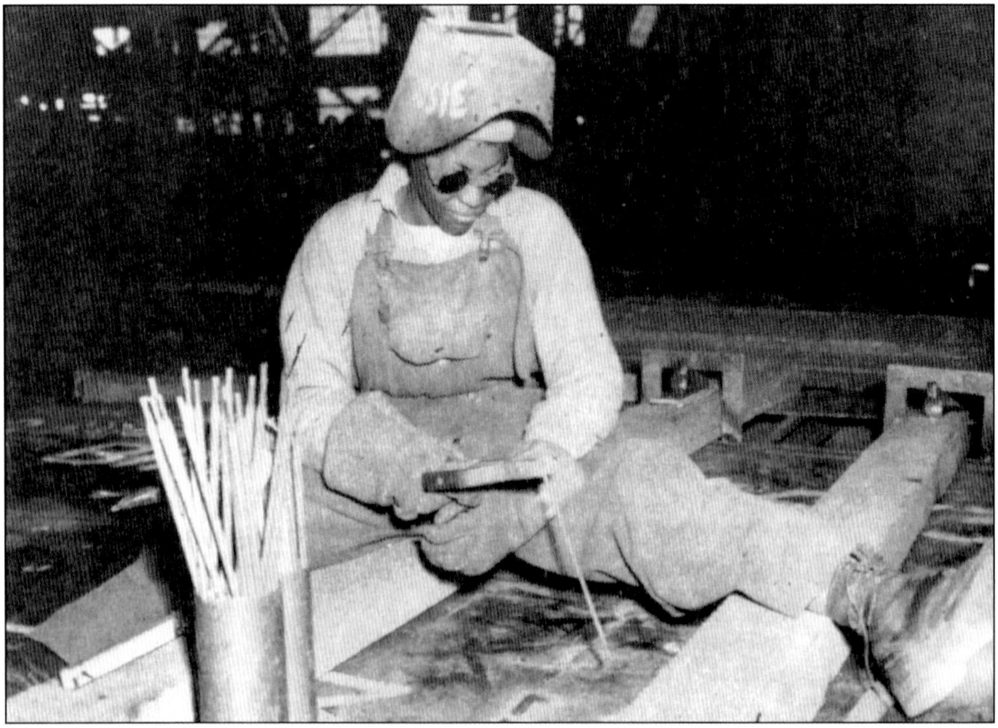

The rapid growth of the war industries and the enlistment of the men into the armed forces created a high demand for workers in a variety of jobs, which black women were willing to fill. This woman welder of World War II and her colleagues helped to satisfy that demand.

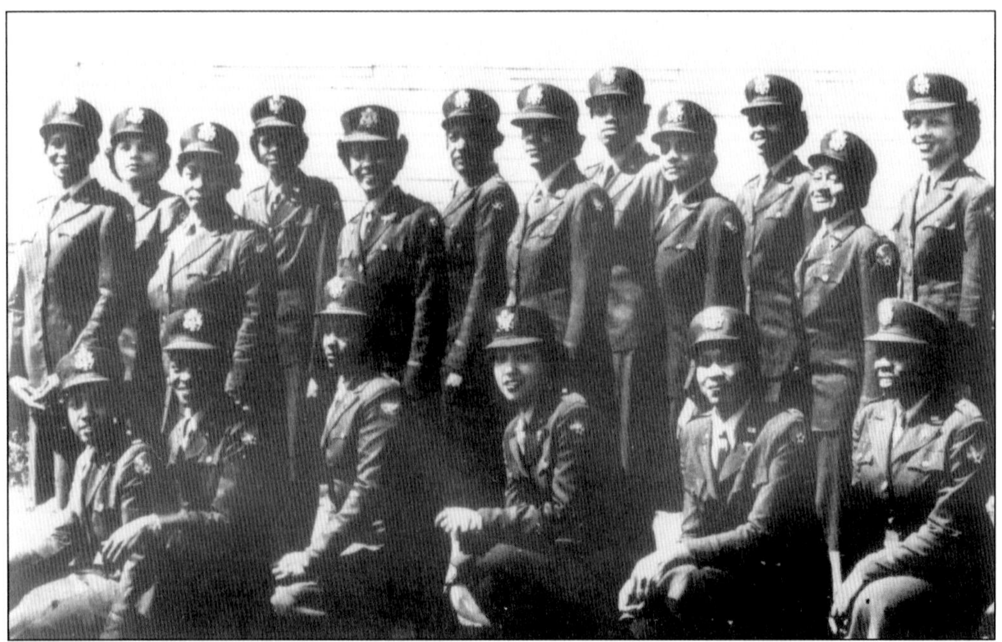

At war's end, these nurses returned to Oakland better trained, more experienced, and ready to serve in local hospitals and clinics.

Willis Ray Woods, an orderly at Stanford University, was killed in an accident on the San Francisco waterfront while working as a longshoreman *c.* 1950.

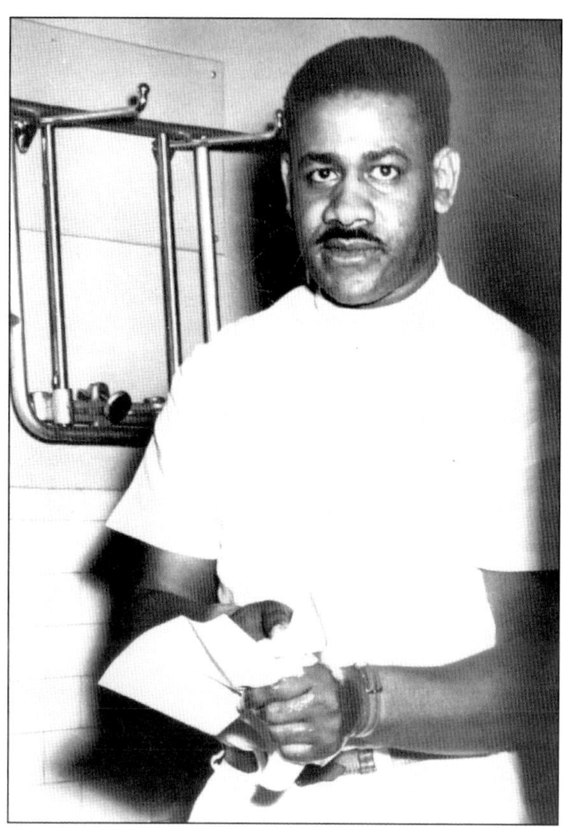

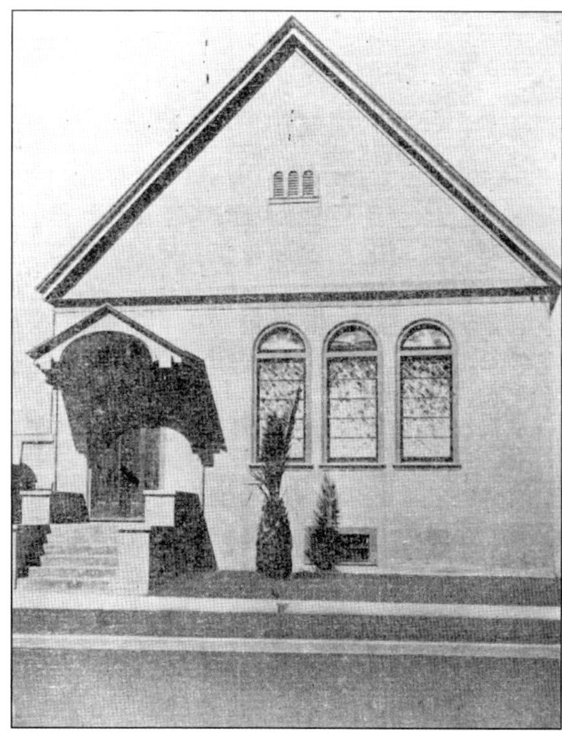

Pictured here is the Beth Eden Baptist Church on Filbert Street between Seventh and Eighth Streets. The members of this congregation were responsible for many community-based service clubs and organizations.

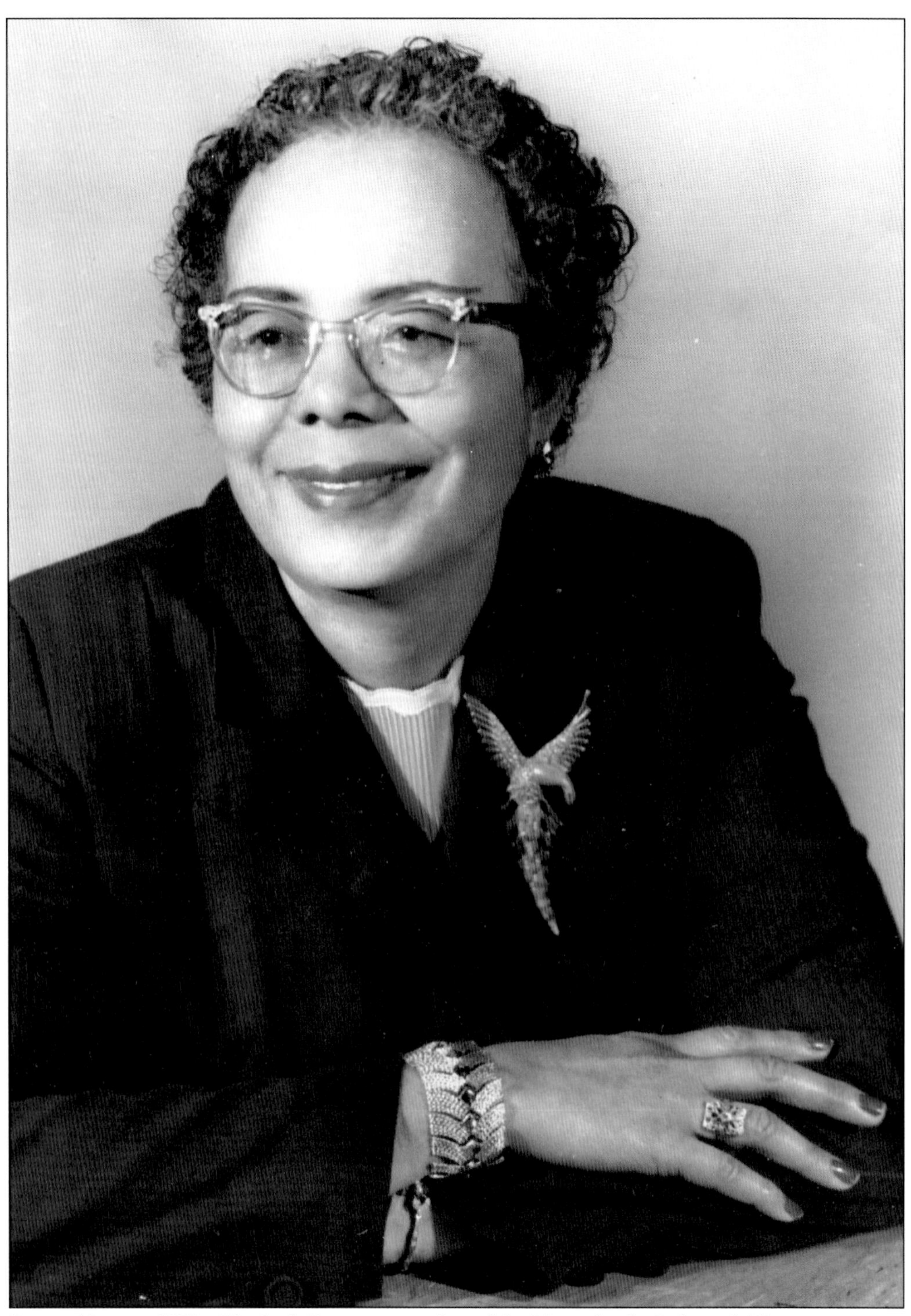

Pictured here in 1959 is Elizabeth Brown, a member of the Home for the Infirmed. The organization was established by a group of local black women, because white retirement homes in the area refused black application.

Francis M. Albrier, the first black woman elected to Alameda Central Committee, was a member of other political action and public service organizations. The Little Citizens Club provided citizenship education for those who had not voted before. She also participated in numerous civil rights activities and broke the color and gender barriers at Richmond Kaiser Shipyards. She passed the welder's test, applied for a position, and was accepted into the union.

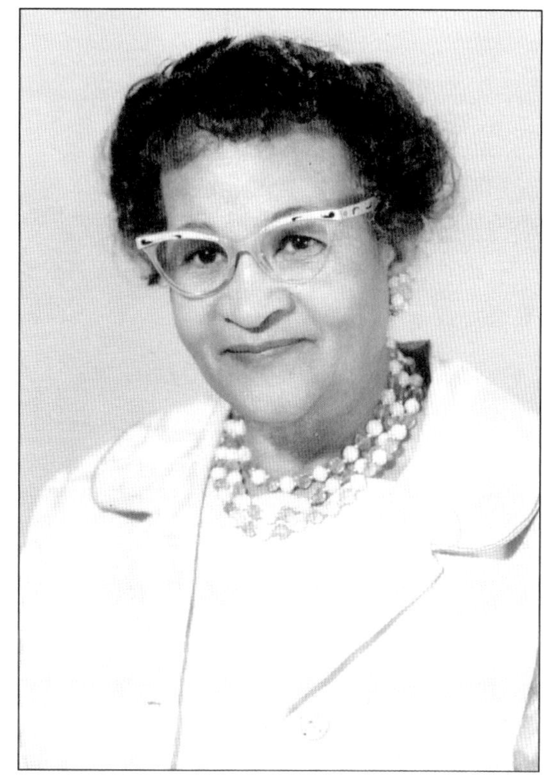

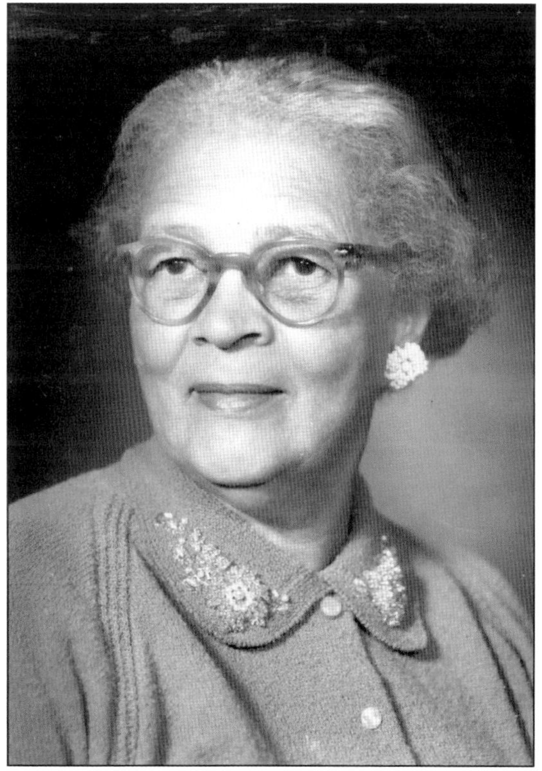

Selma B. Willis spearheaded the rescue of the grave of Delilah Beasley. At her own expense, Delilah, a self-taught historian, meticulously researched her book, *The Negro Trailblazers of California*, which chronicled the worthy achievements of African American. Journalism was her powerful platform to combat racial discrimination in the state.

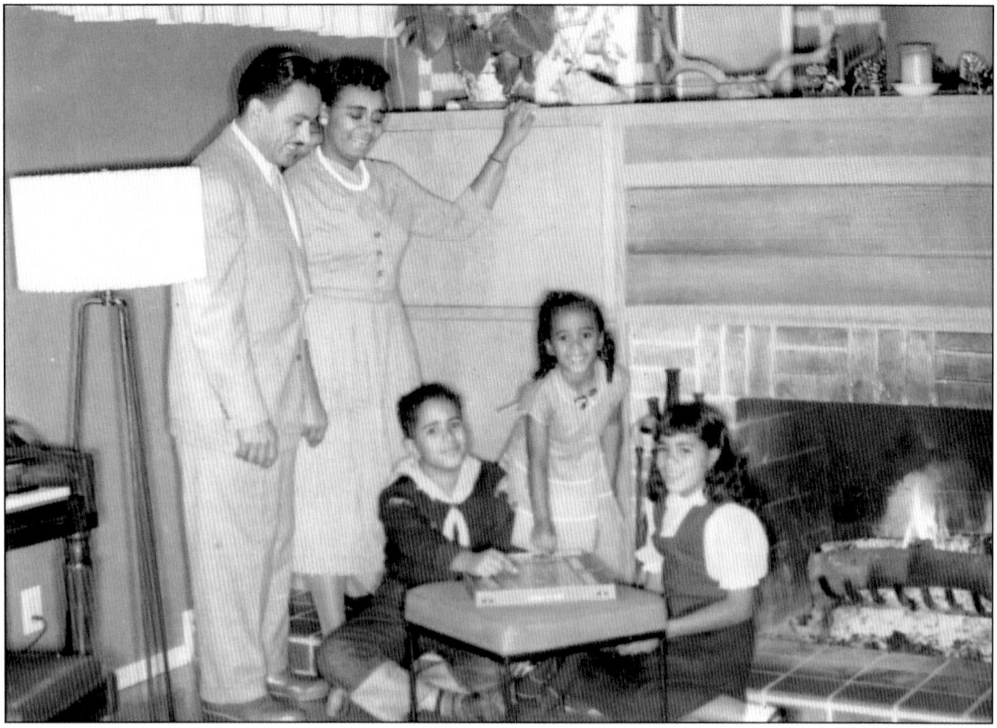

Pictured here is the Mitchell family in their living room in 1954. From left to right are Reverend and Mrs. Mitchell, Henry Jr. (9 years), Muriel (7 years), and Elizabeth (5 years).

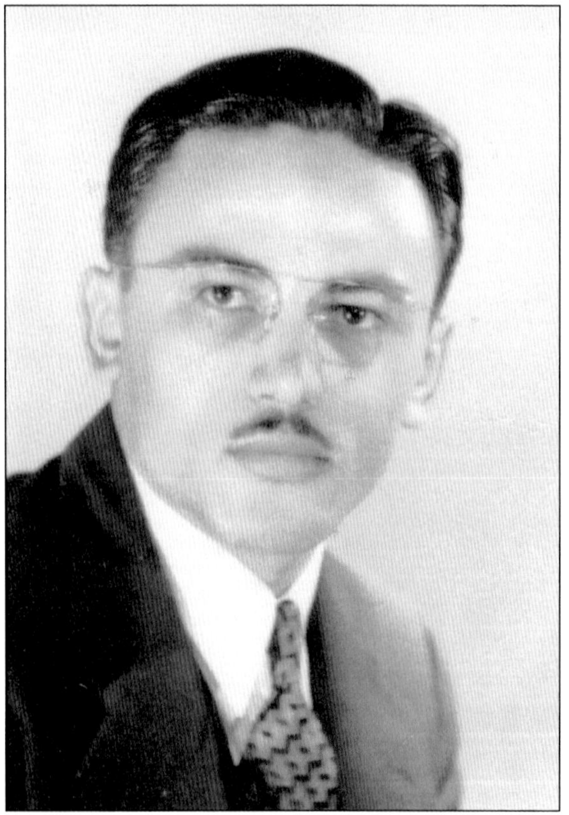

Pictured is Rev. Henry Mitchell in 1945; a family man who took time for the institutions of both his faith and his family.

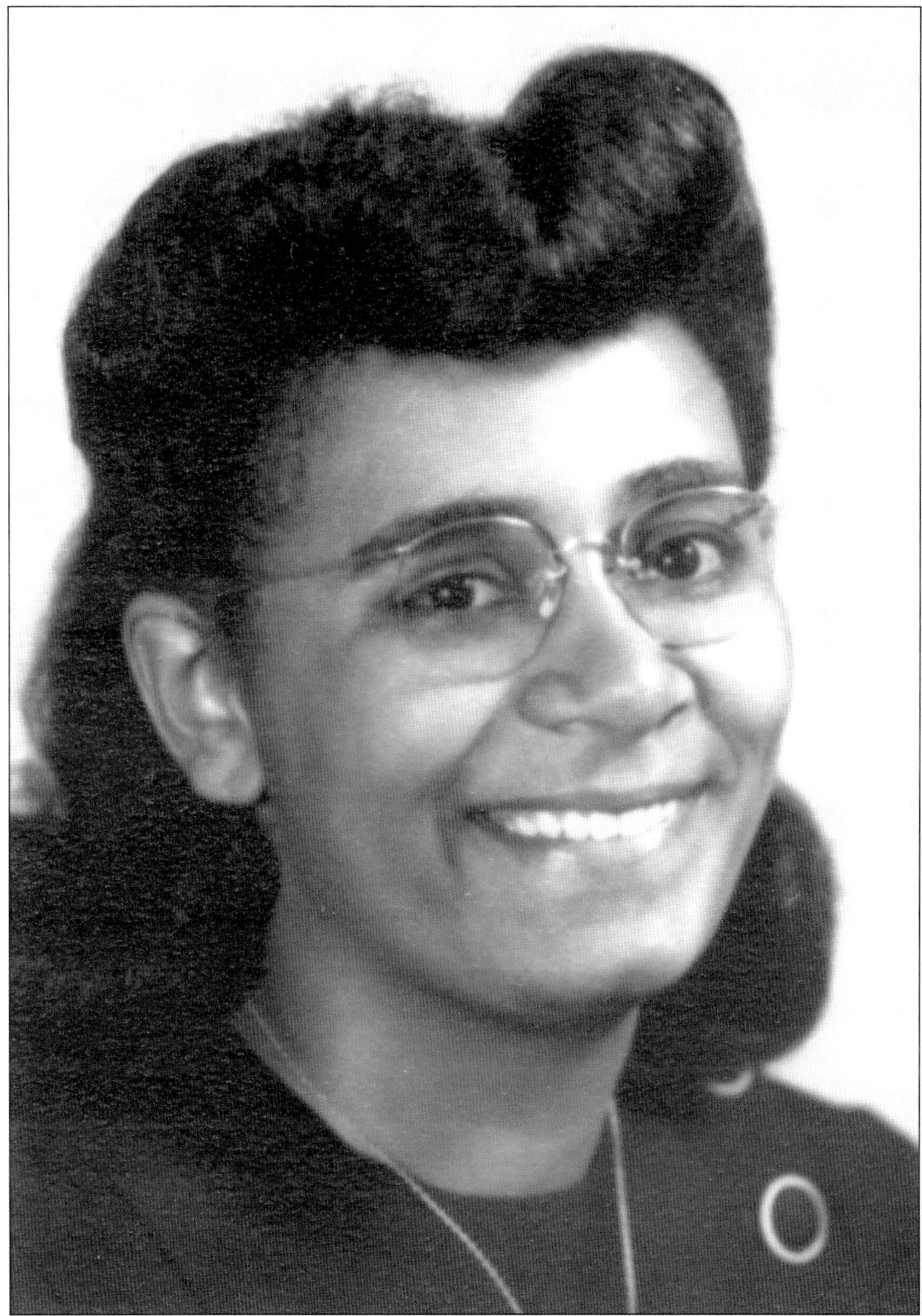

Ella Mitchell, pictured here in 1946, wife of Rev. Henry Mitchell and mother of their three children, was one of many Oakland women contributors to the community.

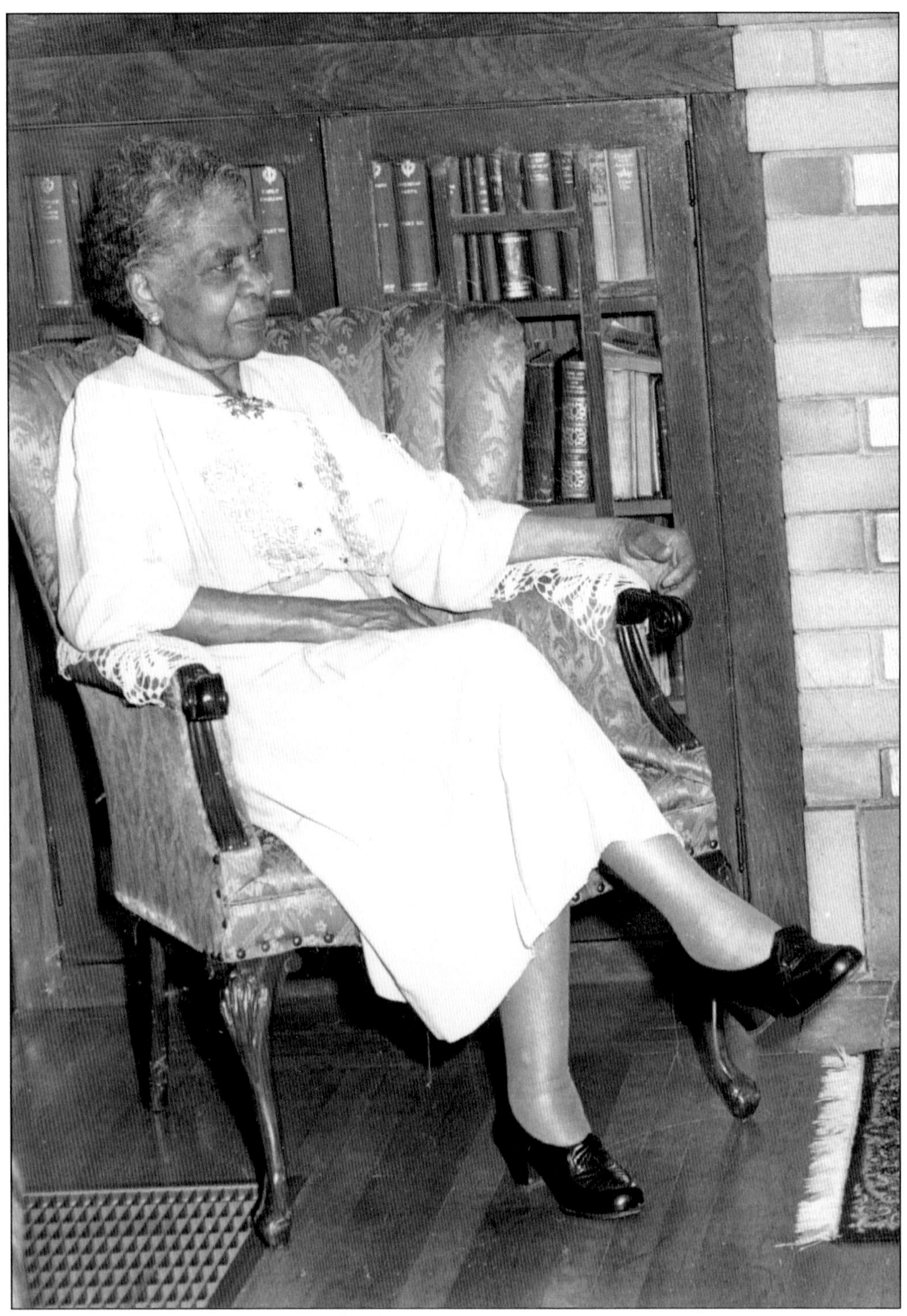

Pictured here relaxing in a chair at her home is Cassie Moten.

Seen here is William R. Moten. Many fathers could only pose in the sitting room on Sunday, because the usual after-work activity was dinner and then it was off to bed.

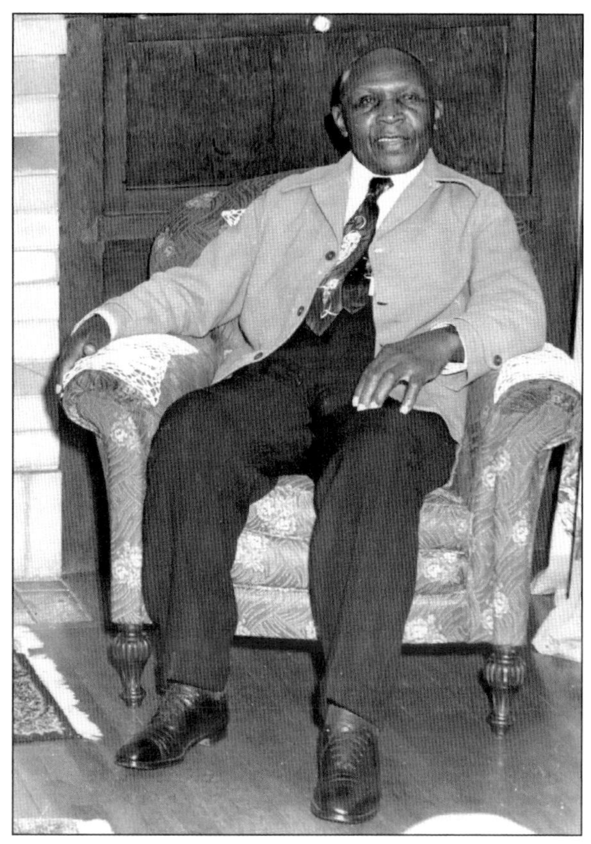

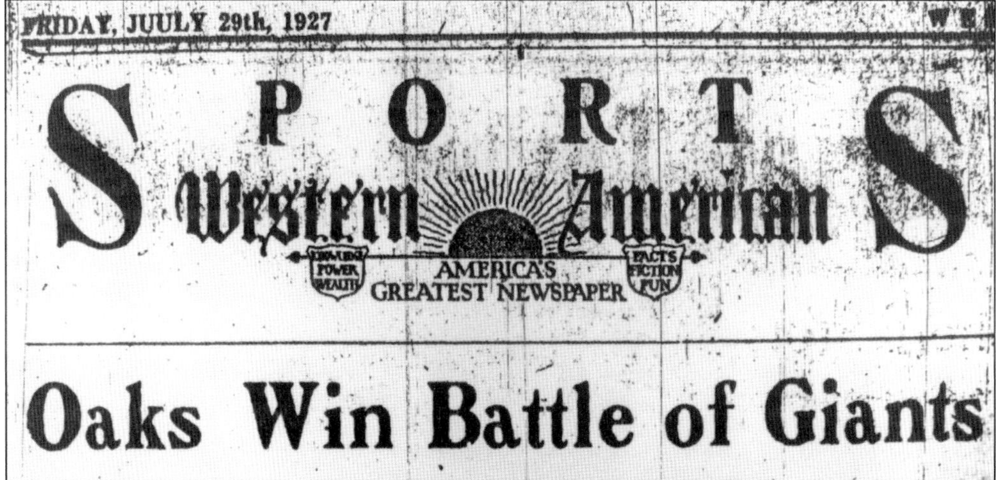

FRIDAY, JUULY 29th, 1927

S P O R T S

Western American

POWER WEALTH

AMERICA'S GREATEST NEWSPAPER

FACTS FICTION FUN

Oaks Win Battle of Giants

On July 29, 1927, the Oakland Royal Giants won the championship and retained possession of the title of Colored Champions of Northern California. America's favorite pastime attracted African American players, teams, and fans from Oakland to the championship game in Vallejo, California.

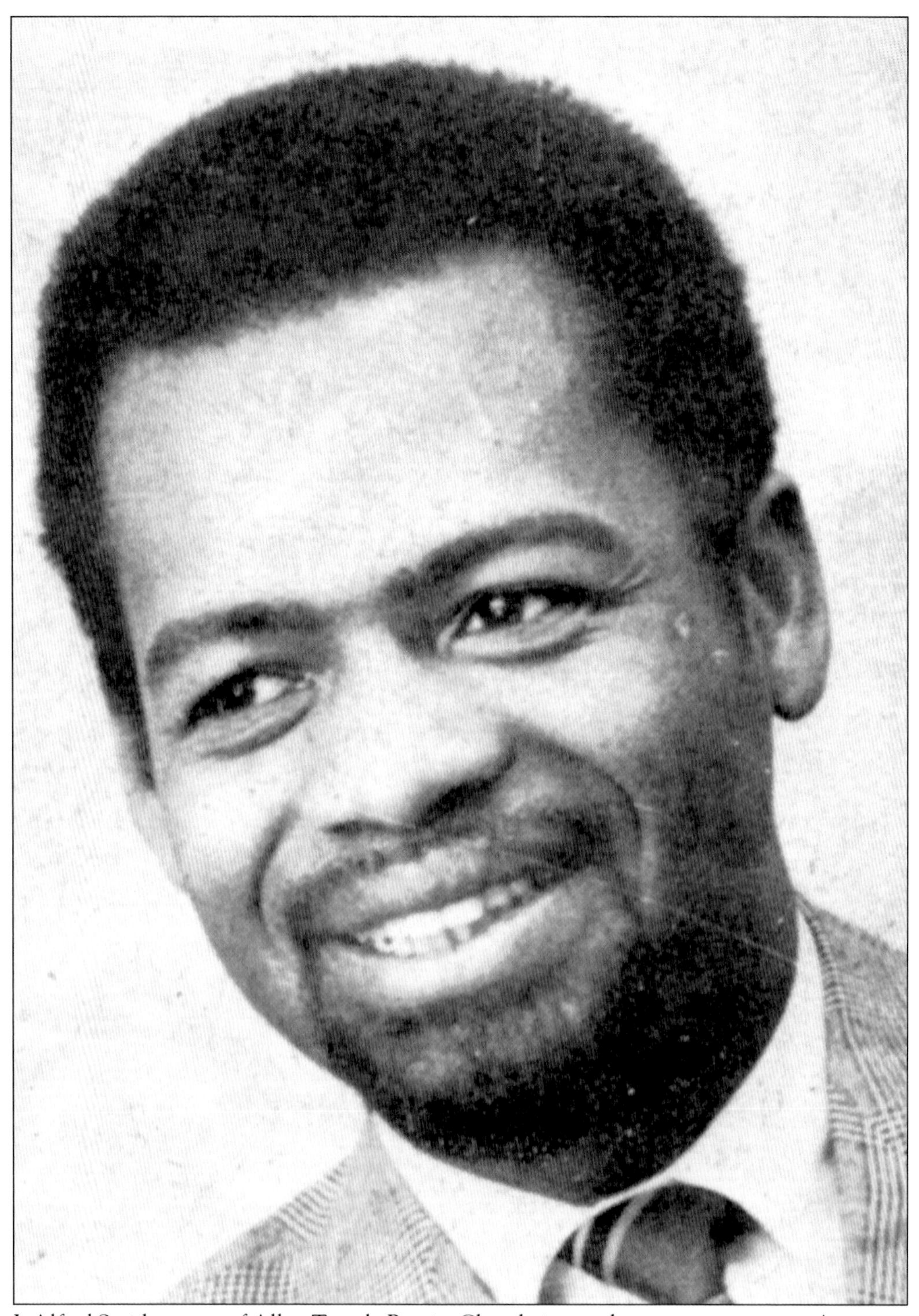

J. Alfred Smith, pastor of Allen Temple Baptist Church, is seen here as a young man. As pastor, Reverend Smith was always a leader in political and social activities.

# *Five*

# West Oakland Blacks Acquire Real Property

*It is almost necessary for you to own your own homes. Rents are high and real estate agents do not care to rent to Negroes.*

—Oakland Sunshine, 1907

By the 1870s, Oakland had become home base for a growing number of Pullman porters and their families. The prestige of their jobs made them stand out as pillars in the West Oakland community. They and others invested in real property for homes, businesses, and churches. As property owners, the dream continued to take shape.

The architecture of West Oakland featured cornices and cupolas, porticos and pilasters, gables and garlands, finials and festoons, and turned balusters and fluted columns. The homes and buildings were a sure indication that African Americans shared in the American dream. The ability to own property with full protection of the law brought a sense of a strong economic backbone and placed West Oakland in a national context.

The perception was that Pullman porters were the backbone of a solid middle class. African Americans in West Oakland believed that with consistent hard work, opportunities to "move-up" were within their grasp, free of physical and psychological threats.

Two facts stand out. The first is that 74 percent of California's black women in the late 1800s could read and write. The second fact is that many of the Pullman porters had earned college degrees and had a "sophisticated porters' education." It is not a surprise, given the economic prowess of this population, that they began acquiring real property.

The growing need to express cultural tastes within these West Oaklanders' homes, worship in church buildings, and socialize in concert halls and benevolent lodges had to be filled. As early as the 1860s, facilities were purchased or rented for Masonic lodges, billiard saloons, bathhouses, newspaper printing offices, and black-operated schools.

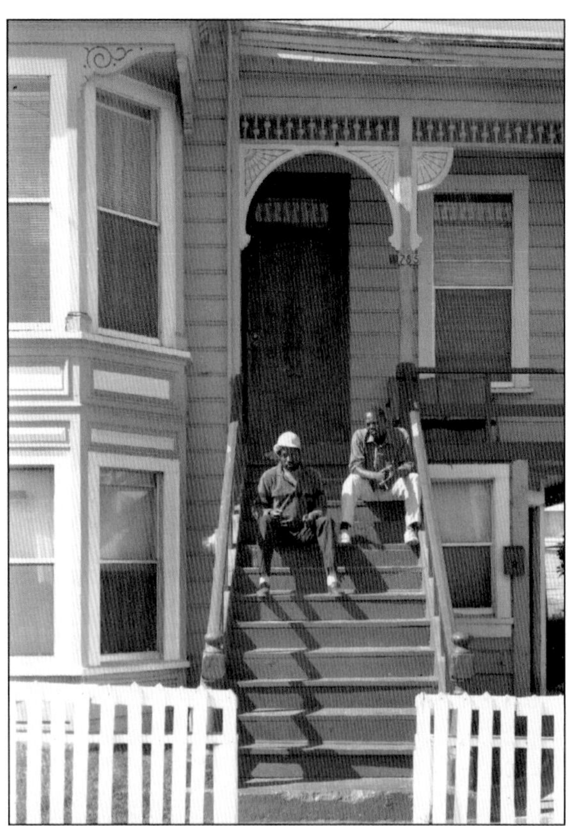

Believed to be the family home, this house, very near Shorey Street, was named after sea captain William Shorey. The Shoreys entertained the great Booker T. Washington in their home during one of his visits to West Oakland.

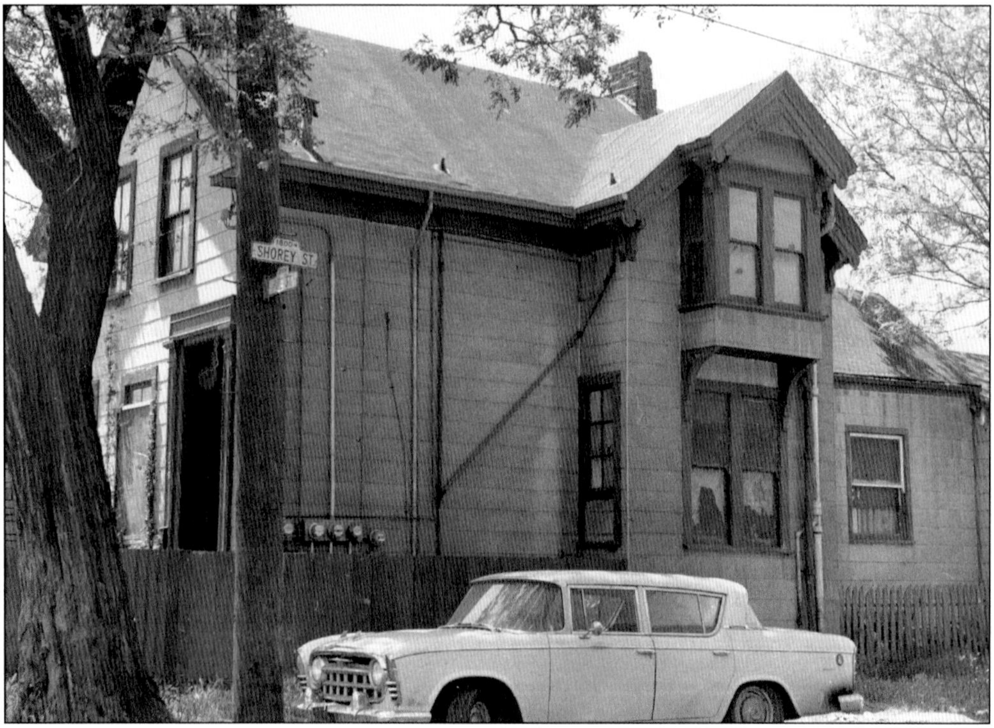

The street sign in this photograph marks the corner of Shorey and Pine Streets in West Oakland. It was renamed to honor the community contributions of both William Shorey and his wife, Samantha.

Here is a close-up of a home at Fifth and Wood Streets. Pullman porters were required to live near the railroad stations in West Oakland and eventually bought homes such as this one in the community.

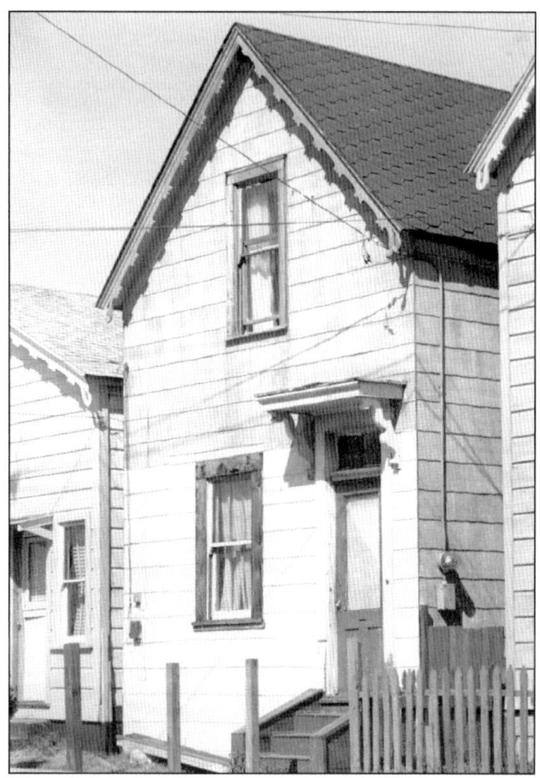

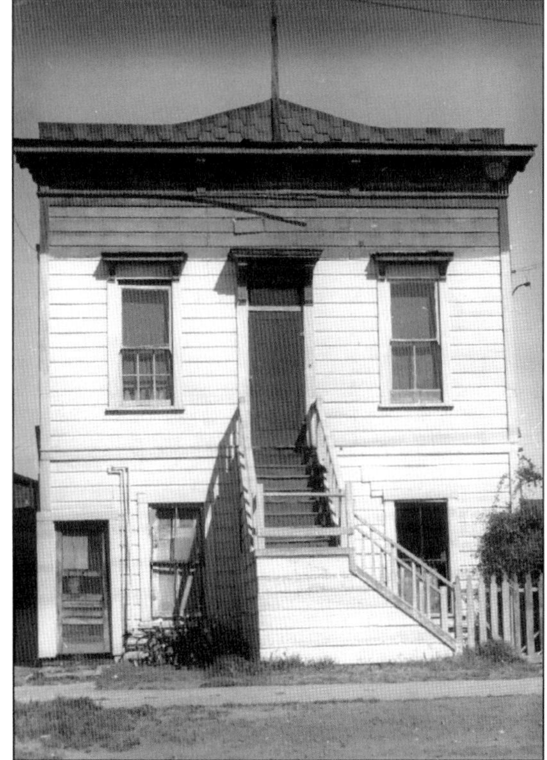

Pictured here is the exterior of a home at Third and Henry Streets. By 1880, there were 593 African American residents in West Oakland. By this time, blacks were living much better than their fathers. In West Oakland, African Americans could adequately feed, clothe, and house their families.

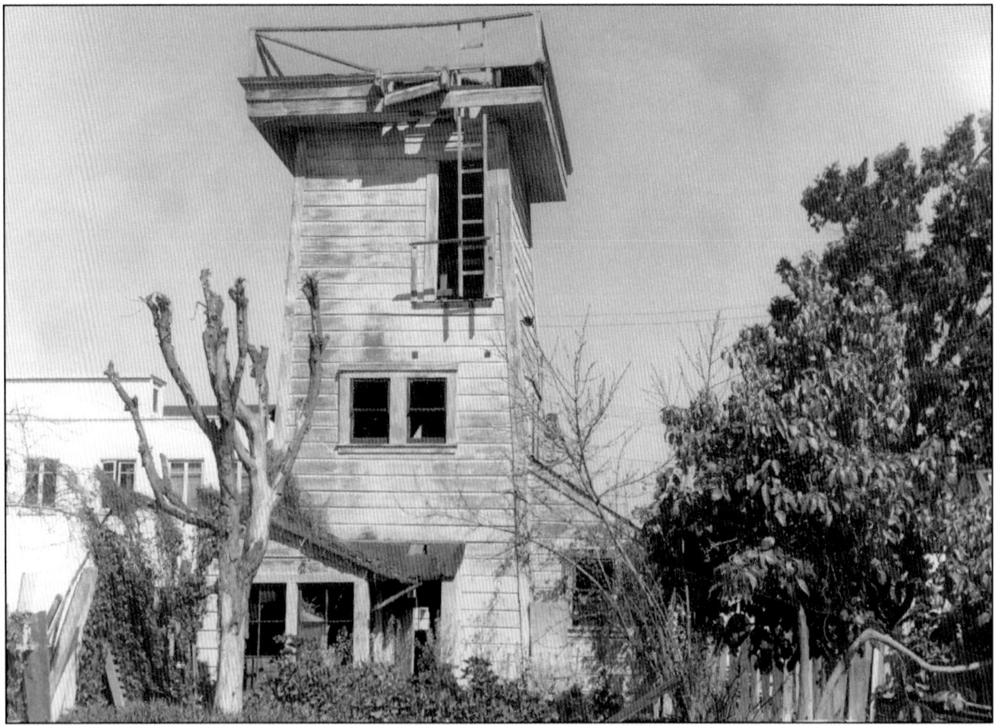

Here is another West Oakland home, this one on Eighth and Adeline Streets, a worn and much neglected structure. The photograph was found in an archive that was once surely the pride of the resident family contributing it.

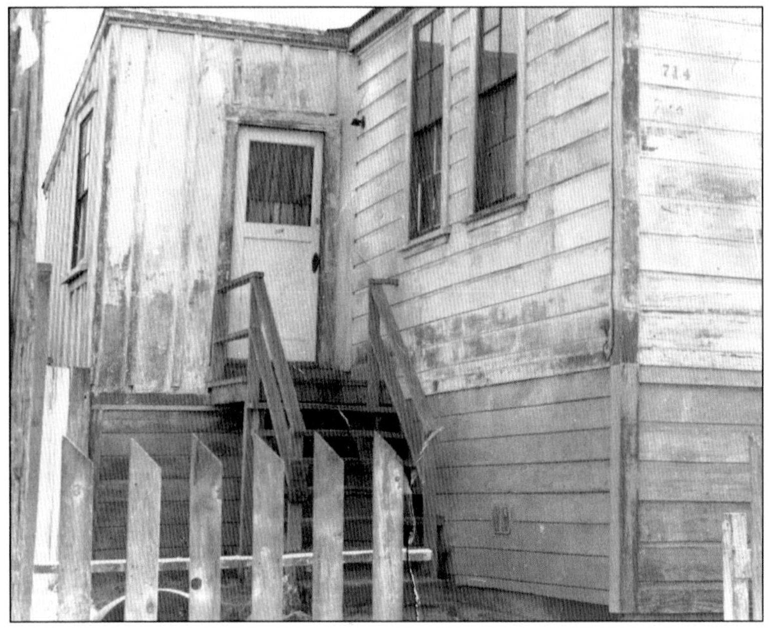


This West Oakland photograph shows a run-down property, which probably once sported a brightly painted white picket fence that pedestrians admired as they walked past.

This house was built by Isaac Flood and was one of the first black residences constructed in Alameda County.

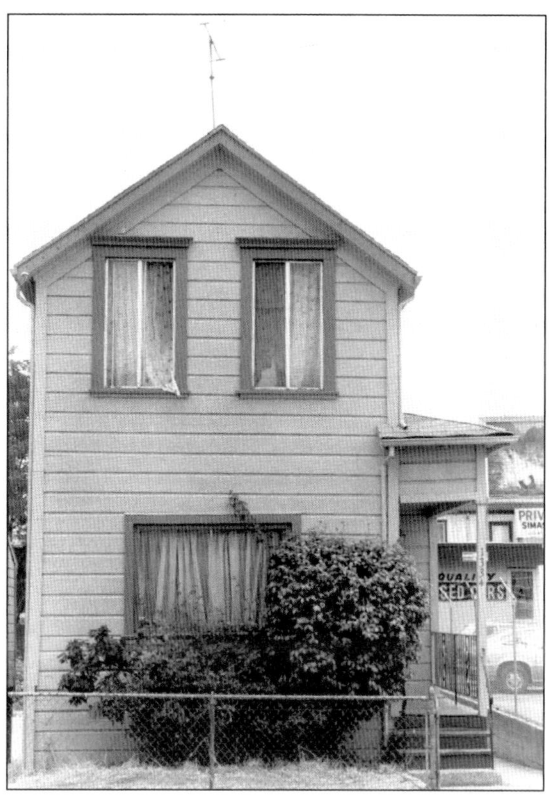

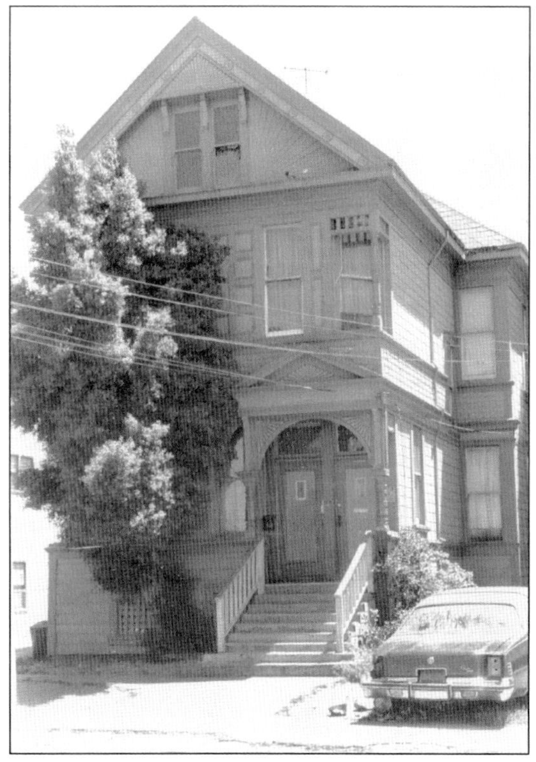

Here is the home of Delilah Beasley at 705 Thirty-fourth Street in Oakland. Delilah wrote of the California blacks' plight that others shied away from, such as the Archie Lee case, the story of Mary Ellen Pleasant, and extensive coverage of the California Colored Conventions.

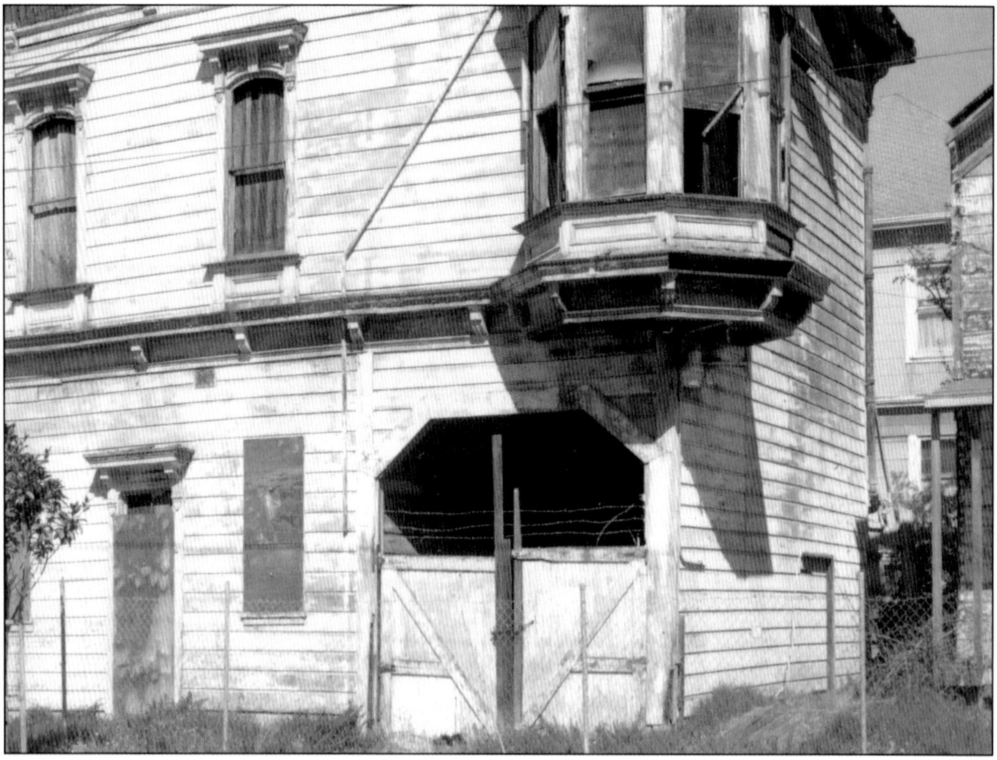

This image shows Liberty Hall at Eighth and Peralta Streets in Oakland, originally called the Western Market Building. Constructed in 1877, it was well known for the sumptuous banquets provided to neighborhood residents for only a few pennies. Liberty Hall was occupied by several black churches. It is said to be the only privately funded renovation project dealing with black history in Northern California.

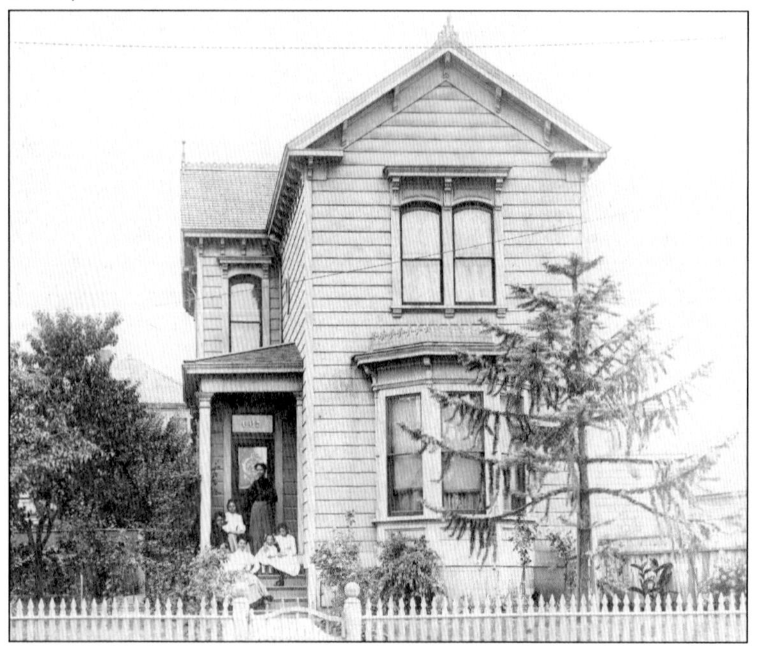

This image shows the home of James Maryatt at 665 Thirty-fourth Street in Oakland, which is now 673–675 Thirty-fourth Street.

This is the 1918 location of the original Fannie Wall Children's Home, located at 1215 Realta Street. The home moved to 815 Linden Street in 1928 and is now the Fanny Wall Child Care Center at 647 Fifty-fifth Street.

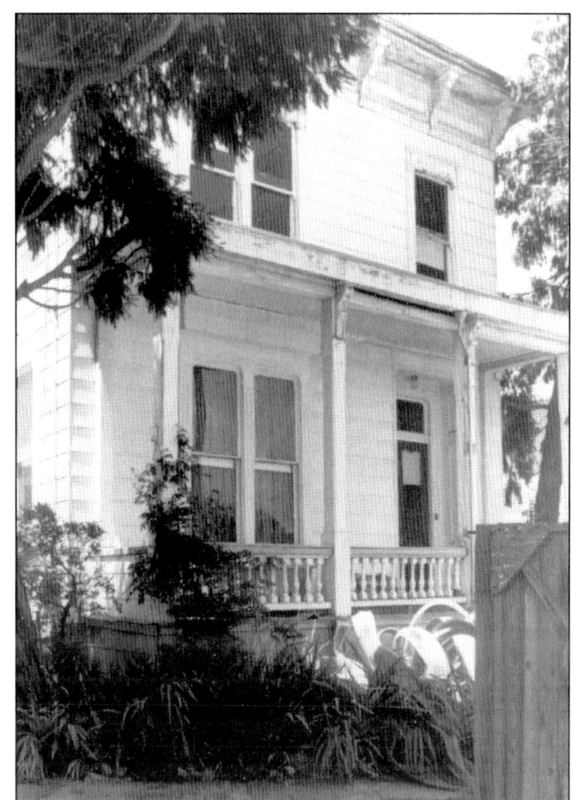

Oakland's first black YWCA, the Linden Branch, was established as a center in 1920 during a period when the main YWCA encouraged the formation of racially segregated branches. A small group of black women, including Melba Stafford and Hettie Tilghman, organized the "center," which later achieved "branch" status in 1923. Linden Branch, located at 828 Linden Street in West Oakland, operated as a community center, offering members religious services and vocational training. The branch, integrated in 1944, became the West Oakland Center.

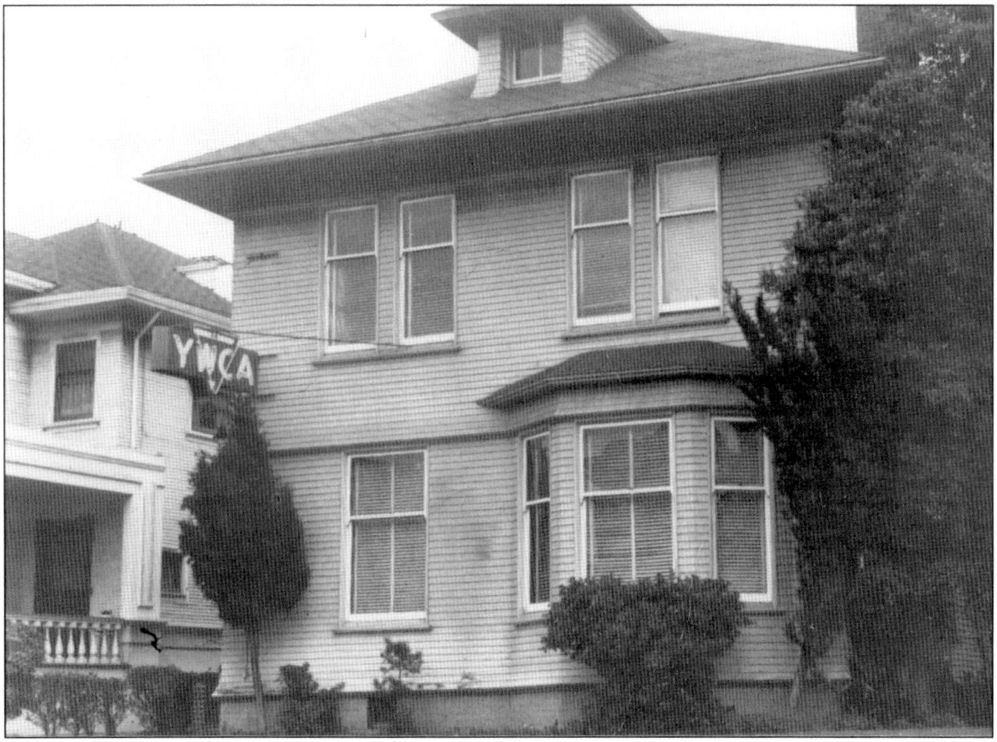

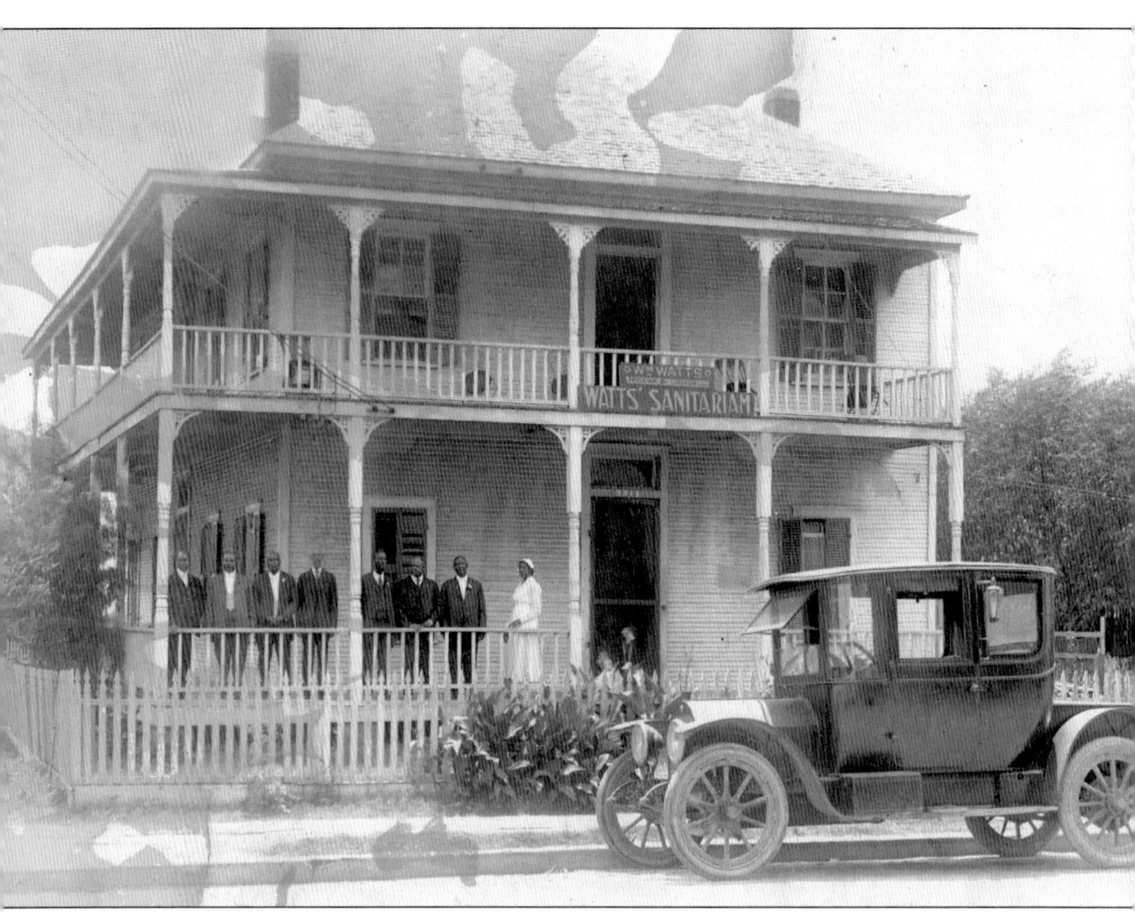


Seen here is the two-story Watts Sanitarium, or the Watts Hospital and Training School for Nurses, a 22-bed hospital and nurse-training campus located at 3437 Harlan Street. A registered nurse was in charge at all times with the students in training.

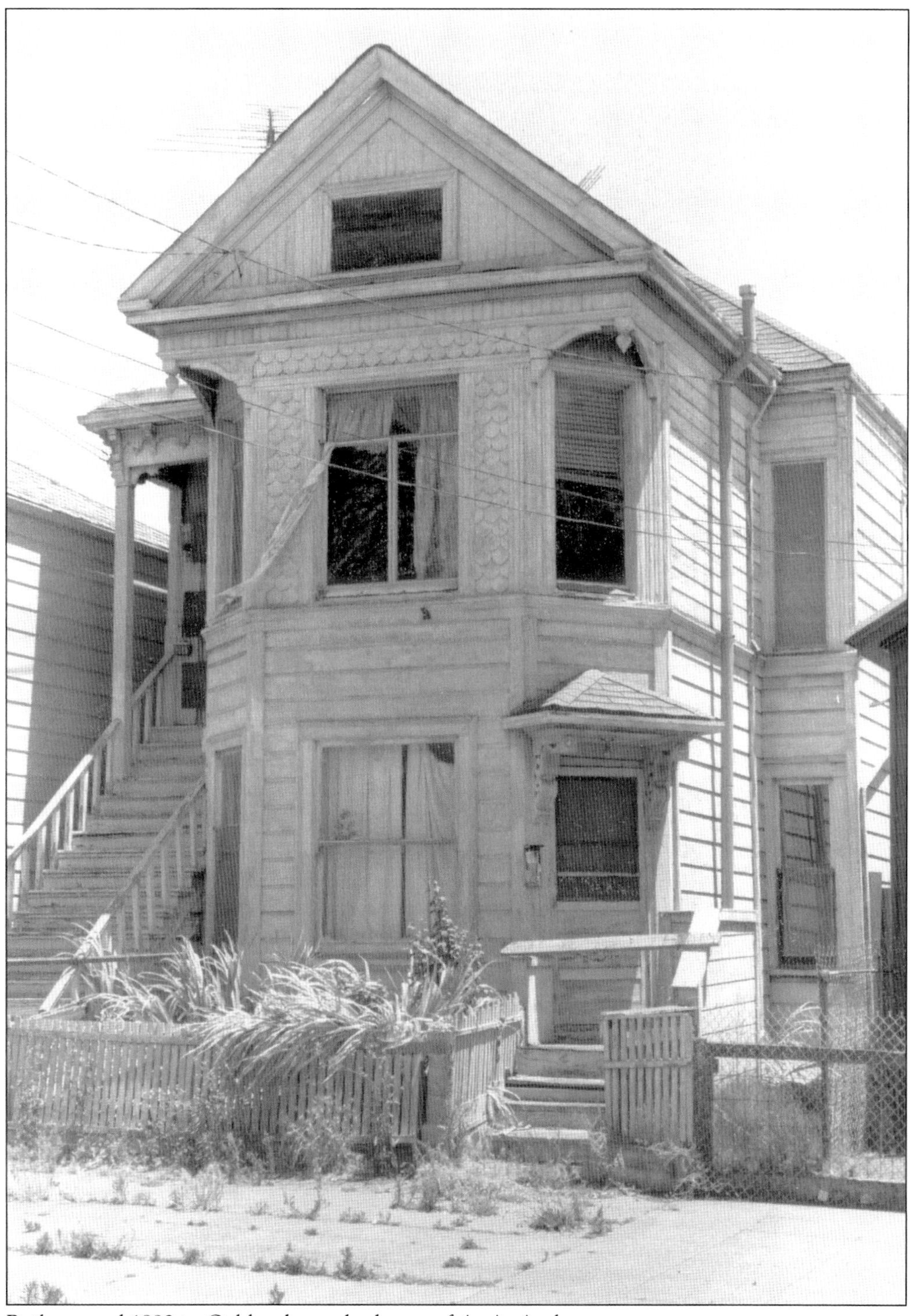

Built around 1892 in Oakland was the home of A. A. Ambrose.

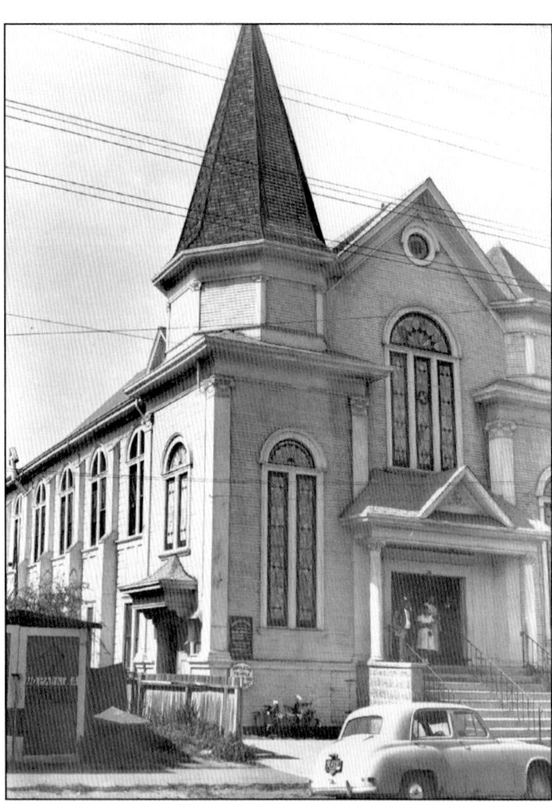

The First AME Church at Market and West (Fifteenth Street) Streets is pictured here in 1945.

Captured some years earlier, the First AME Church is referred to here as the "Second Church." Located between Market and West Streets, it was built in 1884.

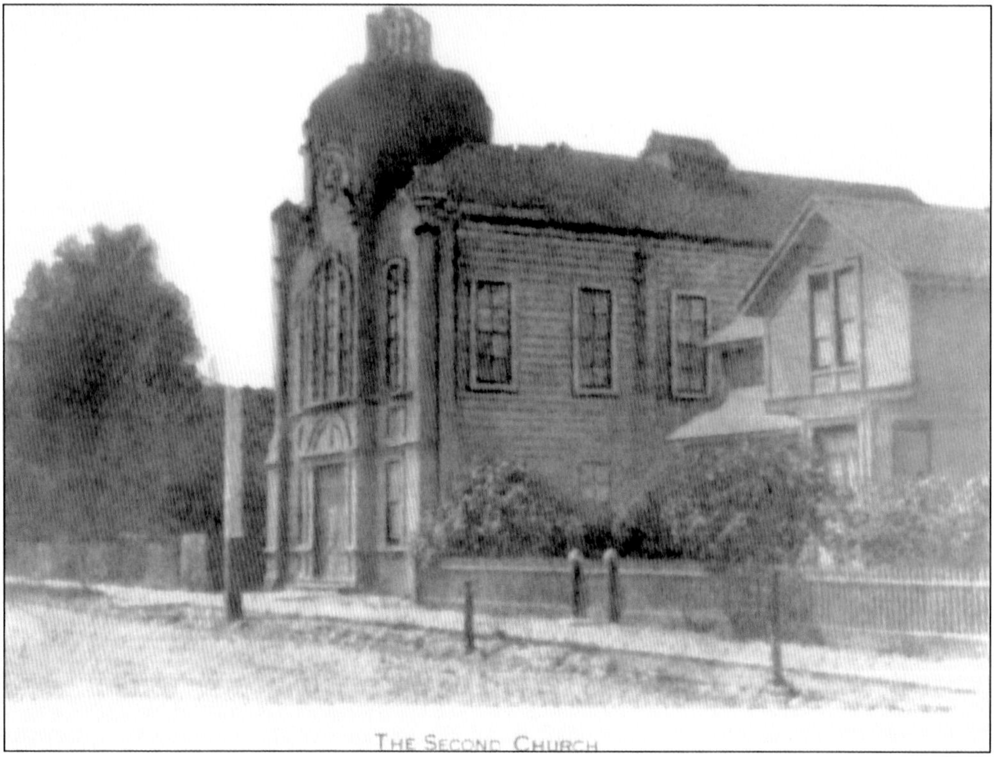

THE SECOND CHURCH

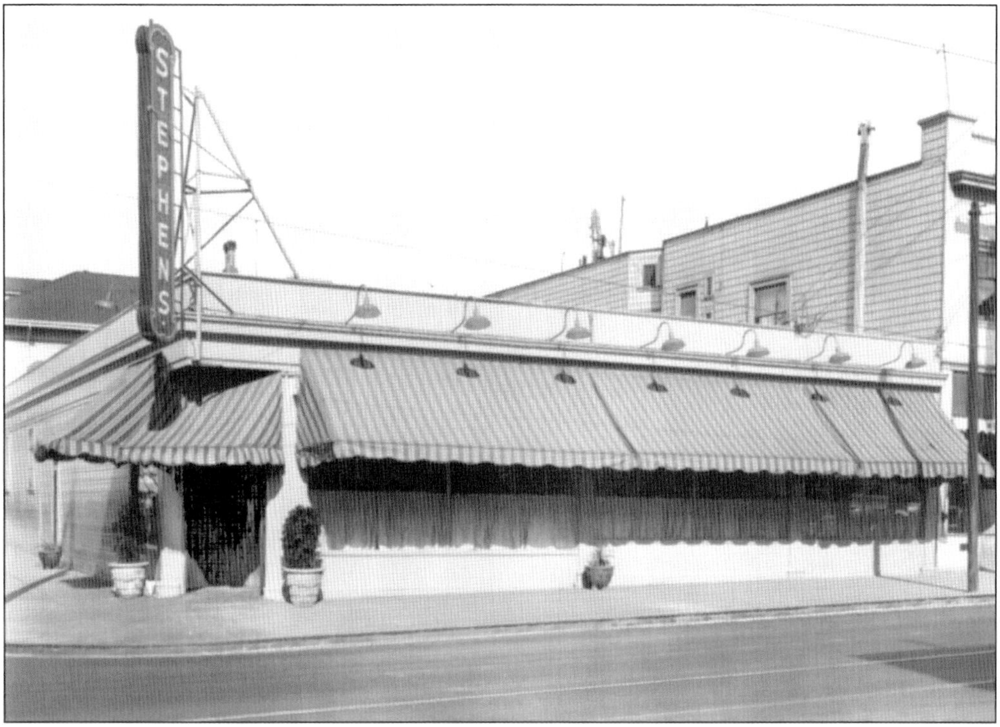

Here is an image of Stephens Restaurant at Second Avenue and Twelfth Street.

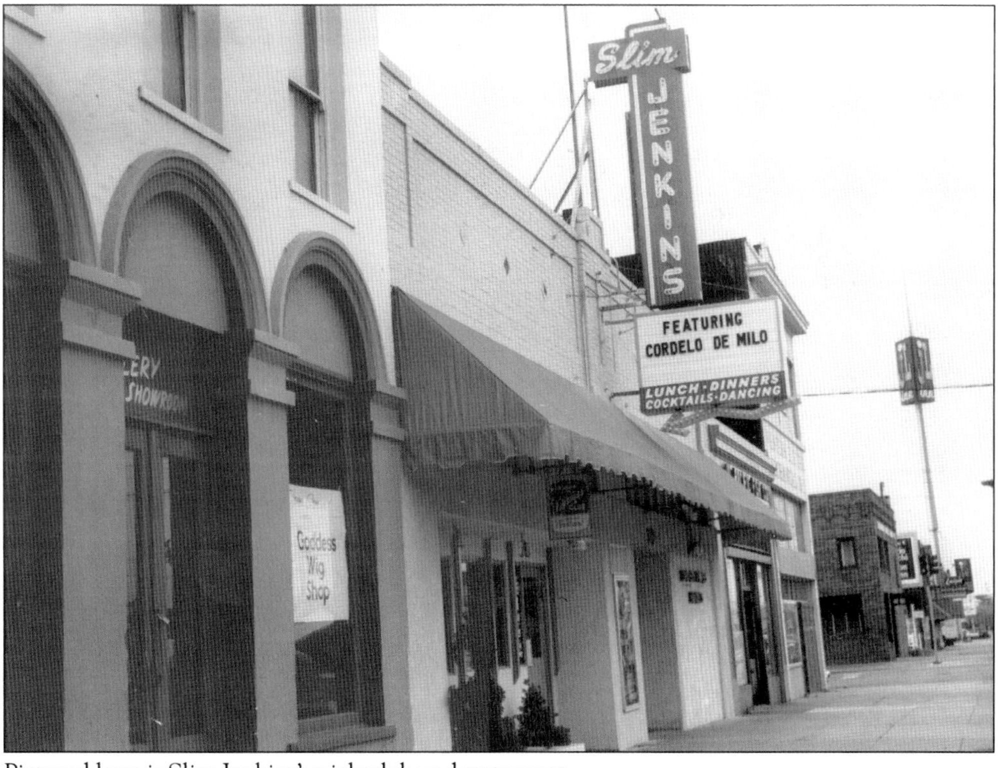

Pictured here is Slim Jenkins's nightclub and restaurant.

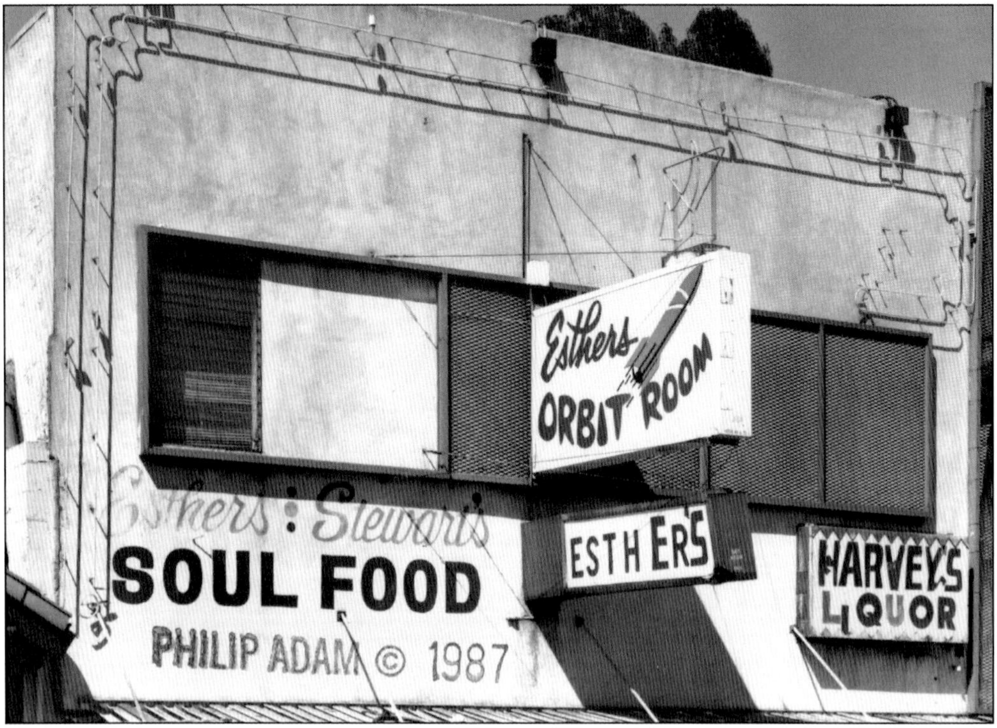

This image shows the renowned West Oakland club, the Esters Orbit Room, where performers of both regional and international fame came to play.

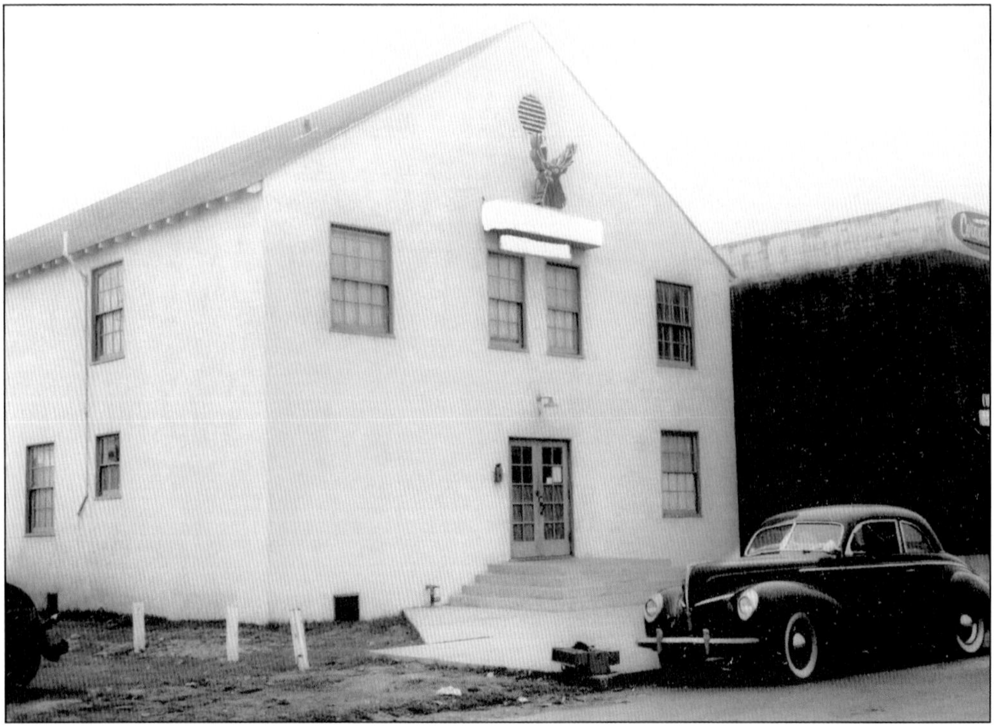

This is the Elks Club Building located in West Oakland.

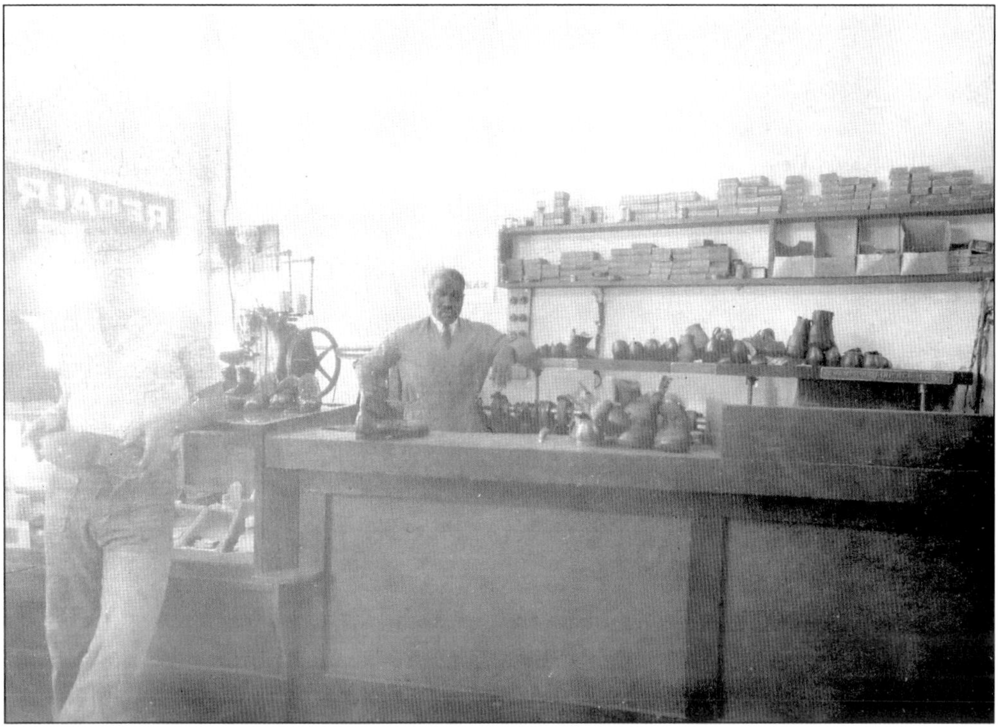

This image shows a shoe repair shop in Jenkins Corner in West Oakland.

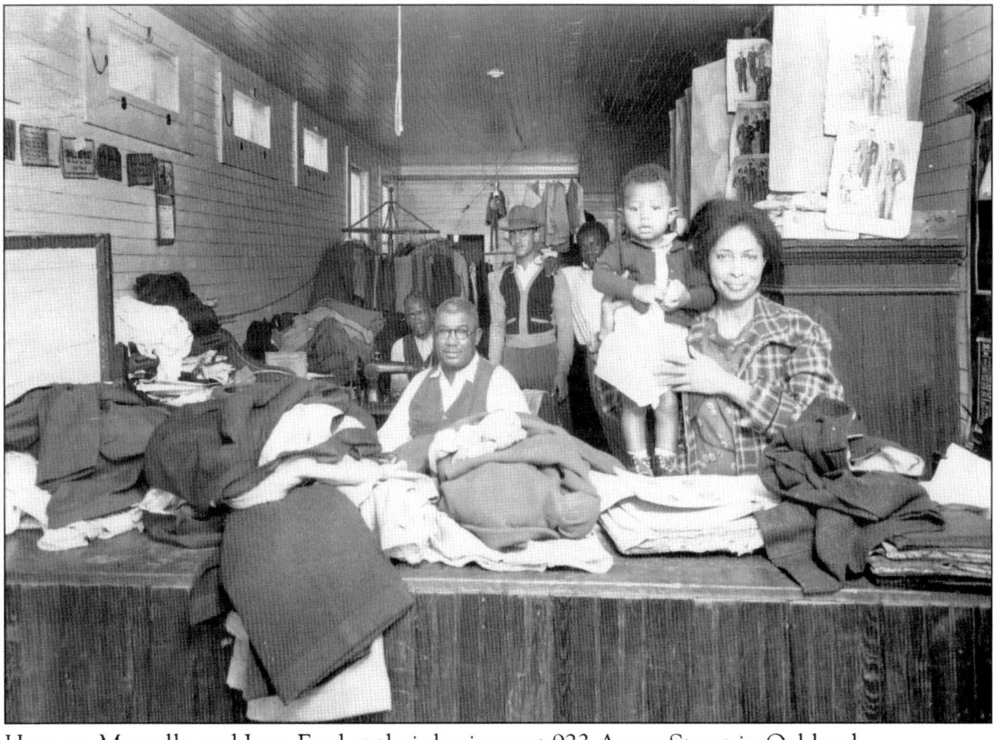

Here are Marcella and Jesse Ford at their business at 923 Apgar Street in Oakland.

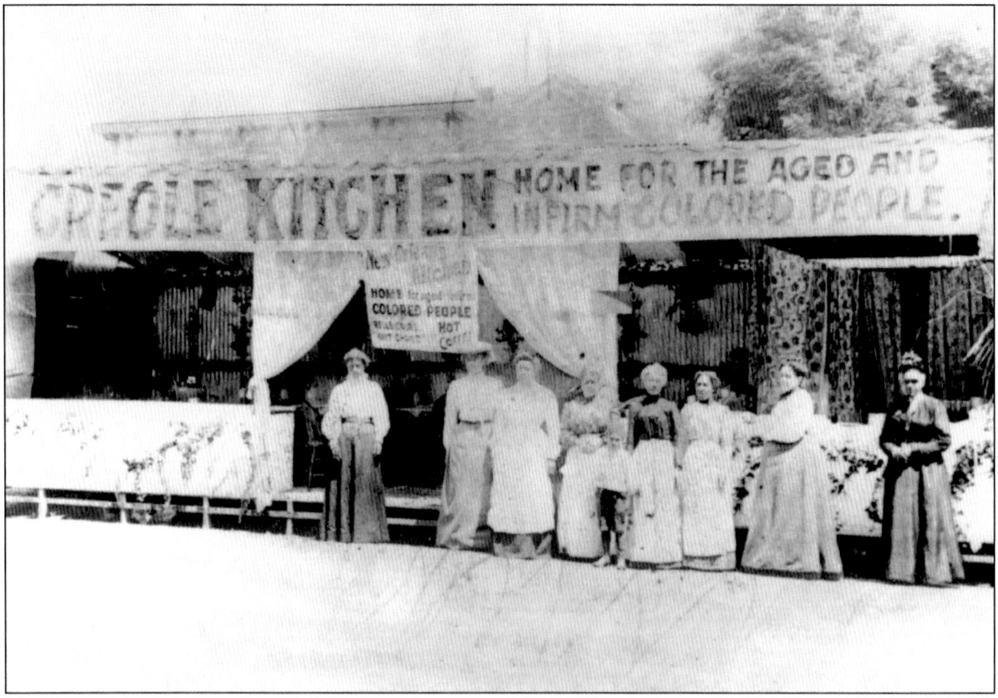

The Home of the Aged and Infirm Colored People opened in 1892. Located at 5245 Harrison Avenue (now Underwood Avenue) near Mills College, the two-story Victorian building originally had 16 rooms and could accommodate 19 residents. The home closed in 1938 after operating for more than 40 years.

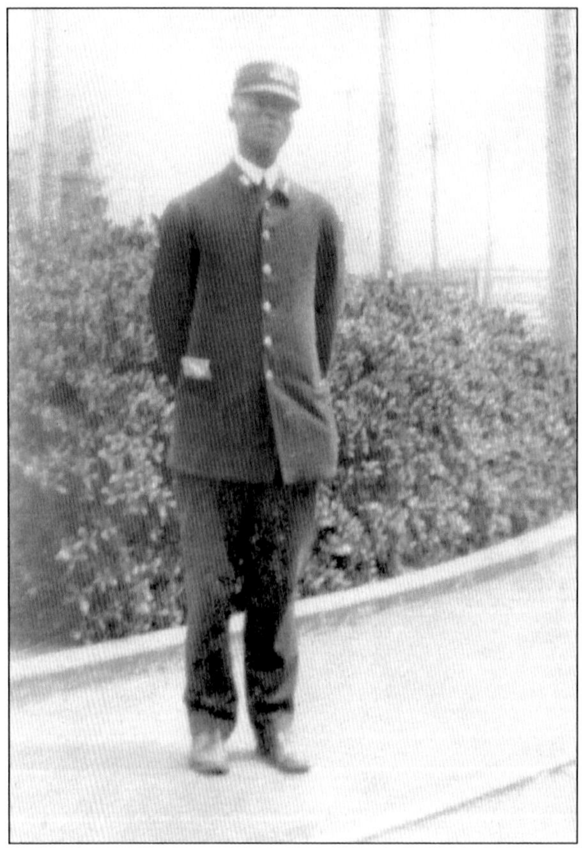

John Davis's family served for three generations as Pullman porters.

John G. Wiggins is pictured here while in Jamaica in the early 1930s. He married a porter's daughter, Elvira Davis.

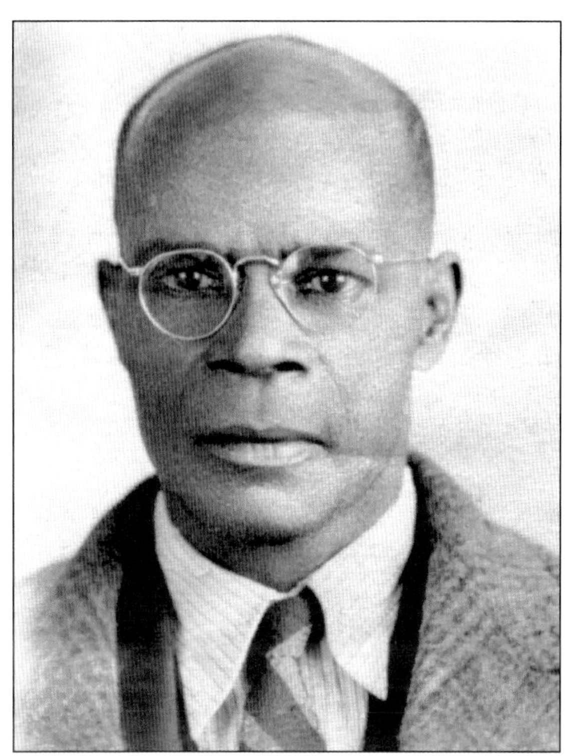

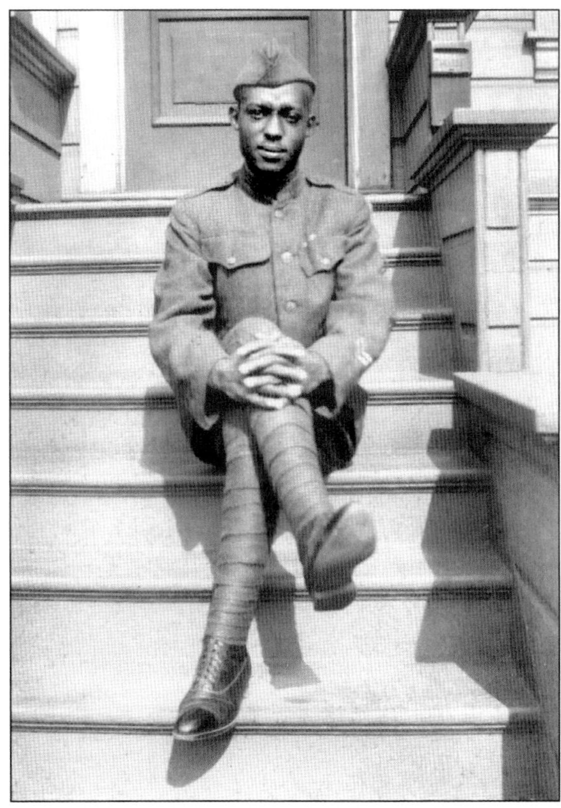

This photograph, *c.* 1919, illustrates the well-kept appearance of this property.

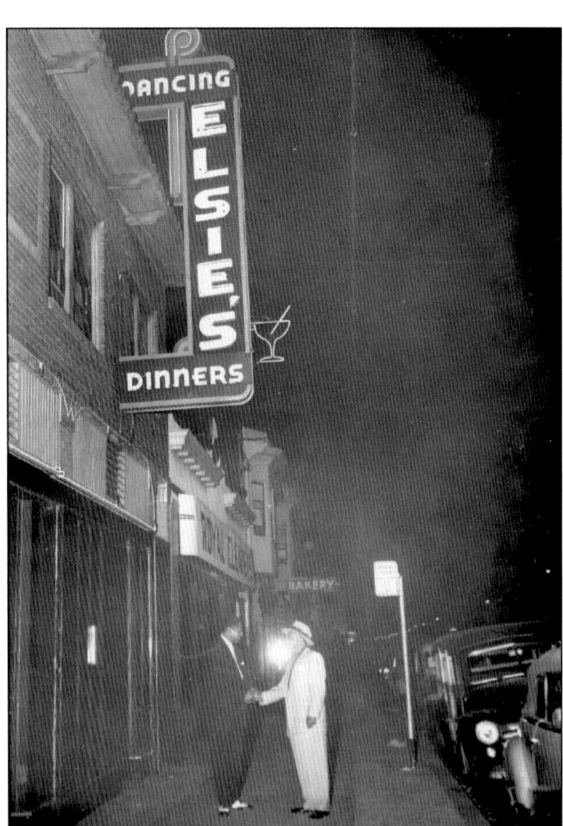


Elsie's Dancing and Dinners was located at Forty-third and Grove Streets.

Prominent Oakland entrepreneur Slim Jenkins created a major splash when he opened Slim Jenkins Cosmopolitan Square, "The biggest little Nite Spot in Northern Calif.," on Wood Street between Seventh and Eighth Streets.

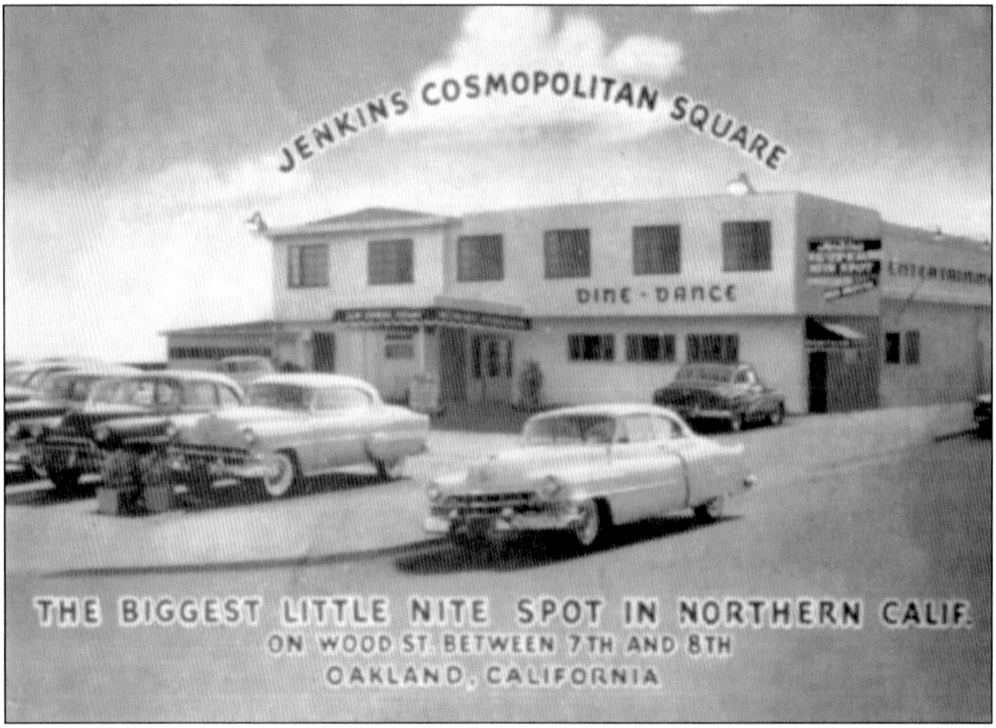

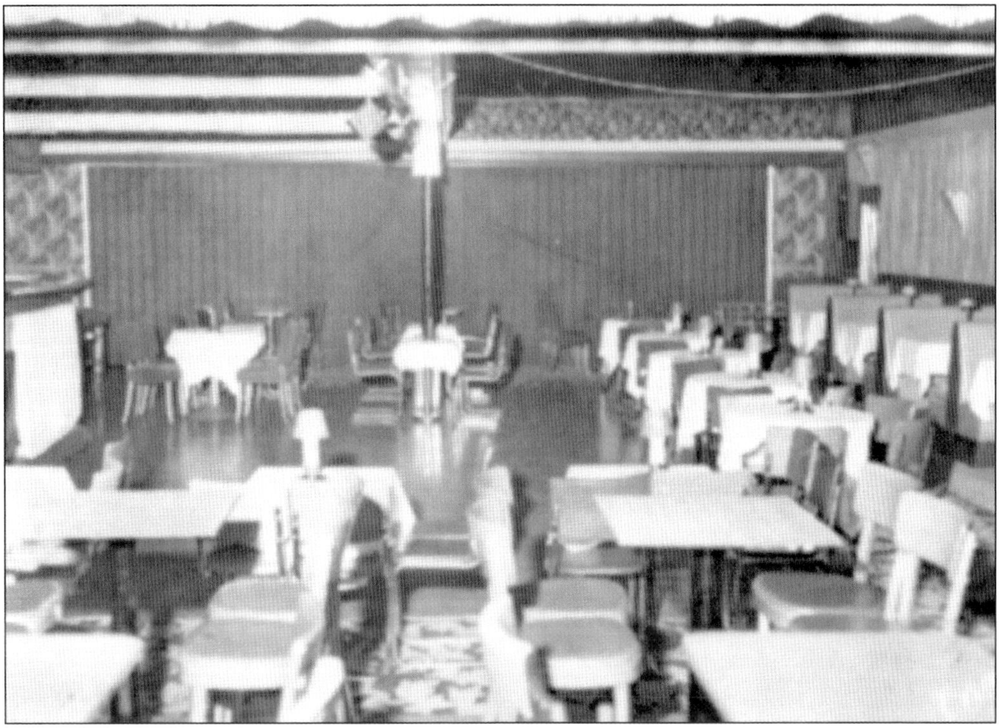

This image shows the interior of the Slim Jenkins cocktail lounge.

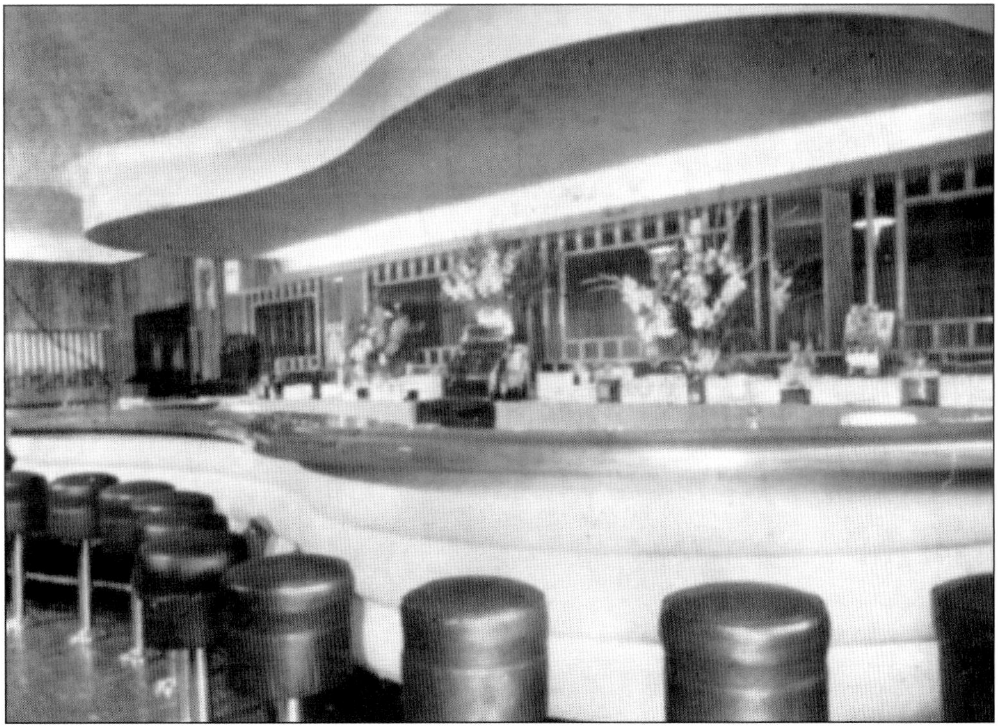

Here is another image of the cocktail lounge interior.

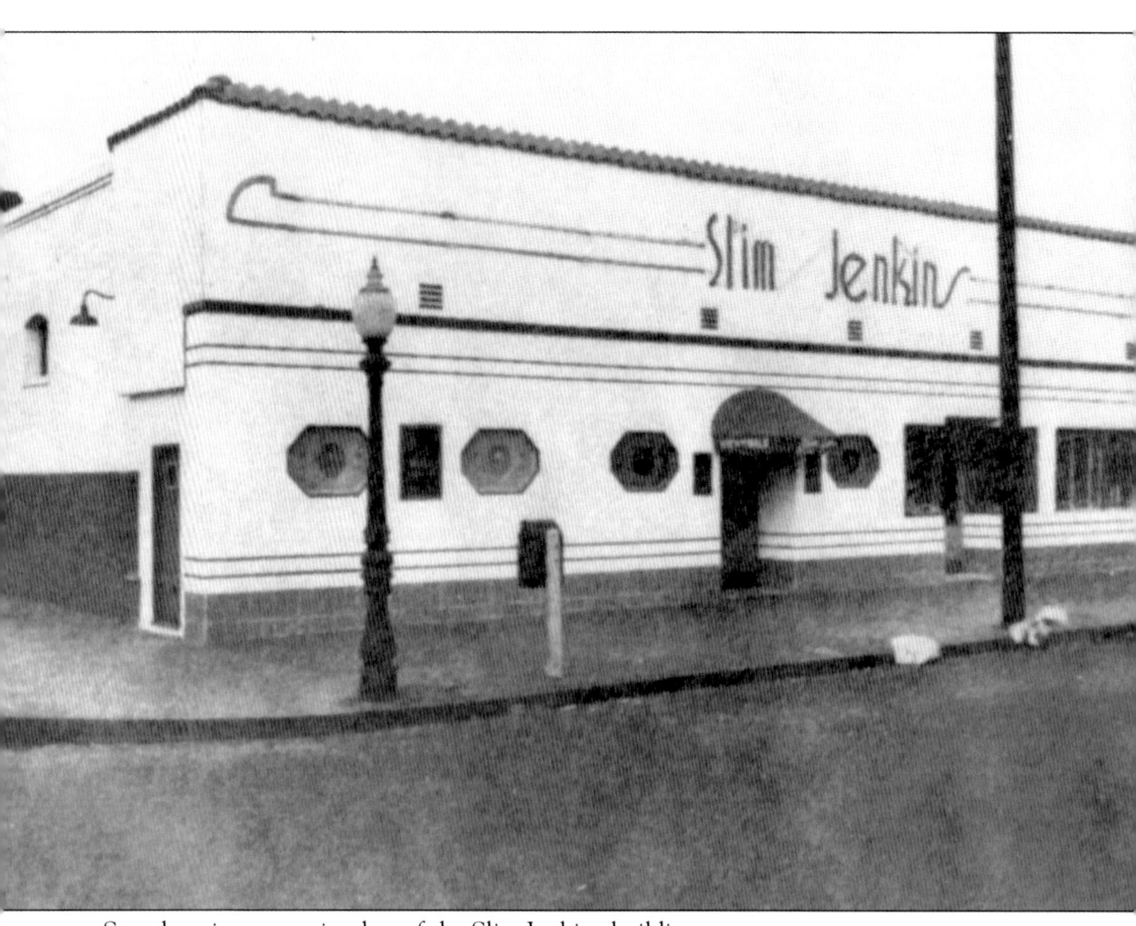

Seen here is an exterior shot of the Slim Jenkins building.

# *Six*

# A Door to New Occupations

In the 1880s, the *Elevator*, a black weekly newspaper published in San Francisco, carried the complaint that blacks applying for jobs as janitors and street cleaners were turned away because of their race. In 1889, John Wilds was the first African American to enter the Oakland Civil Service. In 1892, black delegates petitioned the Board of Police and the Fire Commission to appoint Alonza Young, a black man, to the Oakland police force. He did not get the appointment despite passing the qualifying exam. The process was relatively slow, but persistent, and ultimately successful.

In 1918, Walter Gordon graduated from the University of California, Berkeley. He received a law degree in 1922. He was a campus legend—a football hero, UC Berkeley's first black coach, the first black police officer for Berkeley, and a prominent attorney and effective civil rights advocate.

During this era, Oakland residents opened many new businesses; Marcela Ford was cofounder of the African American Museum and Library at Oakland; Anamis Wills opened the first dry-cleaning operation; Ruth Beckford, a dancer and choreographer, created and taught dance; Joe Johnson, labor historian and author, operated several small businesses; and Cecil Thurston and Ekmer McConnell ran a barbershop.

In 1918, Oakland hired Arthur Sanderson as its first black police officer. In the coming years, the city would appoint African Americans to the fire department as well. In 1926, Ida Louise Jackson, a University of California graduate, was the first black woman hired to teach at Prescott Junior High, the only school assigned black student teachers.

In 1894, Dr. G. B. H. Rutherford began a practice in Oakland; Washington J. Oglesby was the first black man to pass the state bar examination in 1896; and in 1892, George Watkins founded the first black-owned newspaper in Oakland, the *Illustrated Guide*.

African Americans took jobs in retail shops, barbershops and beauty saloons, dress shops, carpentry and painting companies, restaurants, and bars and clubs. Undertaker L. M. Hudson opened a funeral home, Elizabeth Martell operated a board and lodging house, and Strauter and Howard were proprietors of a livery stable. By 1929, there were over 100 black-owned businesses in Oakland.

West Oakland's blacks were entrepreneurs developing the African American dream.

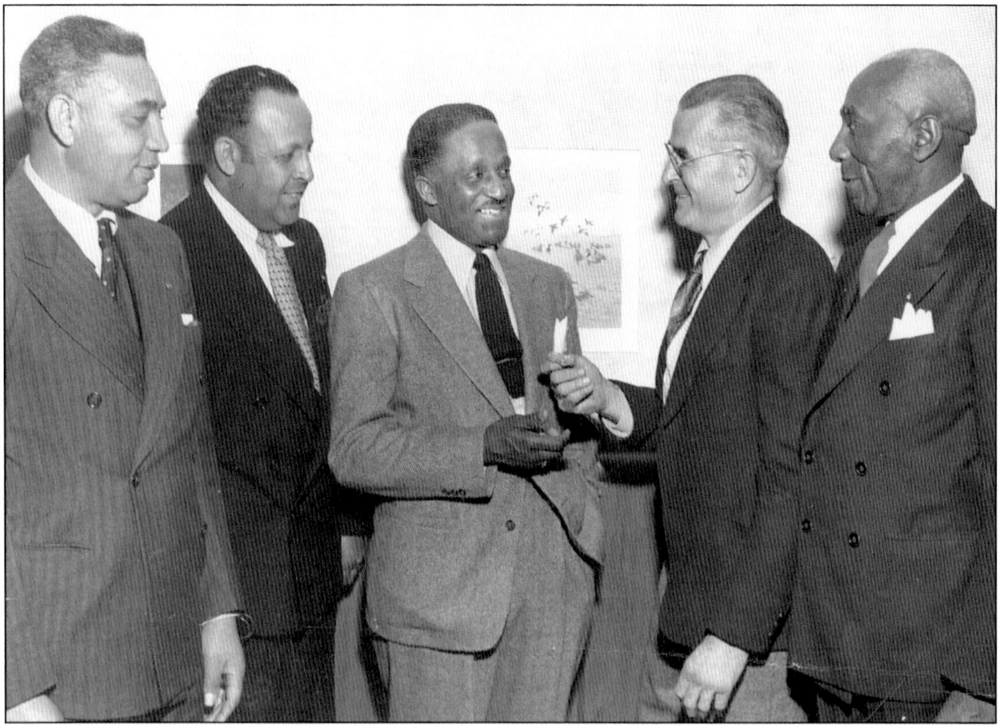

This is Roy Treece, the first black firemen appointed to the Oakland Fire Department in 1920. He was a member of the department until 1971. Treece, a private in the army during World War I, was founder and member of Colonel Young Post No. 269 of the American Legion in Oakland; member of good Hope Lodge No. 29, F&AM, Prince Hall; past grand treasure emeritus of the Most Worshipful Grand Lodge of California; and a member of Queen Ester Chapter No. 4 of the Order of the Eastern Star. Pictured here at Clarence Rhodes's retirement in 1946 are, from left to right, Roy Treece, Royal Towns, Clarence Rhodes, Chief Kispart, and Price Crawford.

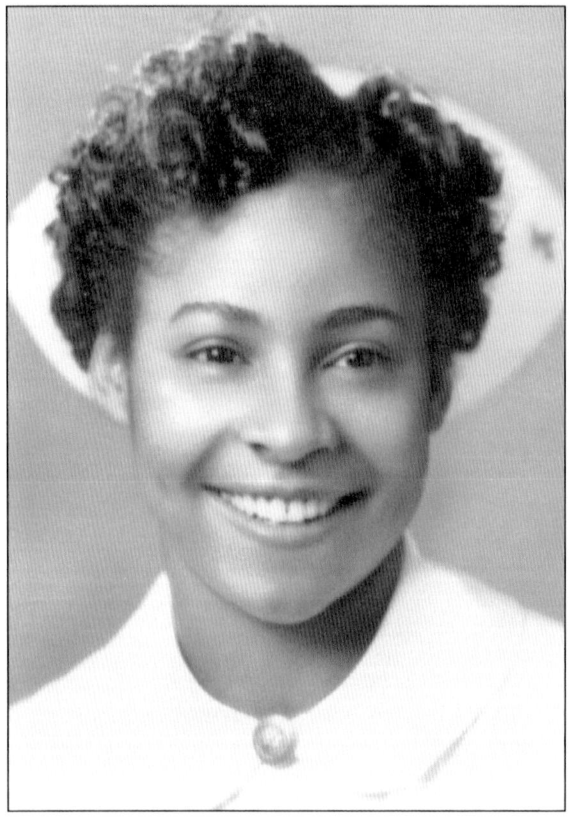

Alice Royals, seen in this 1946 photograph, was the first black nurse in Oakland's public hospital system.

Hilda Tilghman was the first black sales clerk in Safeway Stores and, in 1931, was she promoted to assistant manager.

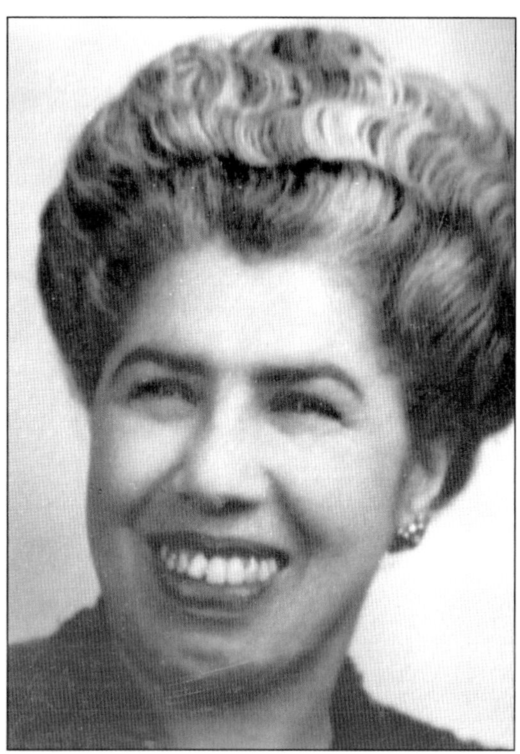

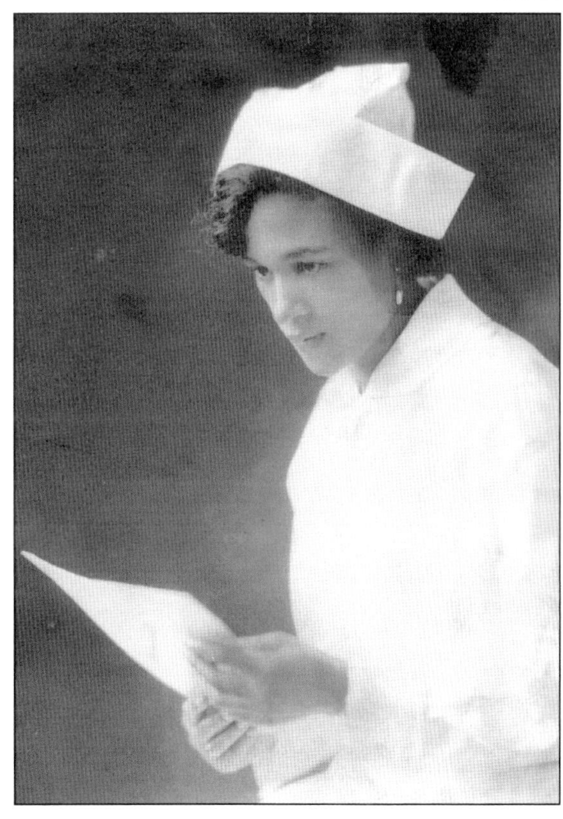

This image from 1916 shows Frances Nedgra, a nurse.

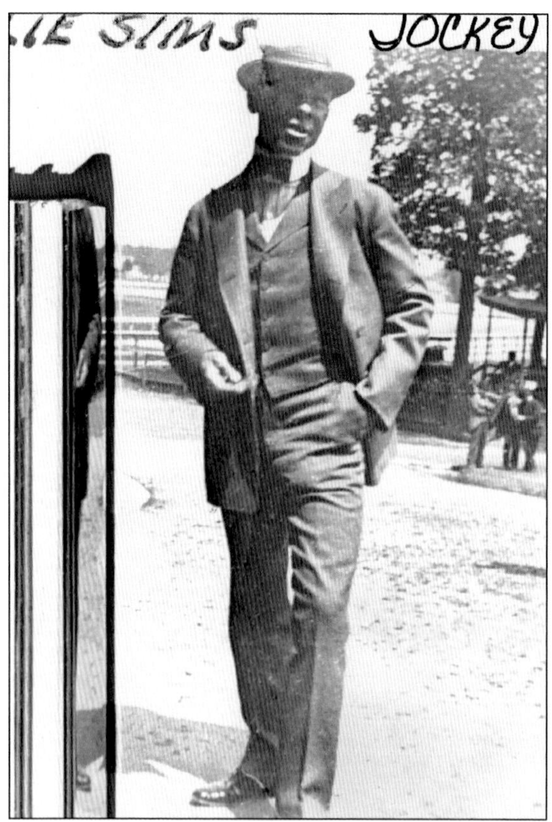


Pictured here is jockey Willie Sims, who won both of his races, in 1896 aboard Ben Brush and in 1898 atop Plaudit, at the Kentucky Derby. He is also the only African American to win horse racing's three Triple Crown events.

This image shows a group of Charm Beauty College instructors and teacher trainees. From left to right are (first row) Willa Cranes, Juanita Caseney, and Mildred Simein; (second row) Ruth Yarbough, Luree Love, and Lillie Webb.

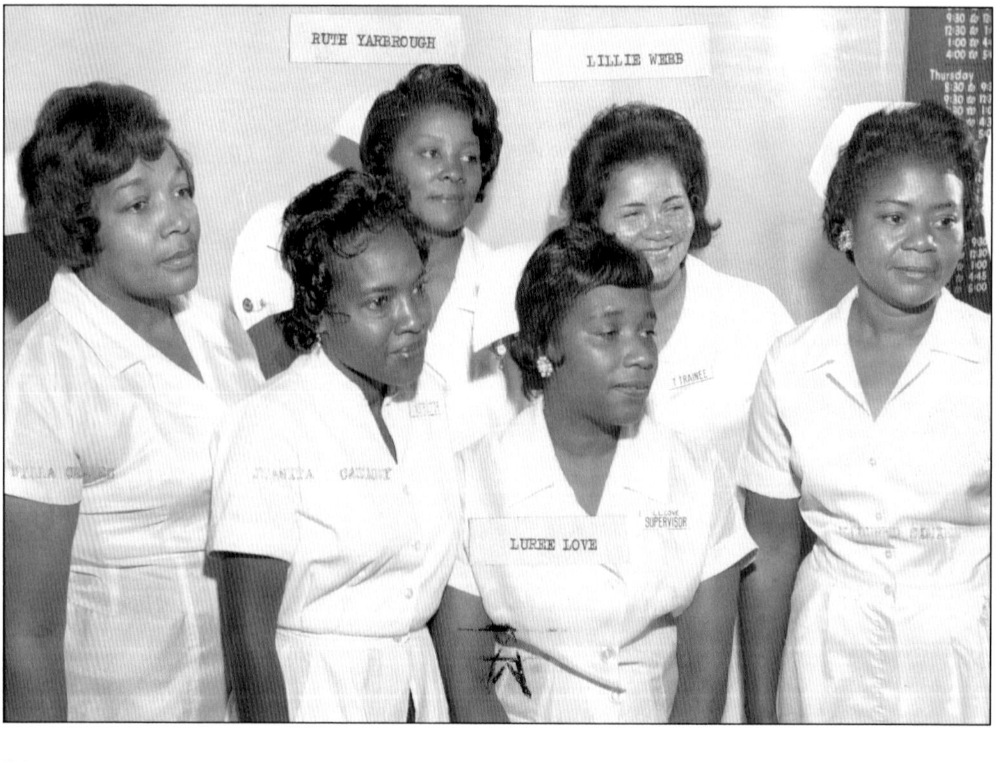

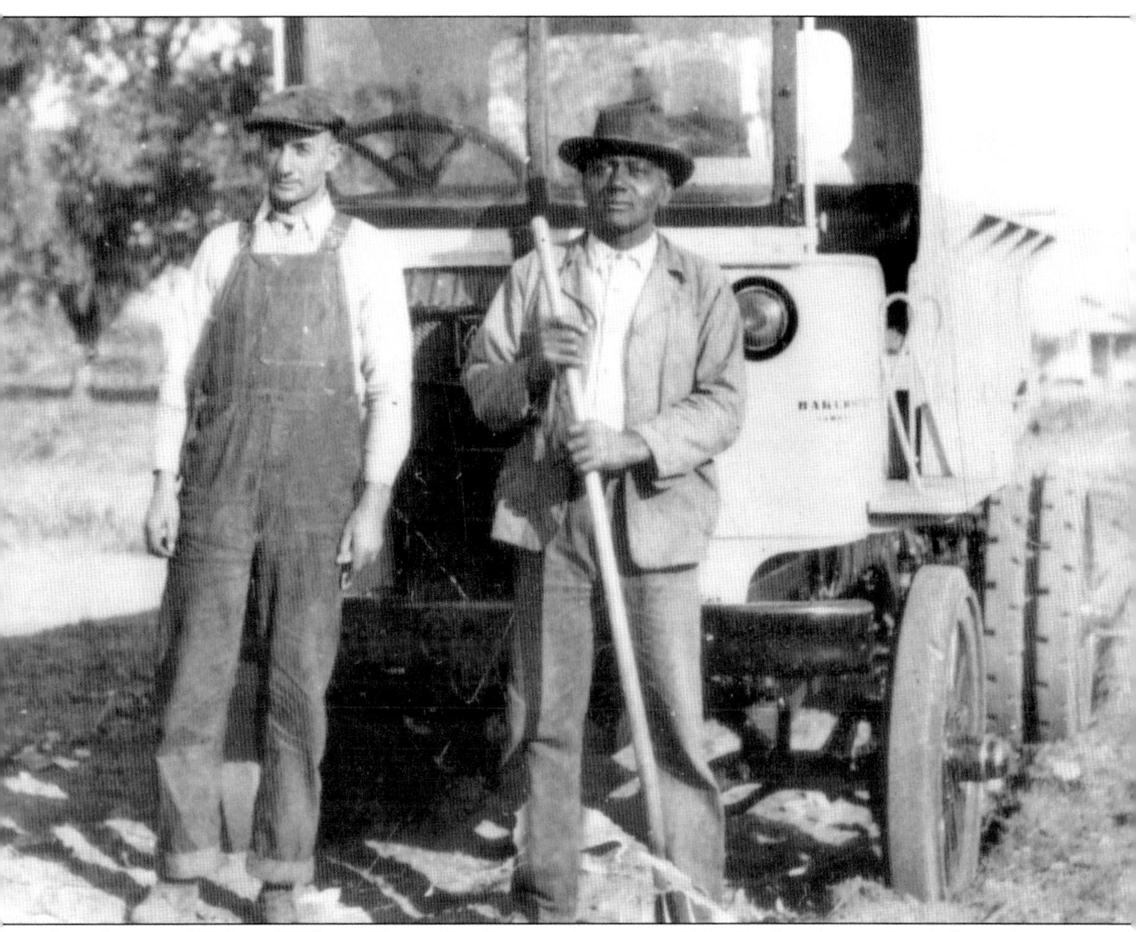

Seen here in 1923 are William Henry Pinckney, a farmer, and Mr. Fitch taking a break from the work at hand.

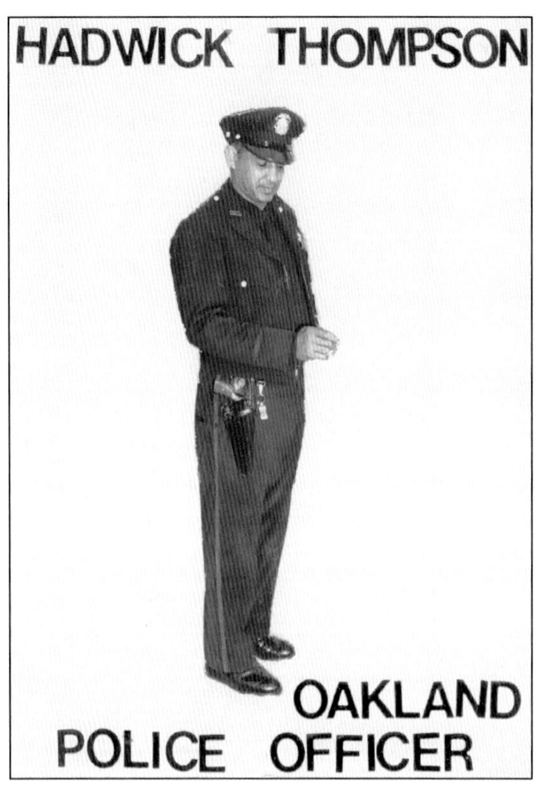


Pictured here is Oakland police officer Hadwick Thompson.

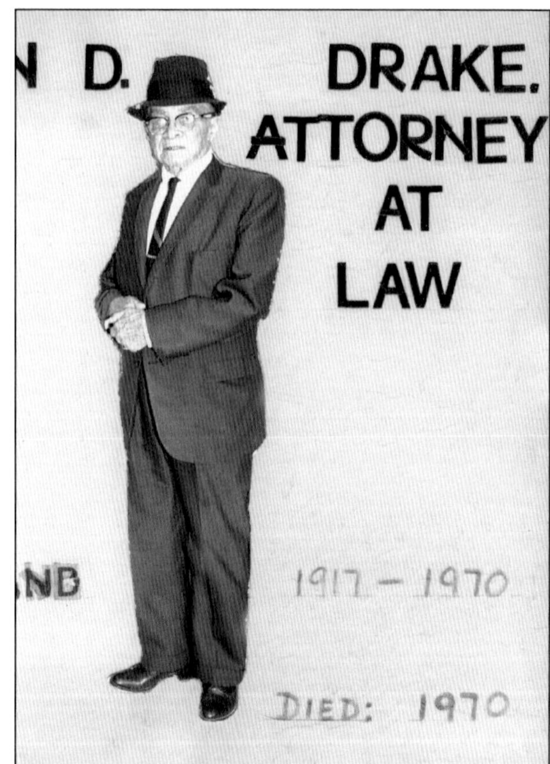


This image depicts John D. Drake, attorney at law, from 1917 to 1970.

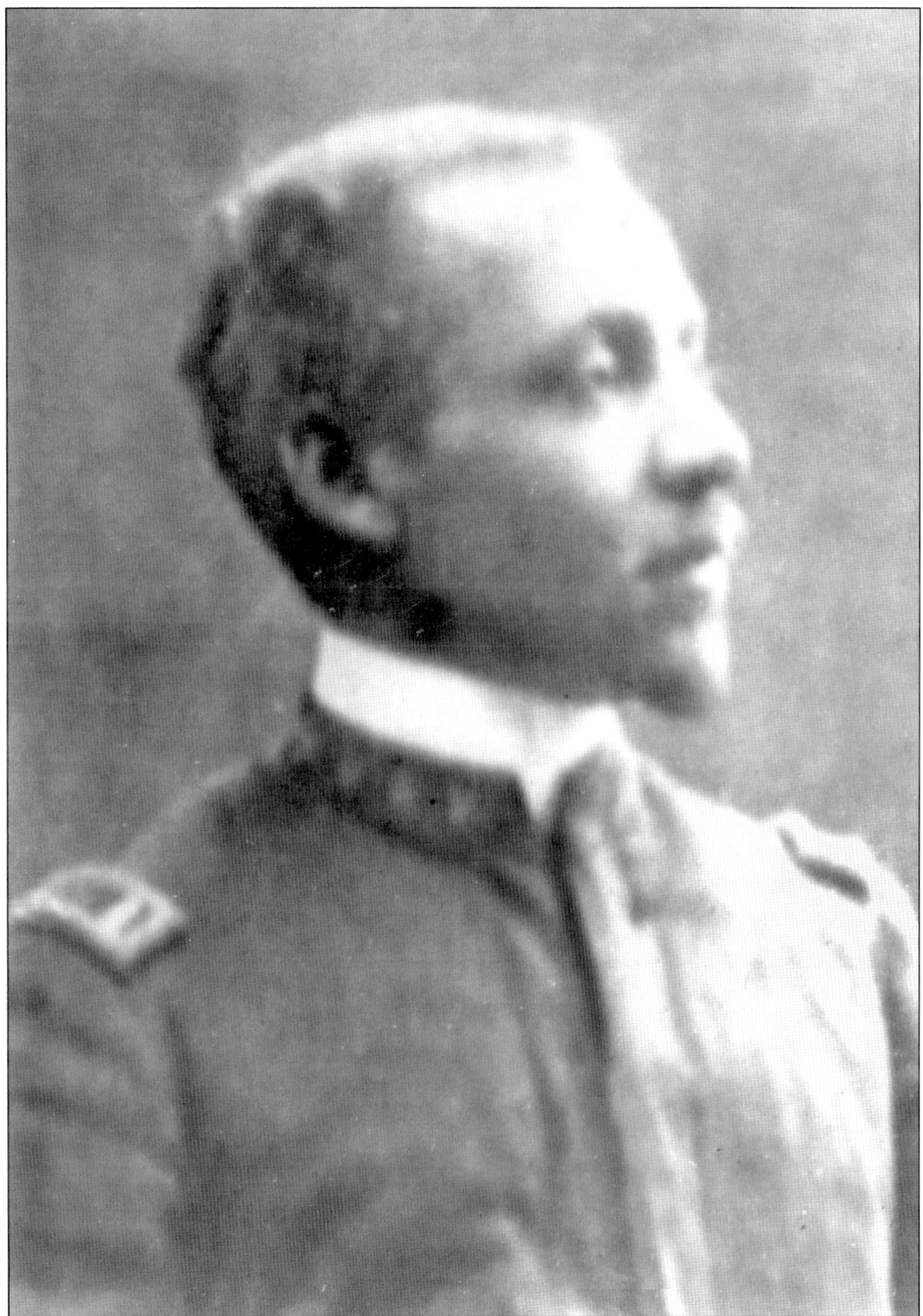

Dr. William Whipple Purnell (1869–1935) served in the Spanish-American War in 1898 as an assistant surgeon. He moved to the East Bay in 1902 and established his medical practice. For several years, he treated residents of the Home for Aged and Infirm Colored People without charge.

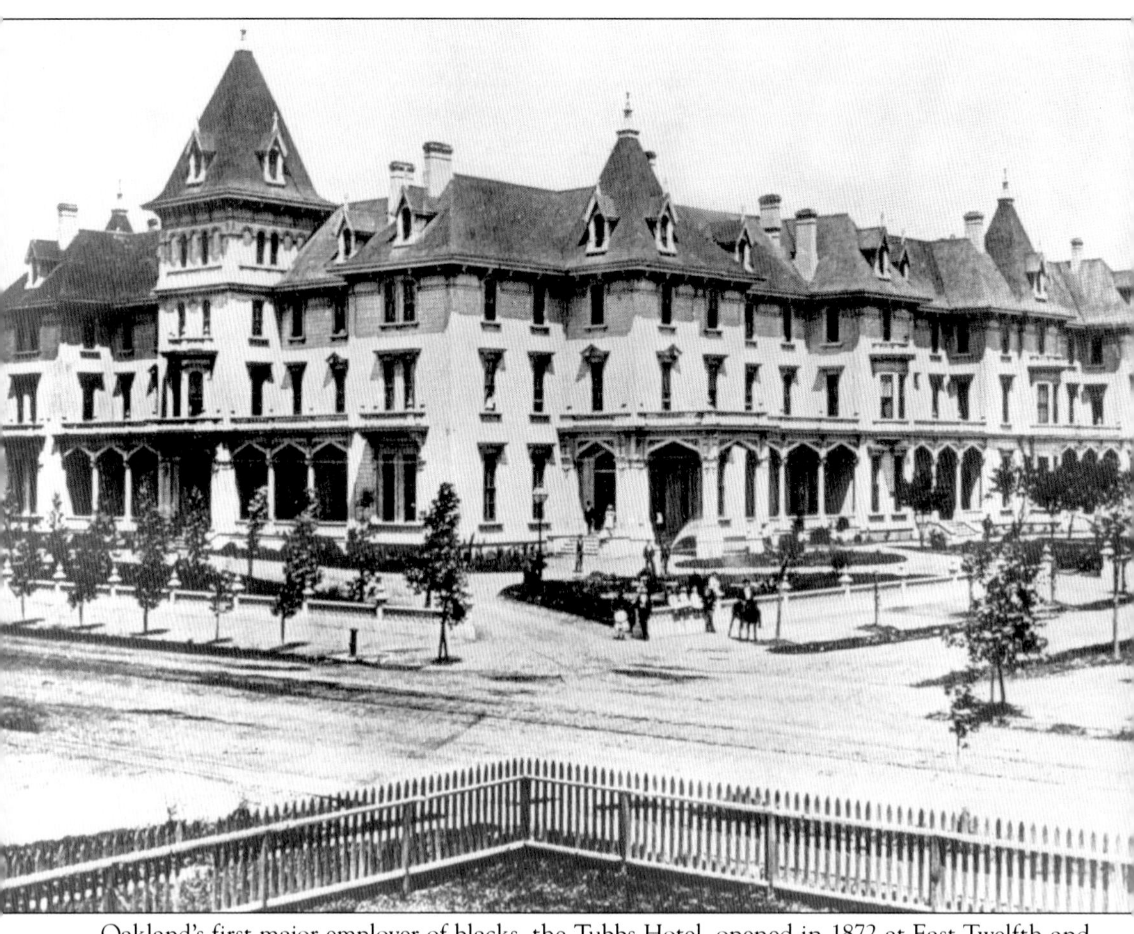

Oakland's first major employer of blacks, the Tubbs Hotel, opened in 1872 at East Twelfth and Fifth Avenues. The hotel employed blacks as stewards. The building burned in 1893.

Pictured here is Ida Jackson, the first black teacher in the Oakland Public School system. She began her career in 1924.

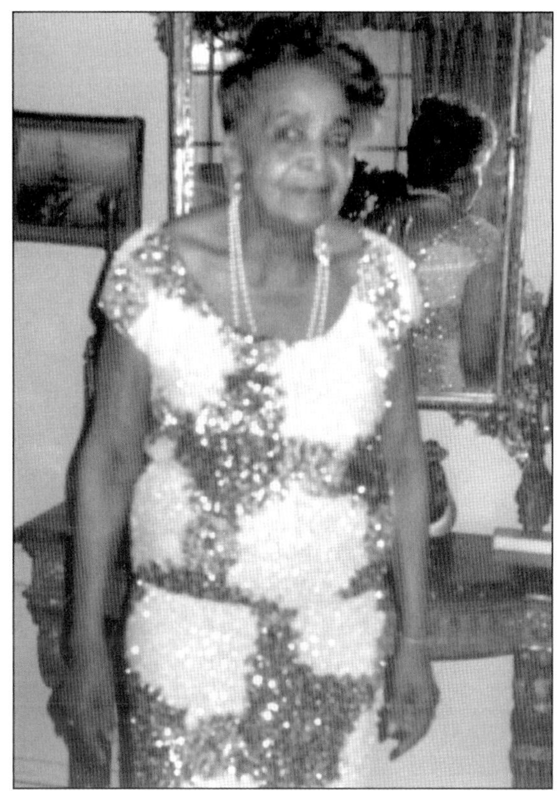

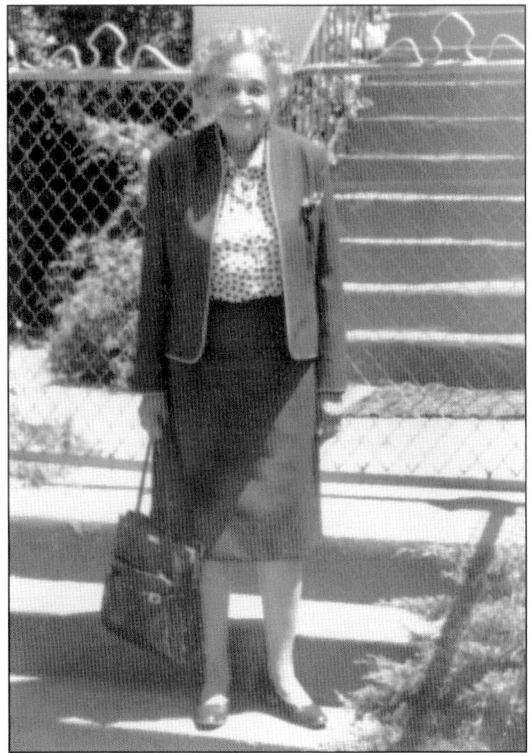

Ida Jackson, pictured here in 1989, was cofounder of the Berkeley Chapter of the Alpha Kappa Alpha sorority. She accomplished one of her goals to become the first black public school principal in Oakland.

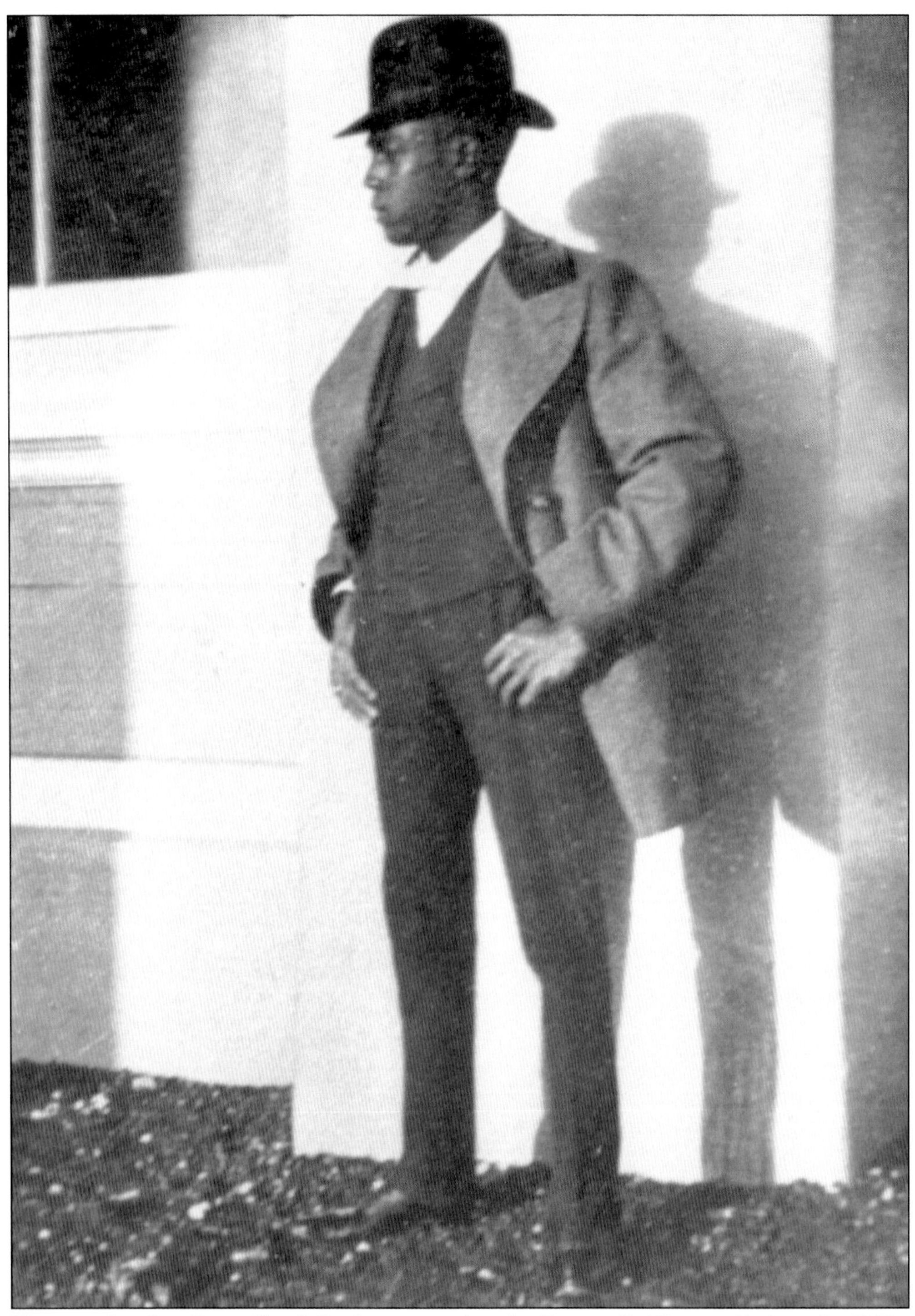

This is jockey Jess "Long Shot" Conley, pictured at the Emeryville Trotting Park in the 1890s. In 1911, he placed third at the Kentucky Derby.

# *Seven*

# ENTREPRENEURSHIP IN OAKLAND

From as early as the 1870s, blacks who bought property were able to realize profits from land ownership, and some of them invested in their own businesses. These businesses were small and offered services their owners had learned as employees in white-owned businesses.

In 1929, over 100 black-owned businesses existed in Oakland. Among them were real estate brokers, barbershops, restaurants and cafes, beauty parlors, billiard and pool parlors, dressmakers, tailor shops, printers, furniture stores, candy shops, auto-repair garages, jewelers, undertakers, insurance companies, and a pharmacy.

In addition to the accompanying photographs, other business names were registered with the city. These include Sylvester Sims's Overland Café, at 1719 Seventh Street; Turf Recreation Hall and Billiard Room, at 1736 Seventh Street on the backside of Jenkins Corner; The Creole Club, c. 1918, on Seventh Street; and the *Oakland Sunshine*, founded in 1897 by city hall janitor John Wilds, which was absorbed by the *California Voice*, established in 1919.

Other black business were the Pacific Coast Real Estate and Employment Company, established in 1907 at 1696 Seventh Street and owned by George Watkins, Oscar Palmer, and William Jackson; the Bay View Reality and Company at Eighth and West Streets, owned by W. A. Butler and W. S. Howard; Smith and Allen Realty Brokers, located at 2327 San Pablo Avenue; E. & L. Bridges, a new and used furniture company; S. R. Hackett and Sons Express Company , a moving business that relocated earthquake refugees into permanent housing in 1915; the L. M. Hudson Funeral Services, located at 953 Eighth Street; the Golden State and Guarantee Fund Insurance Company, which opened in the East Bay in 1928; and the Inter-City Finance Corporation of Alameda County, which provided loans to blacks who had virtually no access to other financial institutions.

The African American dream could not be complete without an investment in one's own economy.

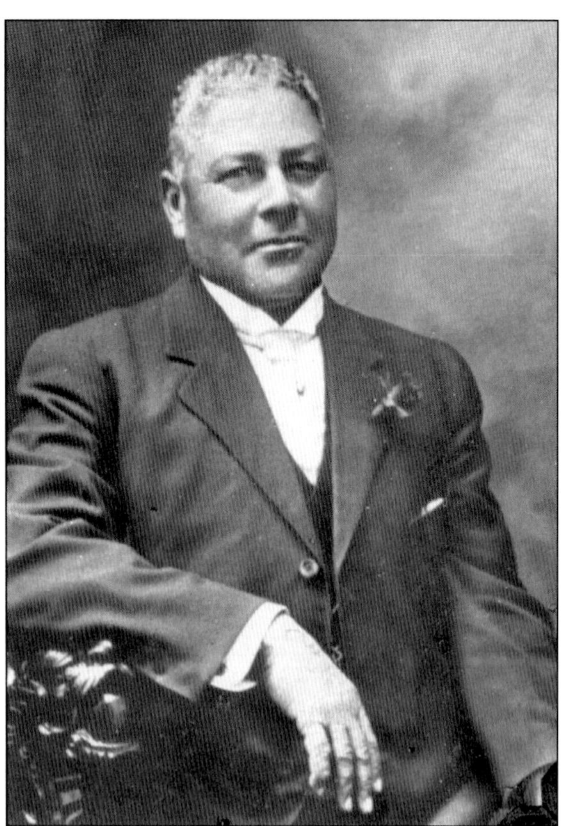

Pictured on January 8, 1901, is the master of whaling vessels, William T. Shorey. He was a director, entrepreneur, and president of the Roachdale Company.

Capt. William T. Shorey, his wife, Julia, and daughters Zenobia and Victoria pose in an Oakland studio around 1900. A third child, William Jr., was born in 1903. As in many other whaling families, Julia Shorey and the children sometimes accompanied the skipper on his voyages.

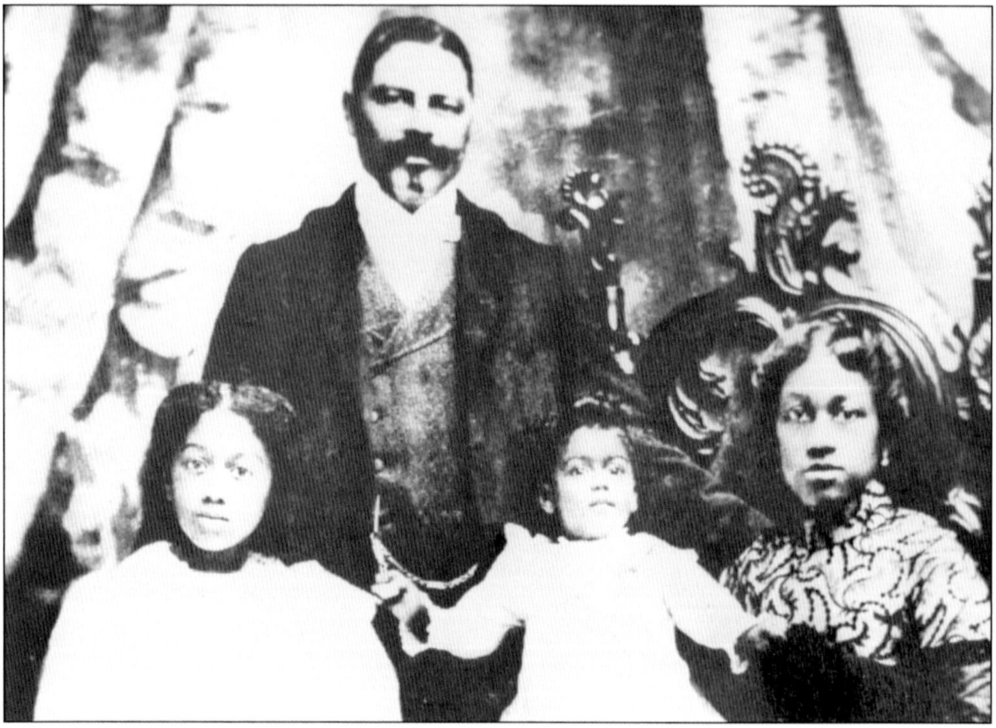

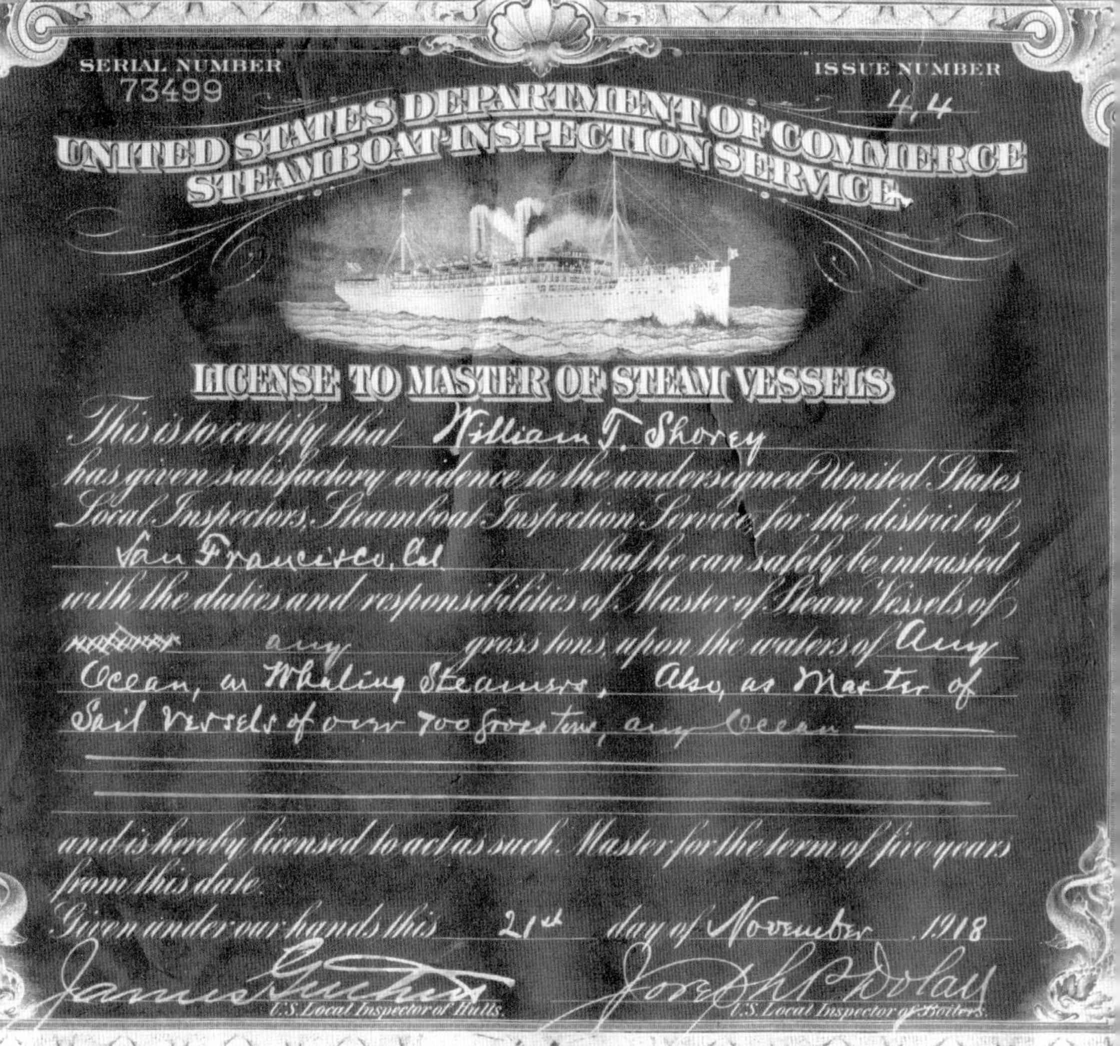

SERIAL NUMBER
73499

ISSUE NUMBER
4,4

UNITED STATES DEPARTMENT OF COMMERCE
STEAMBOAT INSPECTION SERVICE

LICENSE TO MASTER OF STEAM VESSELS

This is to certify that William T. Shorey
has given satisfactory evidence to the undersigned United States Local Inspectors, Steamboat Inspection Service, for the district of San Francisco, Cal that he can safely be intrusted with the duties and responsibilities of Master of Steam Vessels of any gross tons, upon the waters of Any Ocean, or Whaling Steamers. Also, as Master of Sail Vessels of over 700 gross tons, any Ocean —

and is hereby licensed to act as such Master for the term of five years from this date.

Given under our hands this 21st day of November 1918

James Guthrie
U.S. Local Inspector of Hulls.

Joseph P. Dolan
U.S. Local Inspector of Boilers.

Pictured here is a license to master steamboats of any gross tonnage and sail vessels of over 700 gross tons issued to Capt. William Shorey on November 21, 1918.

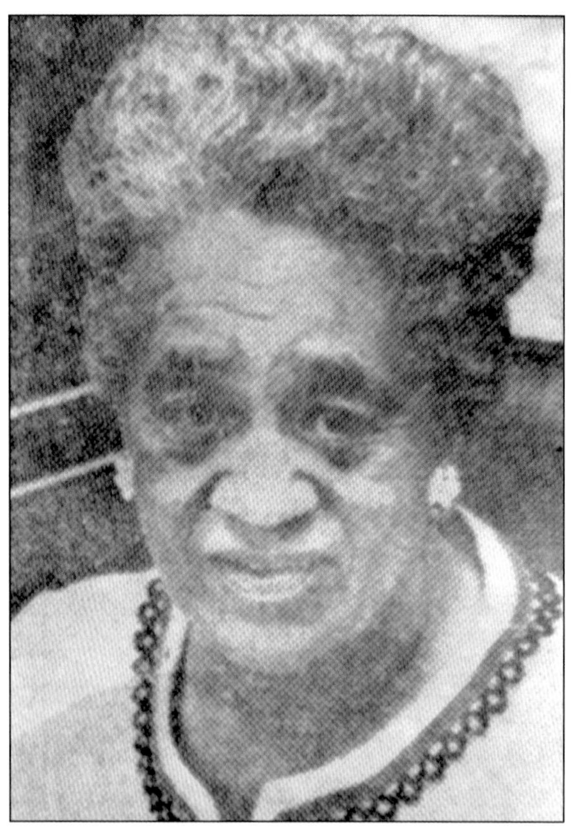

Virginia Stephens submitted the winning name in a contest and is credited with giving the 1915 Panama-Pacific International Exposition in San Francisco the title of the "Jeweled City." The Tower of Jewels was the 435-foot-tall centerpiece of the PPIE. Hung over the building's surface were 102,000 faceted cut-glass "jewels," influencing the name given. Virginia was a cofounder of the Berkeley Chapter of the Alpha Kappa Alpha sorority and realized her dream to be the first black woman admitted to the California Bar.

This is Stephens Restaurant in Oakland.

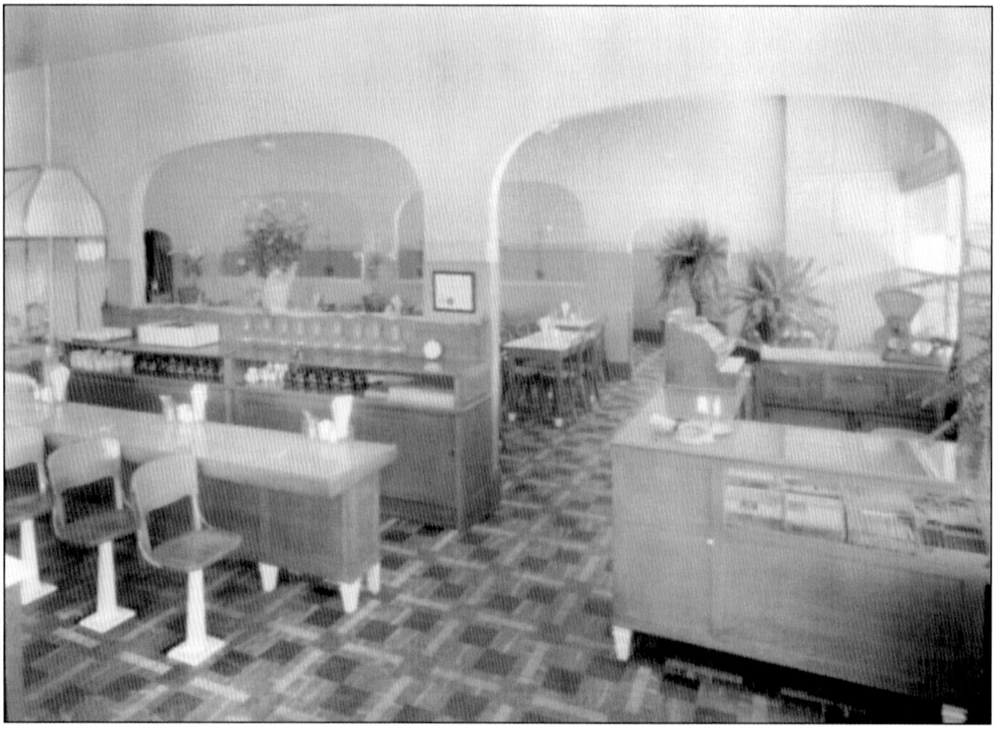

This image shows Virginia Stephens, the mother of Virginia Stephens Coker.

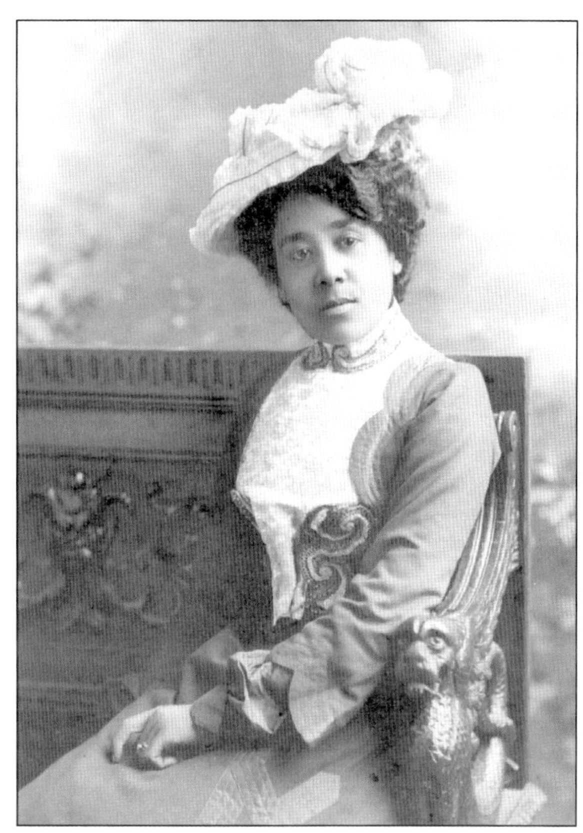

This is an interior view of the new Stephens Restaurant.

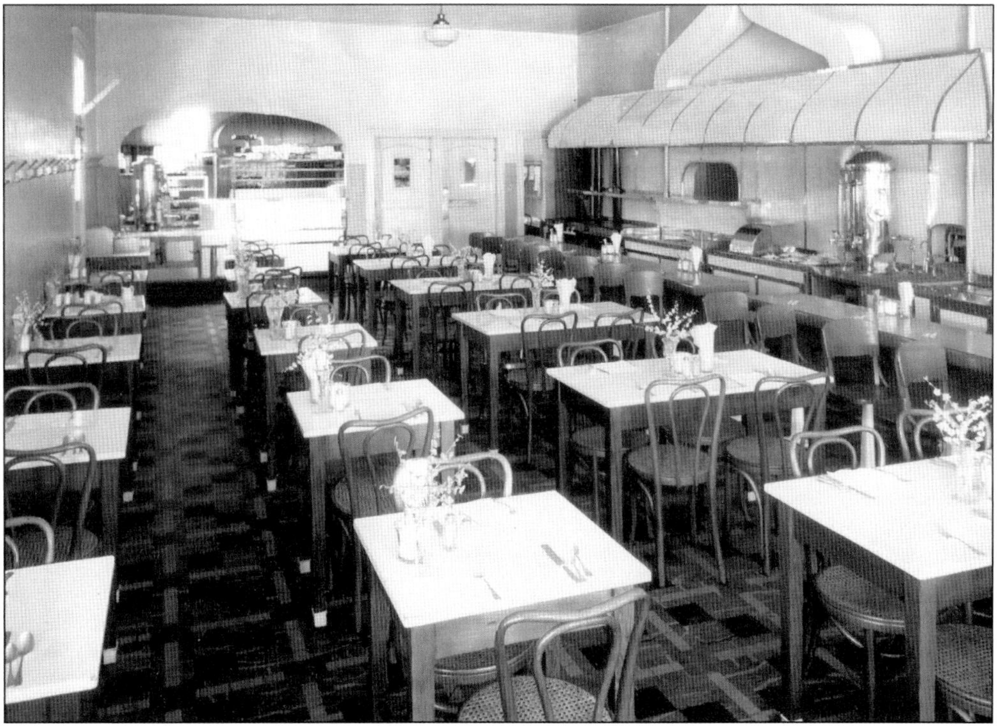

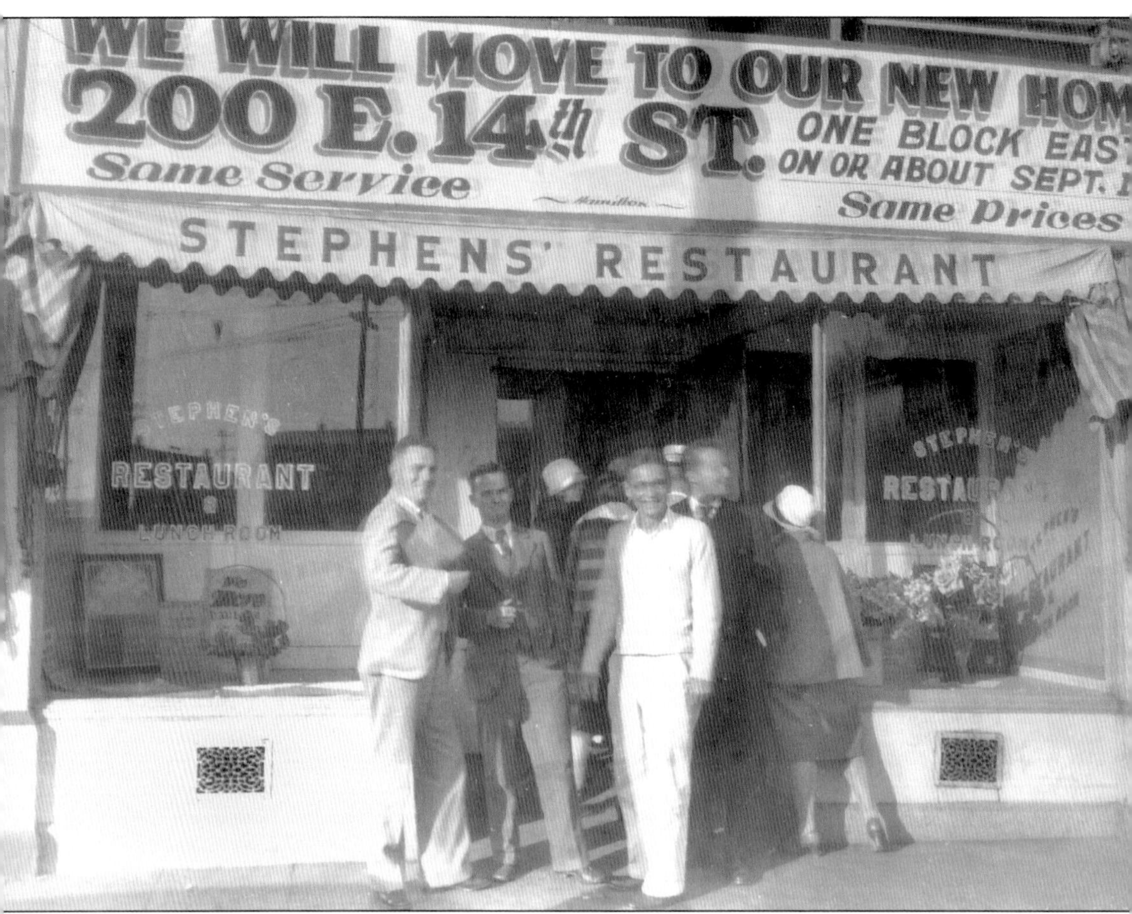


Pictured is Stephens's first restaurant in Oakland, located at Second Avenue and East Fourteenth Street owned by William N. Stephens. At the turn of the century, the Stephens Restaurant at one time served 1,000 meals a day.

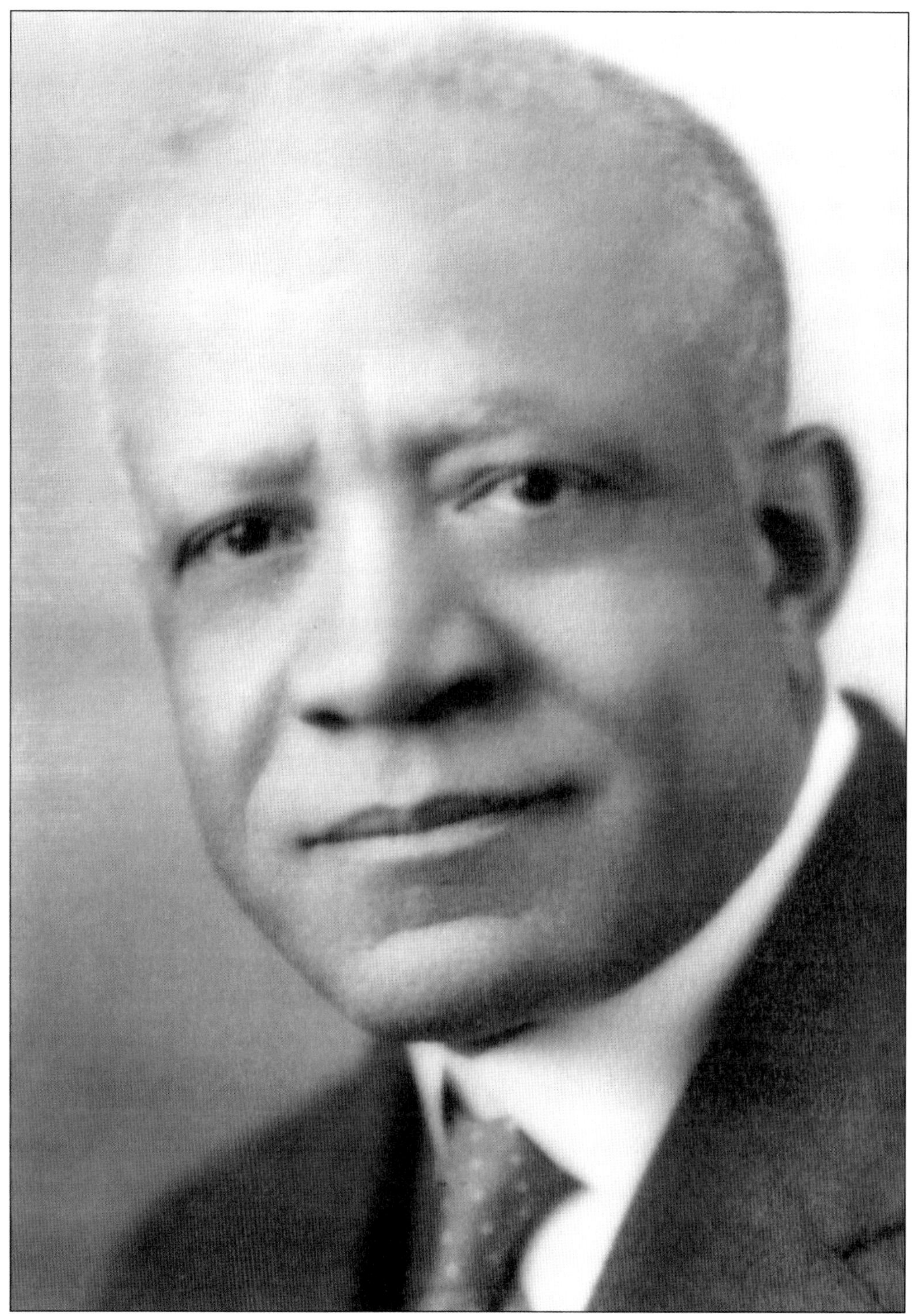

This image is of the father of Virginia Stephens Coker, William Stephens, a successful black Oakland restaurant owner.

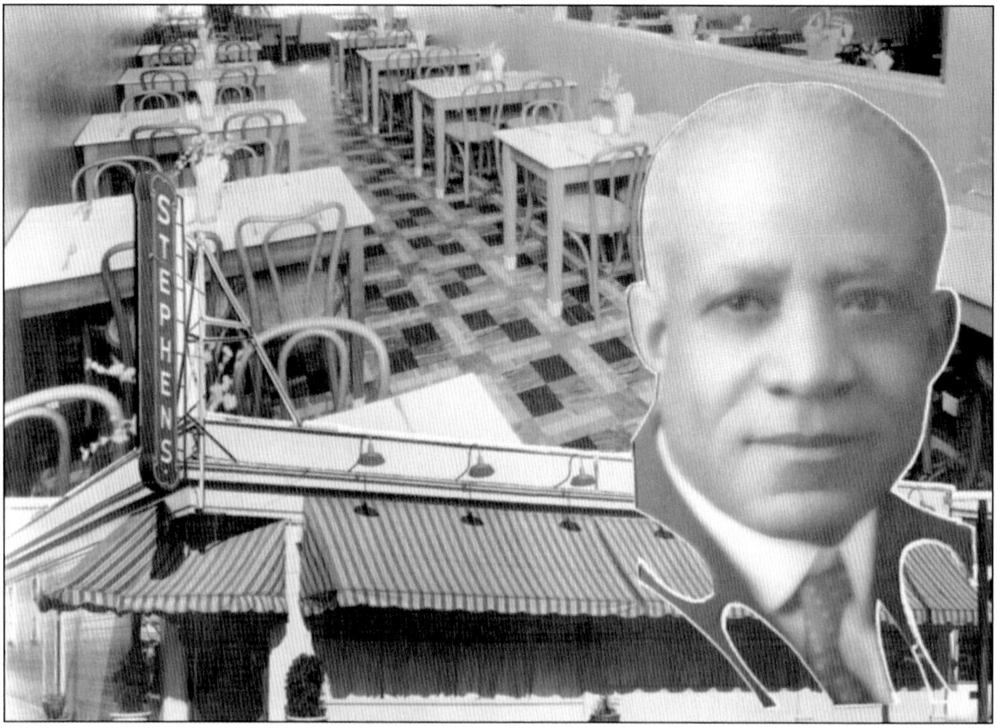

This image depicts William Stephens along with interior and exterior shots of his very successful restaurant.

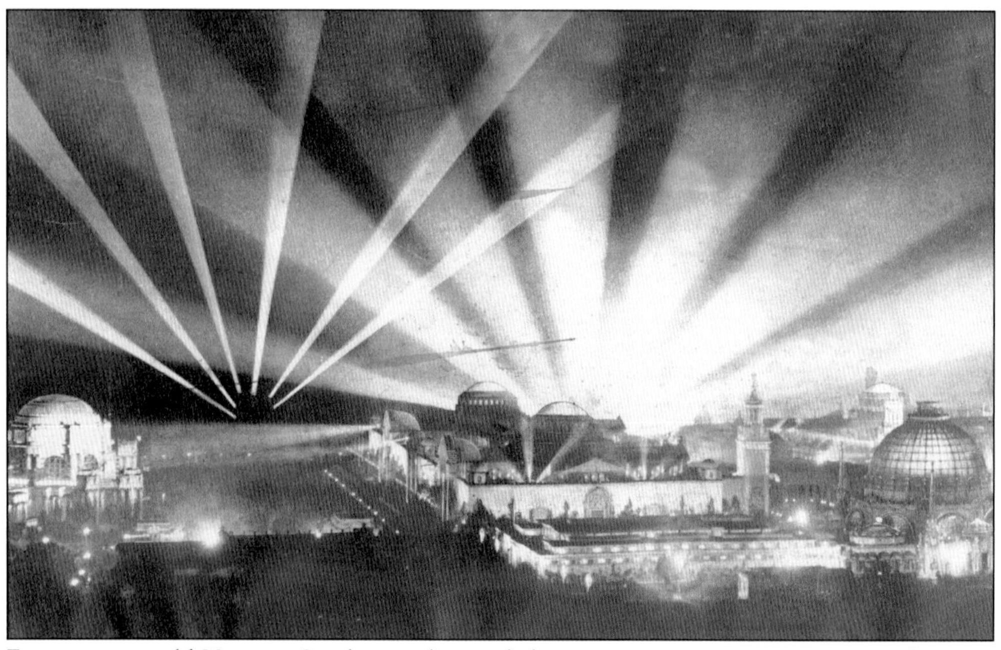

Fourteen-year-old Virginia Stephens submitted the winning entry in a contest to choose a nickname for the 1915 Panama-Pacific International Exposition to be held in San Francisco, deeming it "the Jeweled City." She was invited to the opening ceremonies, an achievement that made all Oaklanders swell with pride.

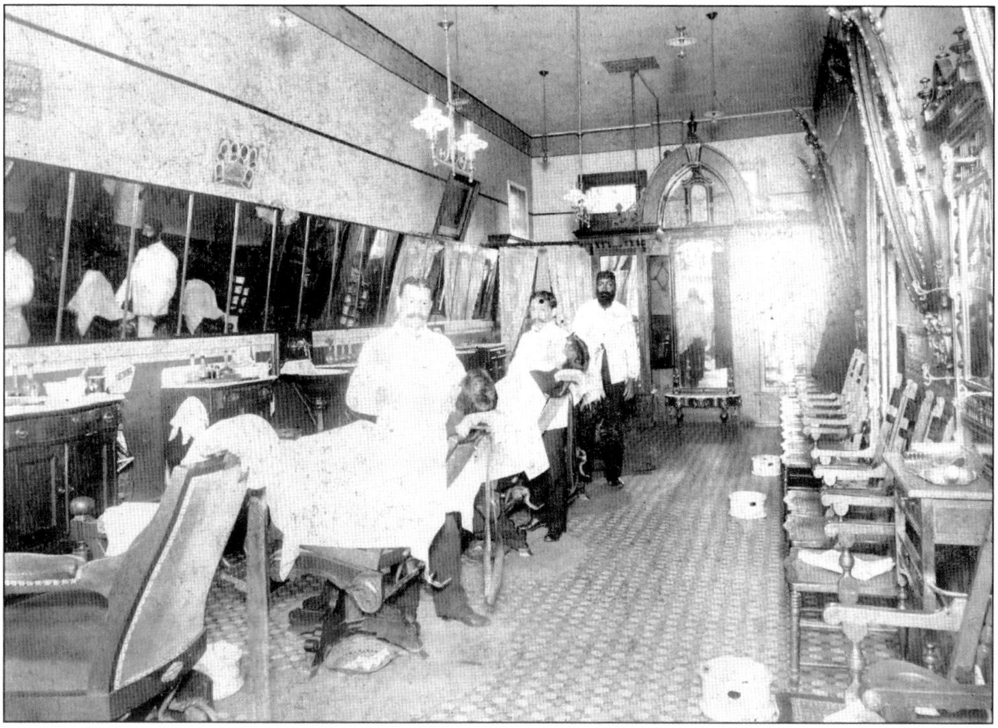

Pictured is the Mint Barber Shop on Broadway, between Ninth and Tenth Streets. William A. Owens was the owner of this shop.

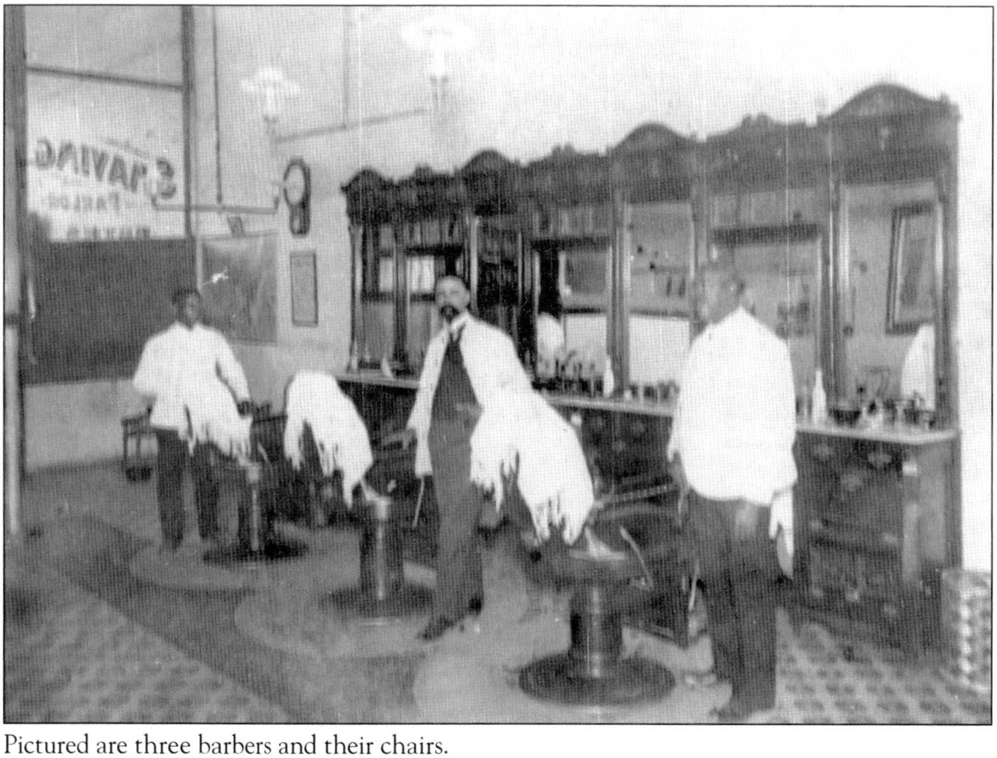

Pictured are three barbers and their chairs.

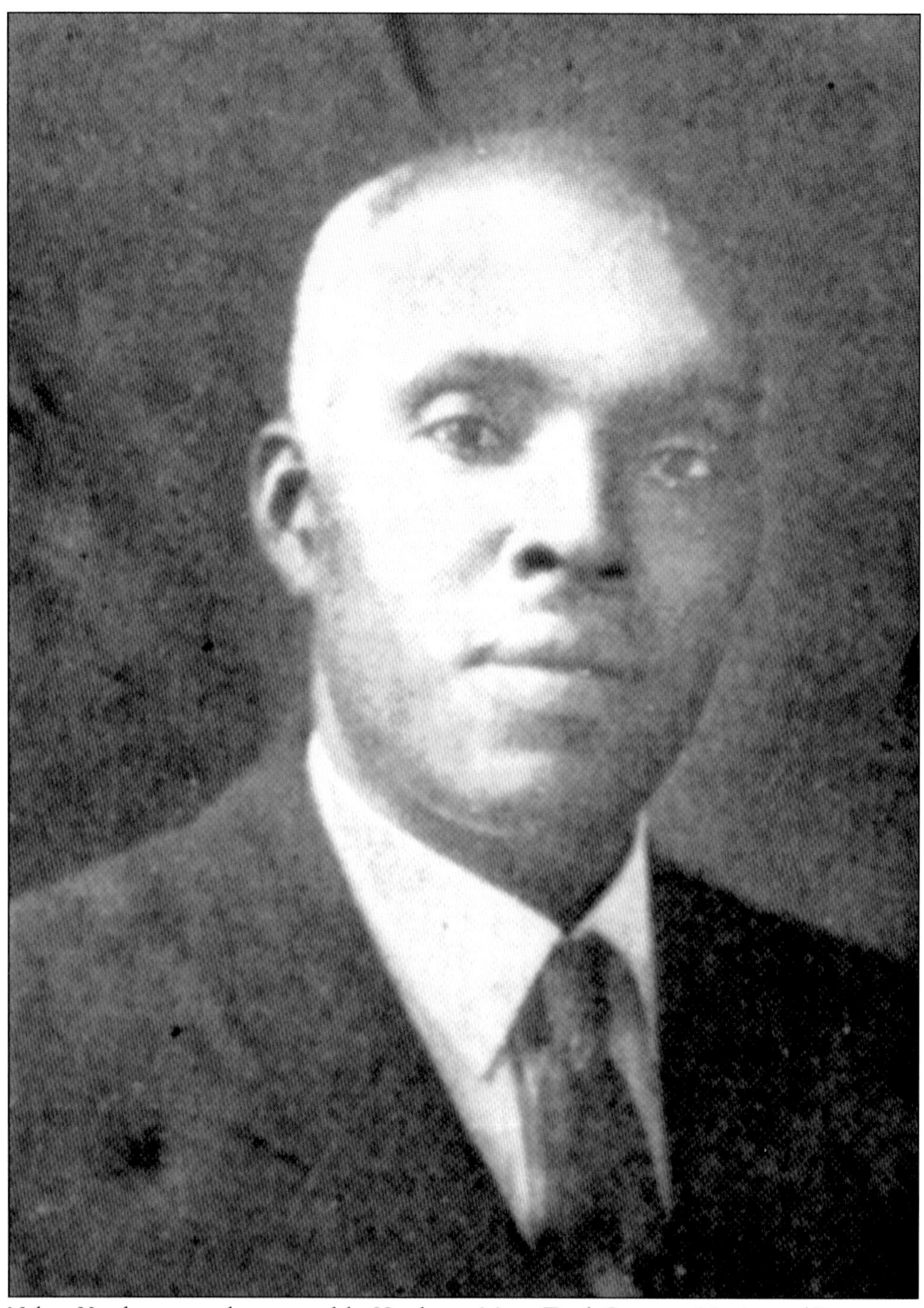

Nelson Henderson was the owner of the Henderson Motor Truck Company Moving and Expressing, located at 405 Eighth Street in Oakland.

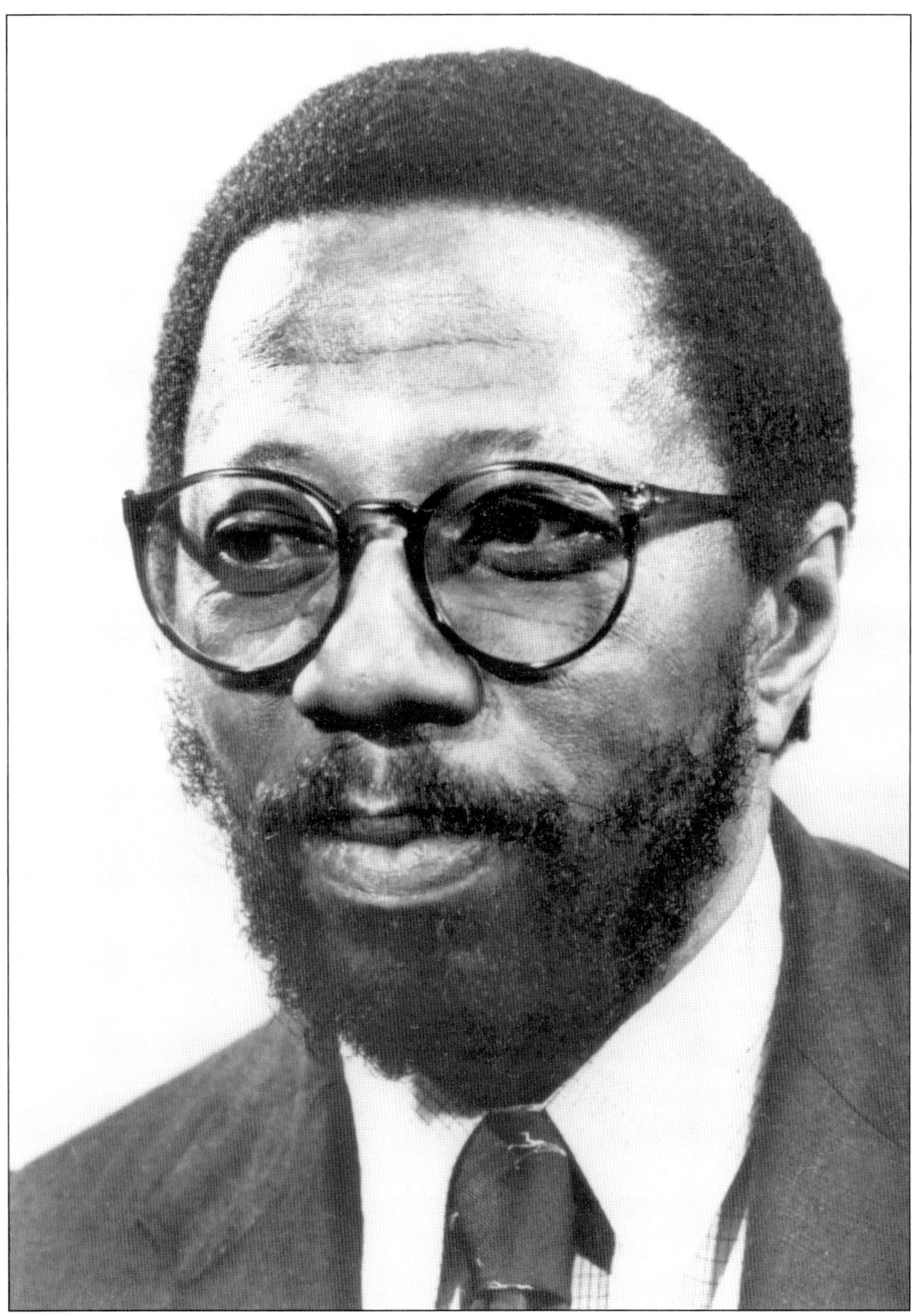

Pictured here is Robert Maynard, the one-time owner, publisher, and editor of the *Oakland Tribune*.

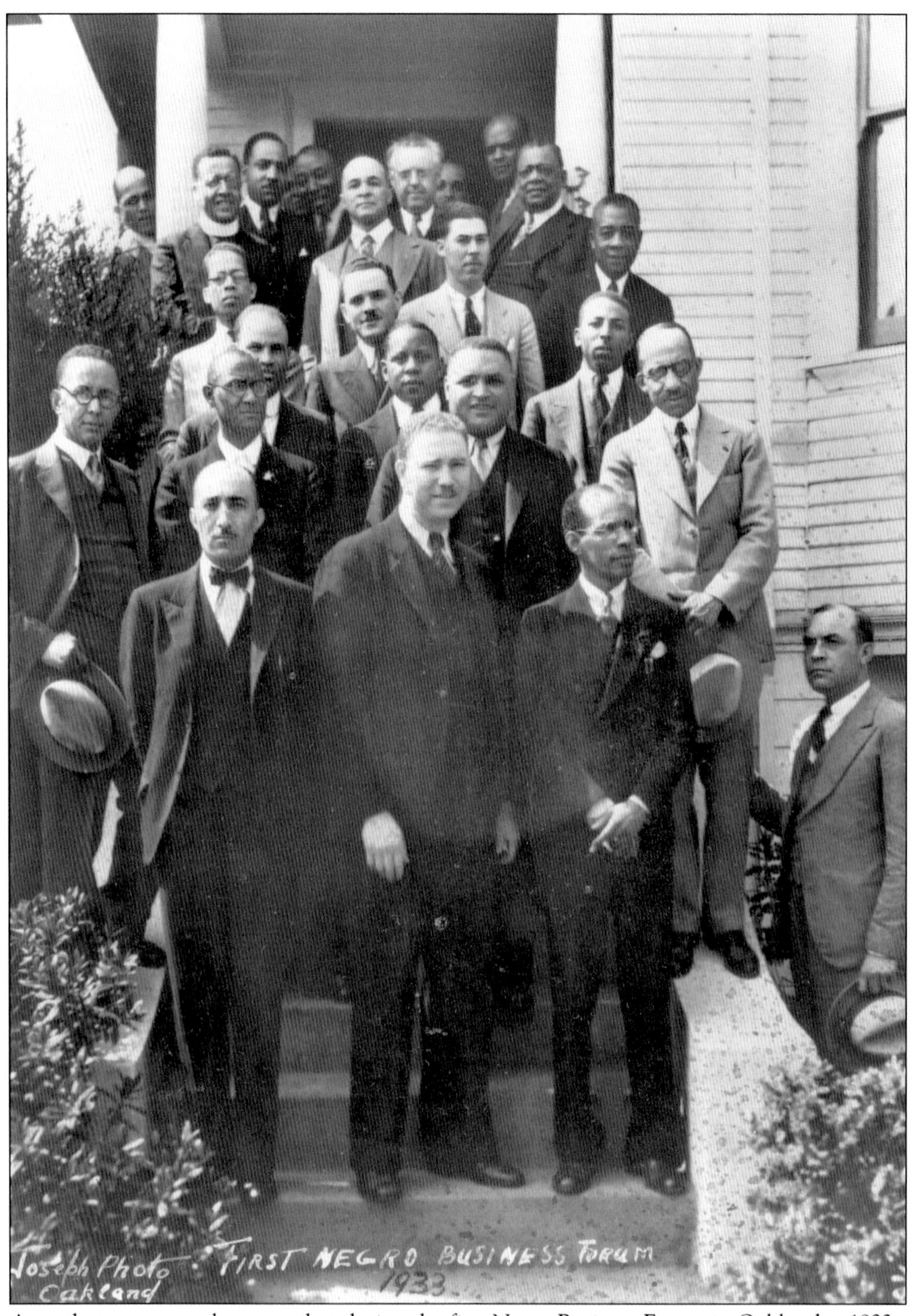

Attendees pause to take a snapshot during the first Negro Business Forum in Oakland c. 1933.

Phil Springer (1874–1952) was the first black man in Oakland to own a taxicab. He was born in Barbados, in the British West Indies, and left home at age 16. At first he operated under a jitney permit in Oakland, but he later had the license changed to a taxicab permit. By 1915, Springer's Cab Company was well established.

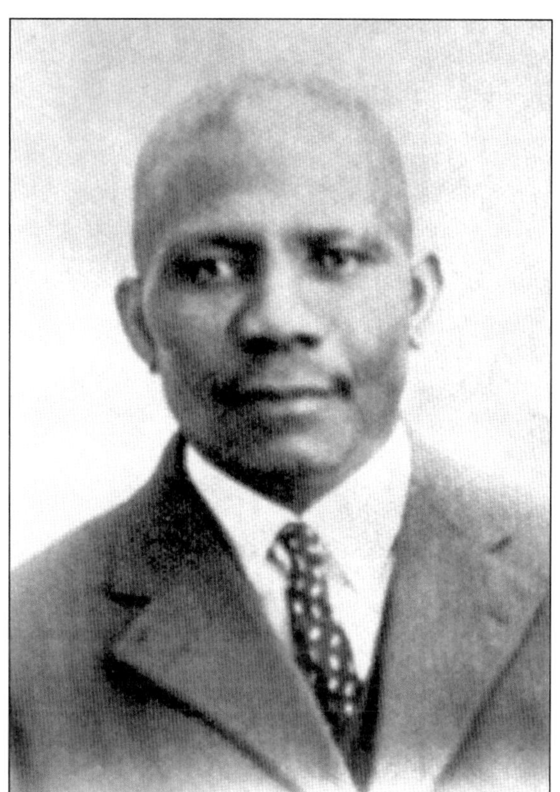

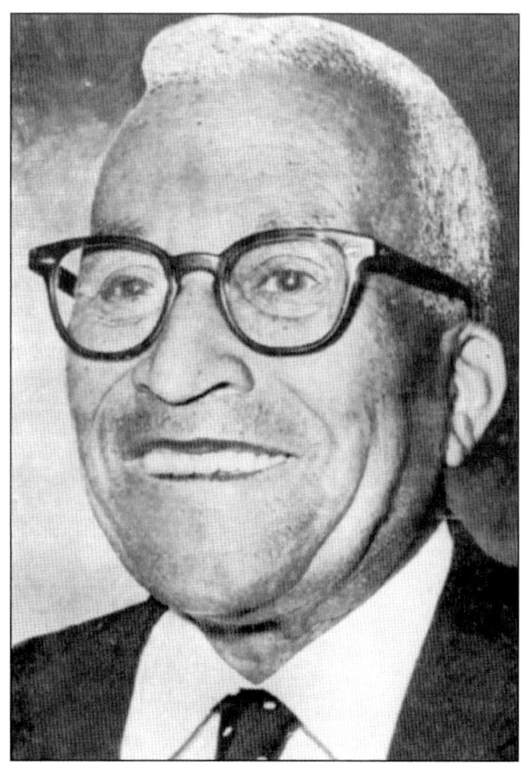

E. A. Daly, seen here, published his own California newspaper in 1960.

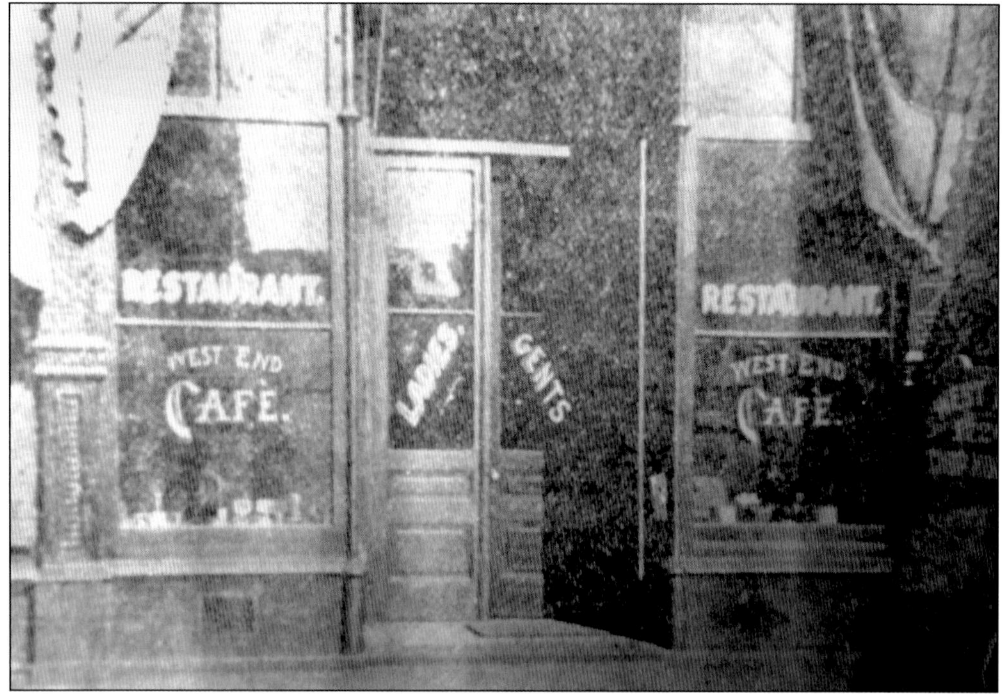


Oakland's first black restaurant opened in 1853. Owned by William Rich, the establishment was located at the foot of Broadway near the estuary. Stephens Restaurant, pictured here, was located at Second Avenue and East Fourteenth Street.

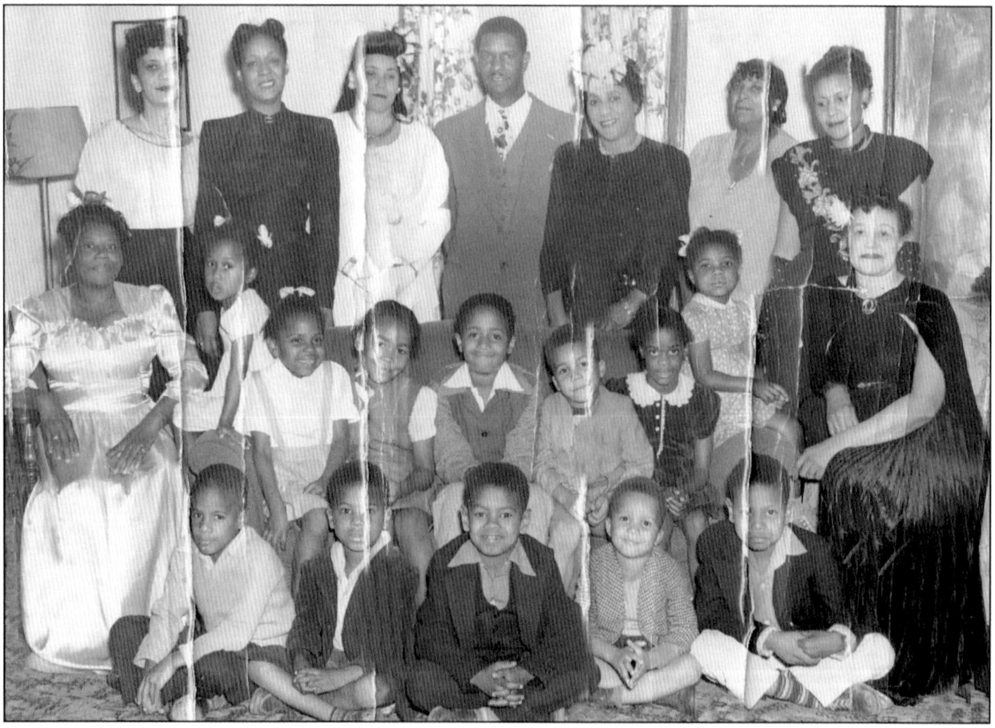

This image is of the Fanny Wall Day Nursery staff and children in October 1947.

The Pacific Coast Stock Raising and Farming Company was Oakland's first black corporation, which started in 1884.

OAKLAND'S 1ST BLACK CORPORATION

1884 1884

**Pacific Coast Stock Raising and Farming Company.**

[INCORPORATED MAY 21, 1884.]

CAPITAL STOCK, $5,000

Divided into 1000 shares, of the par value of $5.00 each.

PRINCIPAL OFFICE, OAKLAND, CAL.

BOARD OF DIRECTORS.

JAS W. WASHINGTON, JOHN A. WILDS
JOHN W. SMITH, W. H. STEWART Jr.,
HORACE M. WILDS.

| | |
|---|---|
| JOHN W. SMITH, - - | President |
| W. H. STEWART, - | Vice-President |
| JOHN A WILDS, - - - | Treasurer |
| HORACE M. WILDS, - - | Secretary |
| J. W. WASHINGTON, - | Superintendent |

The Company buys and sells all kinds of live stock; buys, sells, leases, rents and mortgages lands, and does all things necessary to be done for the purpose of carrying on the business of stock raising and farming. Shares sold on installments if desired. For particulars, apply to the President or Secretary of the Company, No. 1298 Broadway, or 1275 San Pablo Avenue, Oakland, Cal.

Elevator July 3, 188[illegible] p.

Emanuel F. Joseph was the official press photographer for the *Pittsburgh Courier*, *California Voice*, *San Francisco Examiner*, and the *Post Enquirer*. He died in 1979.

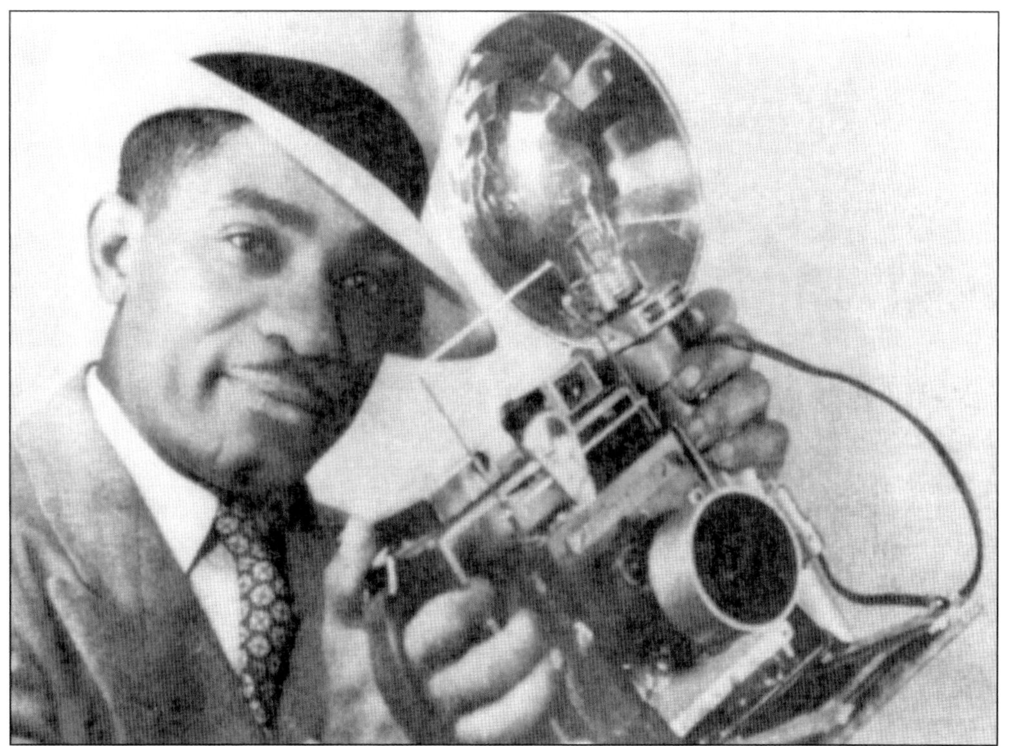

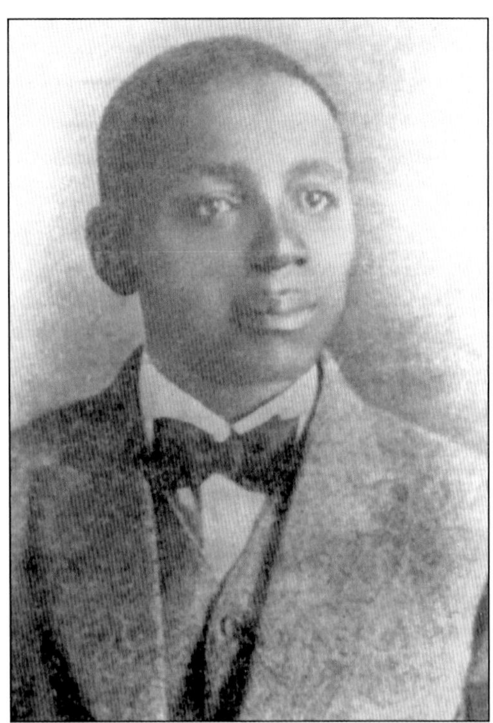

L. Errol Marshall, the owner of a black newspaper, was founder and editor of the *California Voice*.

129242

ARTICLES OF INCORPORATION

of

THE ETHIOPIA CREDIT UNION

KNOW ALL MEN BY THESE PRESENTS: May 15, 1928

That we, the undersigned citizens and residents of the State of California, do by these presence hereby voluntarily associate ourselves together for the purpose of incorporating a credit union under the laws of the State of California:

AND WE DO HEREBY CERTIFY:

FIRST: That the name of said corporation shall be "THE ETHIOPIA CREDIT UNION".

SECOND: That the principle place of business of said corporation shall be at the City of Oakland, County of Alameda, State of California.

THIRD: That the par value of the membership certificates shall be Ten Dollars, ($10.00), each.

FOURTH: That the name and address of the incorporators and the number of shares held by each is as follows:

James R. Ross, 2030 Chestnut St., Oakland, Calif., ten shares;
C. H. Rice, 1033 Poplar St., Oakland, Calif., ten shares;
T. J. Jefferson, 923 Center St., Oakland, Calif., ten shares;
Walden Banks, 1375 Twelfth St., Oakland, Calif., ten shares;
Henry W. Smith, 1505 Union St., Oakland, Calif., ten shares;
Charles S. Truehill, 2011 Linden St., Oakland, Calif., ten shares;
Claude J. Davis, 1543 Prince St., Berkeley, Calif., ten shares;
Robert Green, 2429 Post St., San Francisco, Calif., ten shares;
B. Chrisman, 1622 Stuart St., Berkeley, Calif., ten shares;
W. J. D. Thompson, 1530 Seventh St., Oakland, Calif., ten shares;

FIFTH: That the term for which said corporation shall exist shall be fifty (50) years from and after date of its incorporation.

1-

Pictured here are the 1928 Articles of Incorporation for the Ethiopia Credit Union.

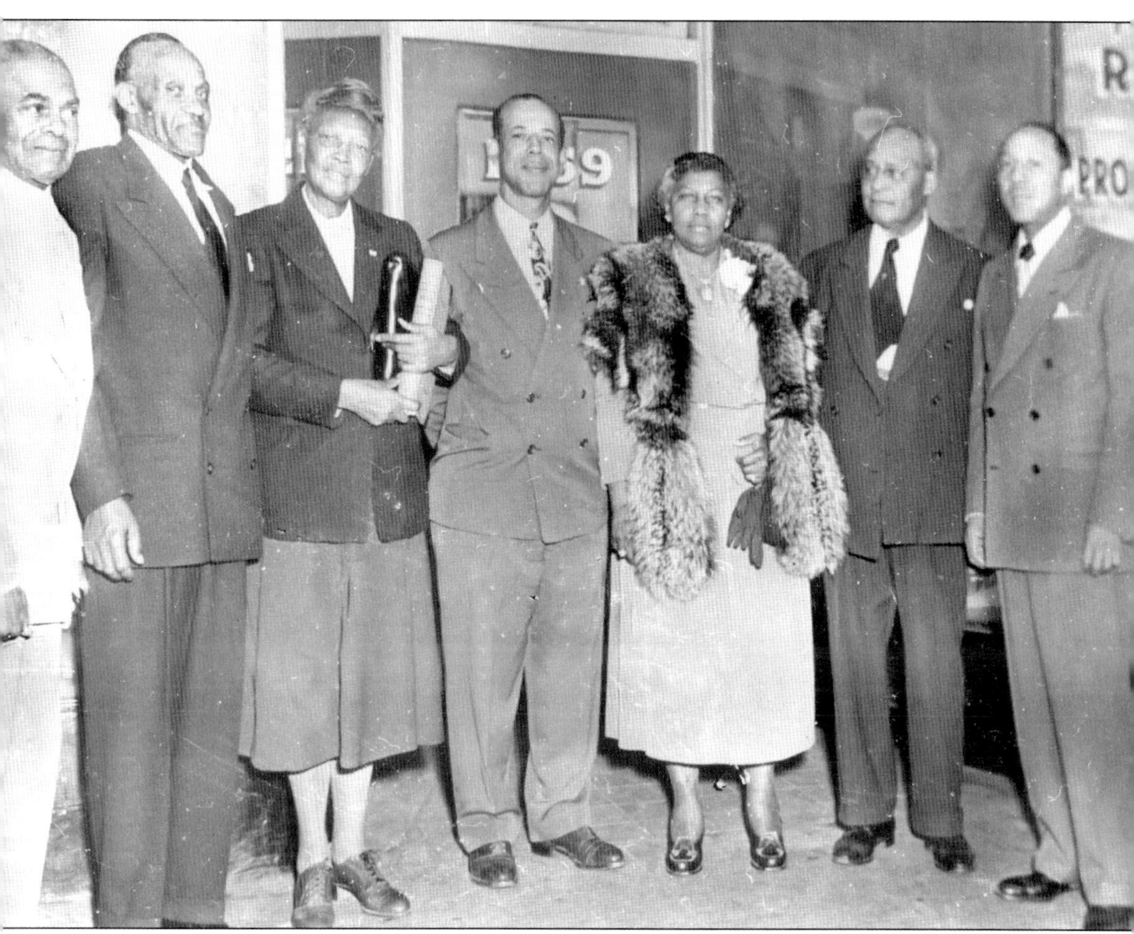

In 1952, the board of directors stand in front of this hotel and business office building at 1559–1563 Seventh Street in Oakland to celebrate its mortgage burning.

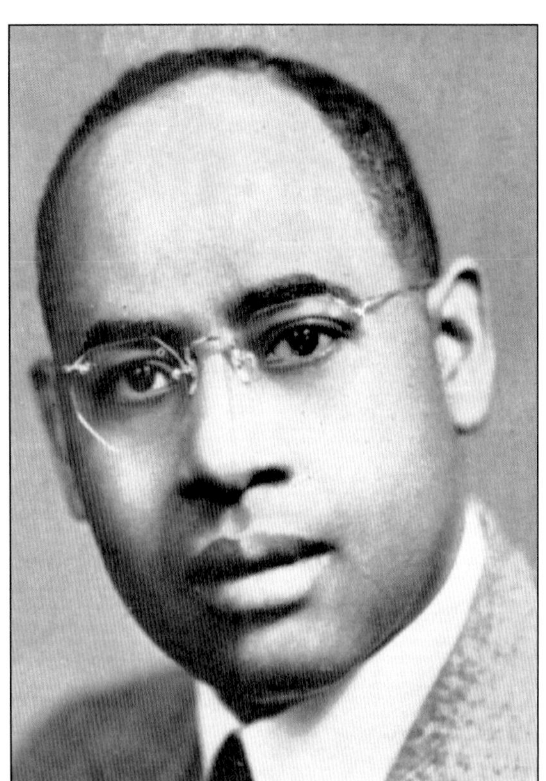

Slim Jenkins, pictured here, was one of Oakland's most well-known entrepreneurs.

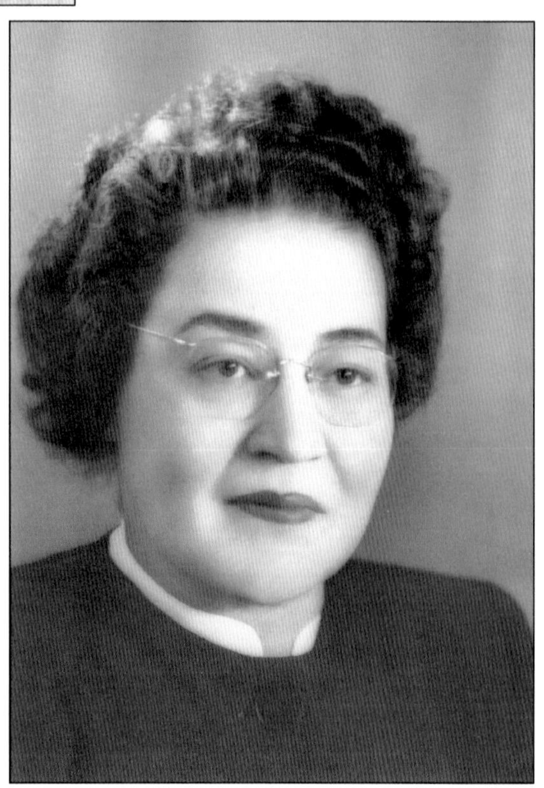

This image depicts Mrs. Elsie Jenkins, Slim's wife.

# *Eight*

# Leisure-Time Activities

Time off of work was usually spent getting the family in the car and driving to visit relatives still living back home. West Oaklanders, proud of their new, wealthier lifestyle, also spent time off in a new variety of leisure-time activities.

Socializing meant dressing for the occasion and getting out of the house. These activities included card games, driving in the country, swimming, and snow skiing.

A "family and friends" picnic always promised hot dogs, hamburgers, barbecued pork and beef ribs, and potato salad. The best outings always had "red soda water" and homemade barbecue sauce. Family potlucks drew a crowd because it was a certainty that only the cooks' best dishes would be on the table.

Traditions from "back home" were maintained, as weekend hunting and fishing hobbies were brought to California. Hunting was mostly reserved for the men, but fishing was open to anyone. The catfish found throughout the streams, rivers, and deltas of the area was usually served up at any fish fry.

When the railroad dominance gave way to the highway system, and more people could afford cars capable of cross-country travel, families increased visits to "back home" locations. Those able to invest in cameras took photographs of sights recorded along the way.

The African American dreamscape, different than the total concept of the American dream, became a reality for many West Oakland residents.

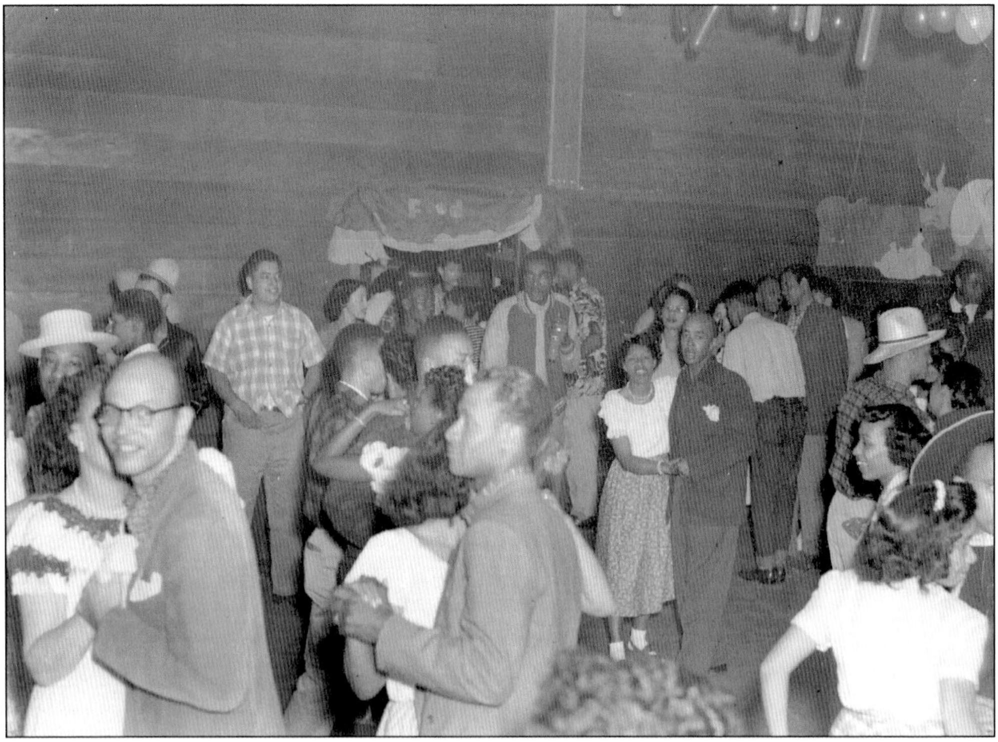

This is an image of a Women's Barn Dance at the North Oakland YMCA in 1949.

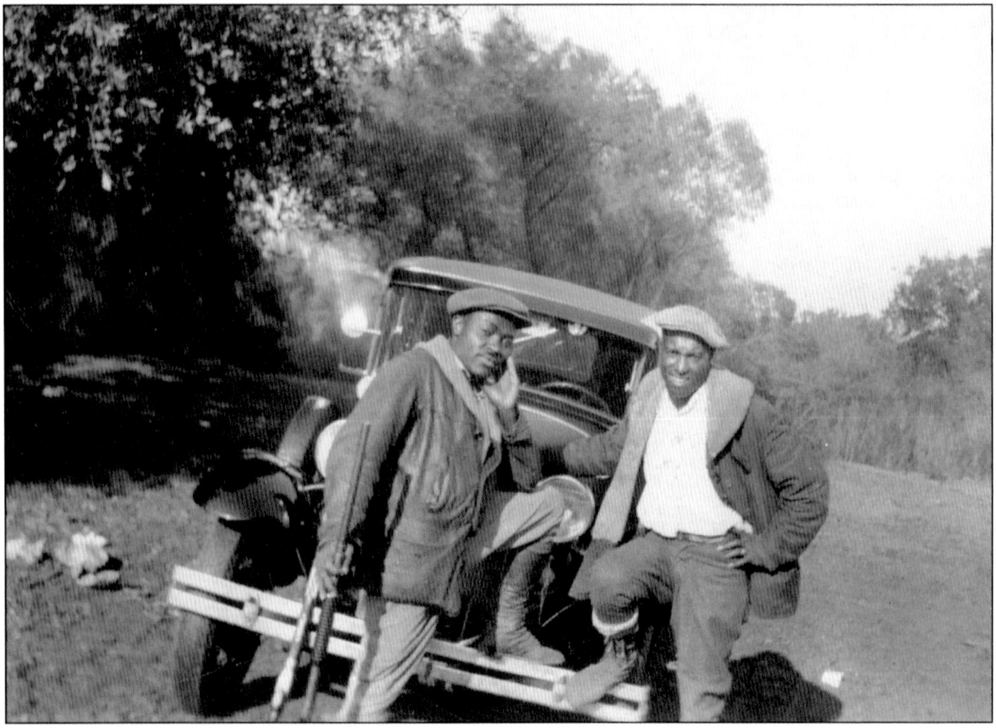

Here two men pose in front of their car, preparing for a day of shooting at the Rod and Gun Club.

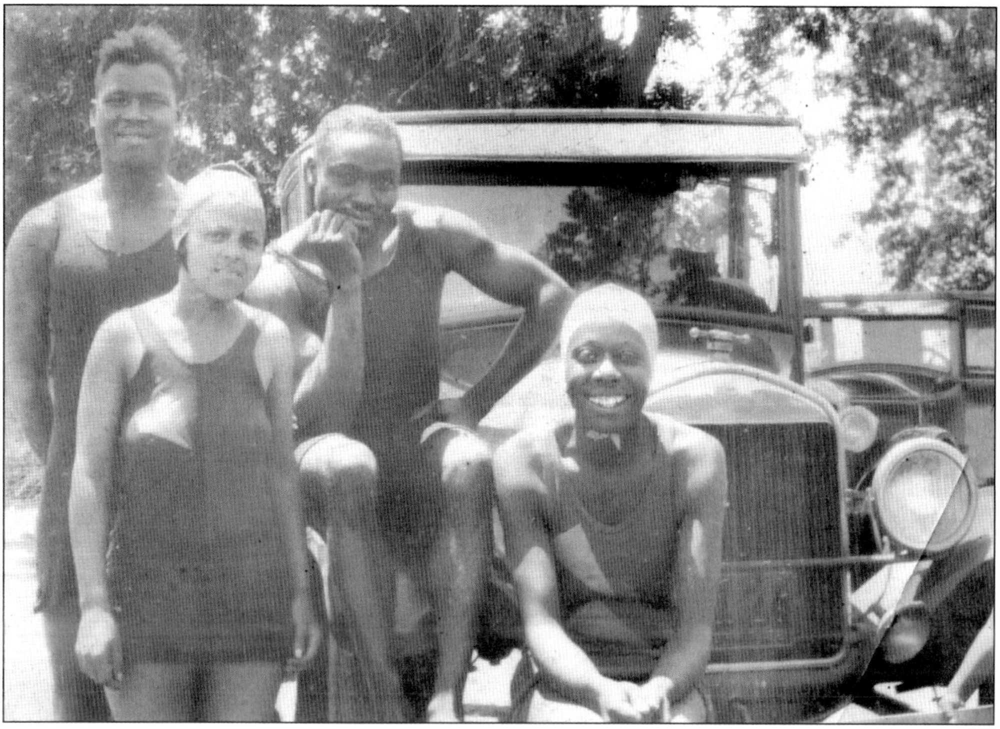

In 1932, this group, posing in front of their car, is ready to go swimming.

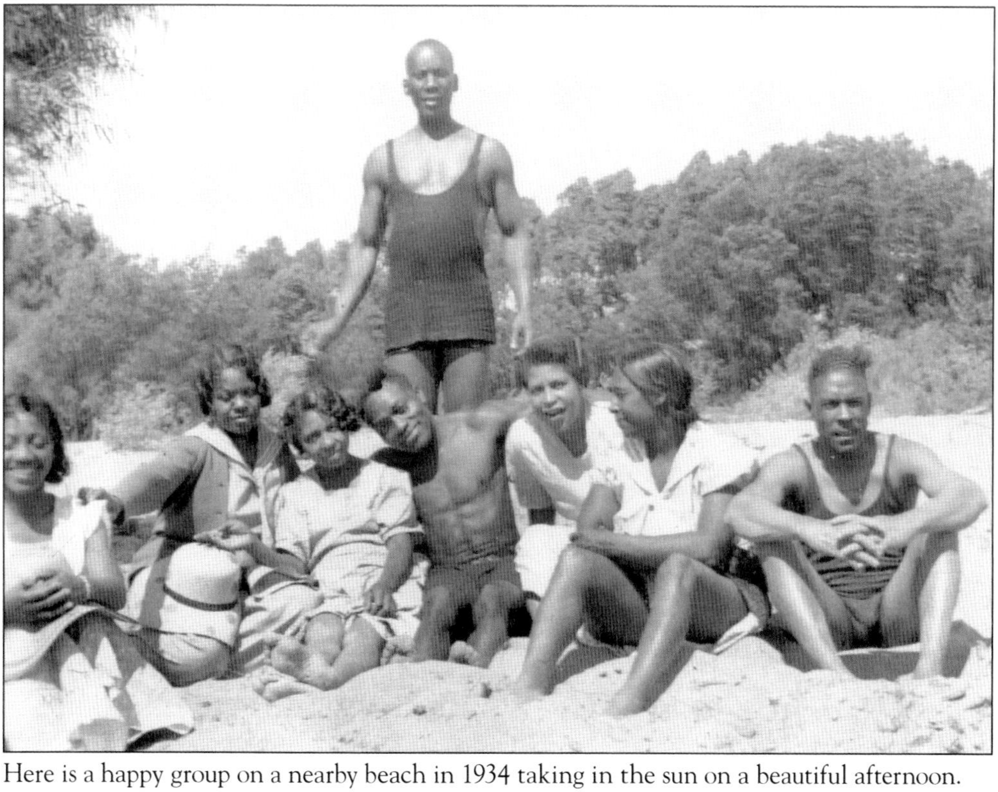

Here is a happy group on a nearby beach in 1934 taking in the sun on a beautiful afternoon.

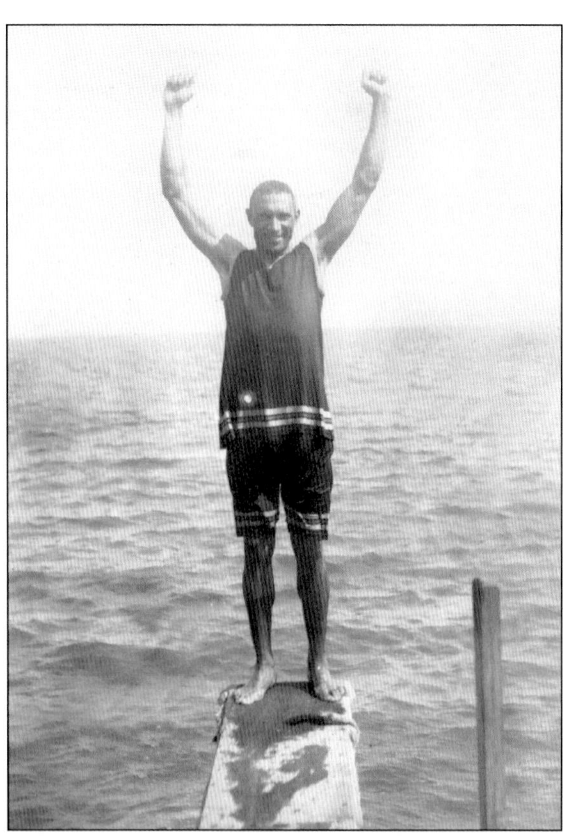

This unidentified swimmer posing at a diving pier shows off one leisure-time activity. This photograph is from an AAMLO collection.

This image shows locals on a skiing trip in Khyber, California. This was an unusual and costly leisure-time activity for West Oakland African Americans and was only possible in middle-income families.

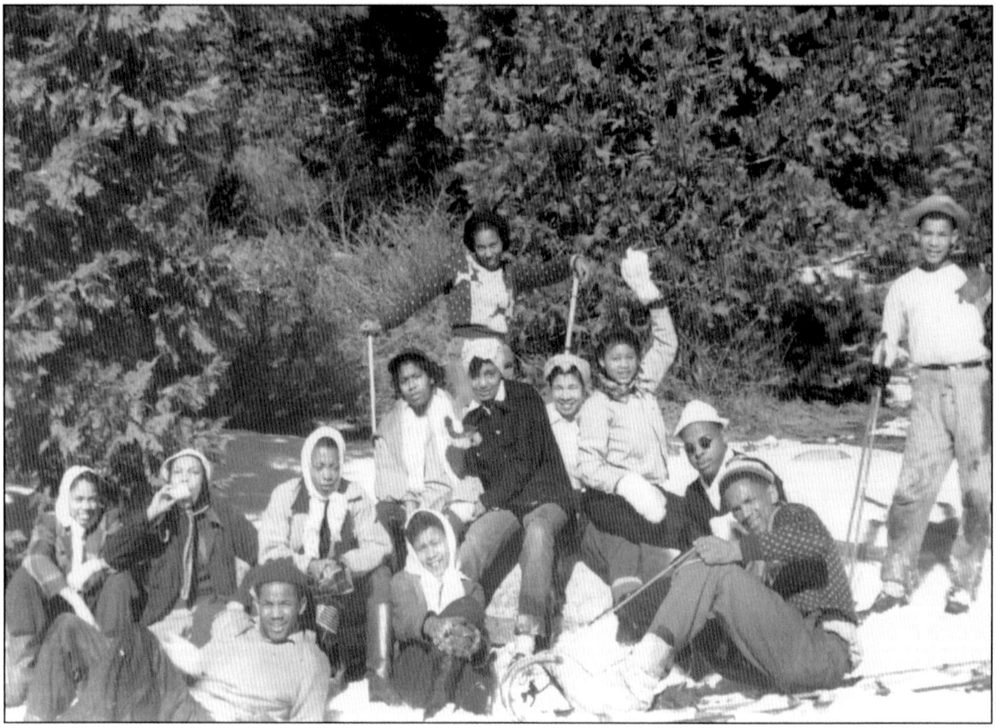

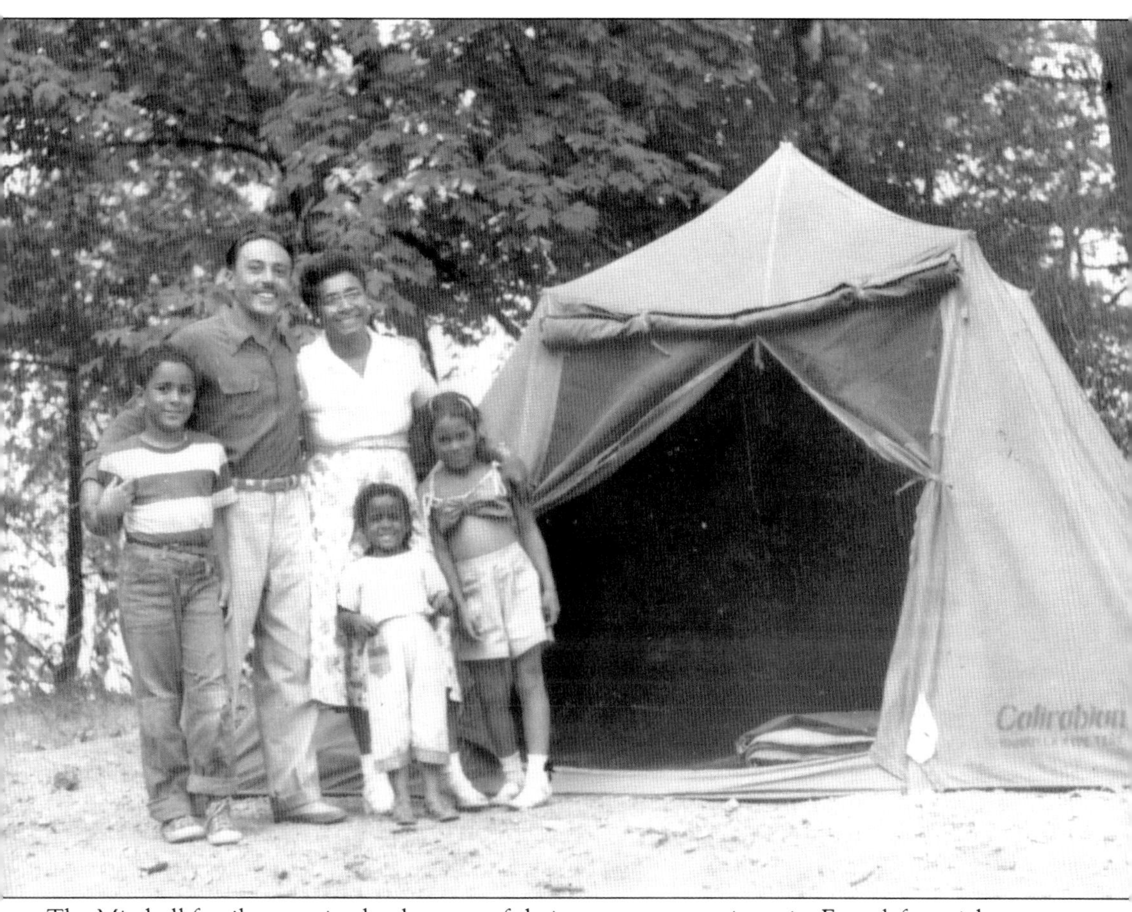

The Mitchell family poses in the doorway of their tent on a camping trip. From left to right are Henry Jr., Henry Sr., Elizabeth, Ella, and Muriel.

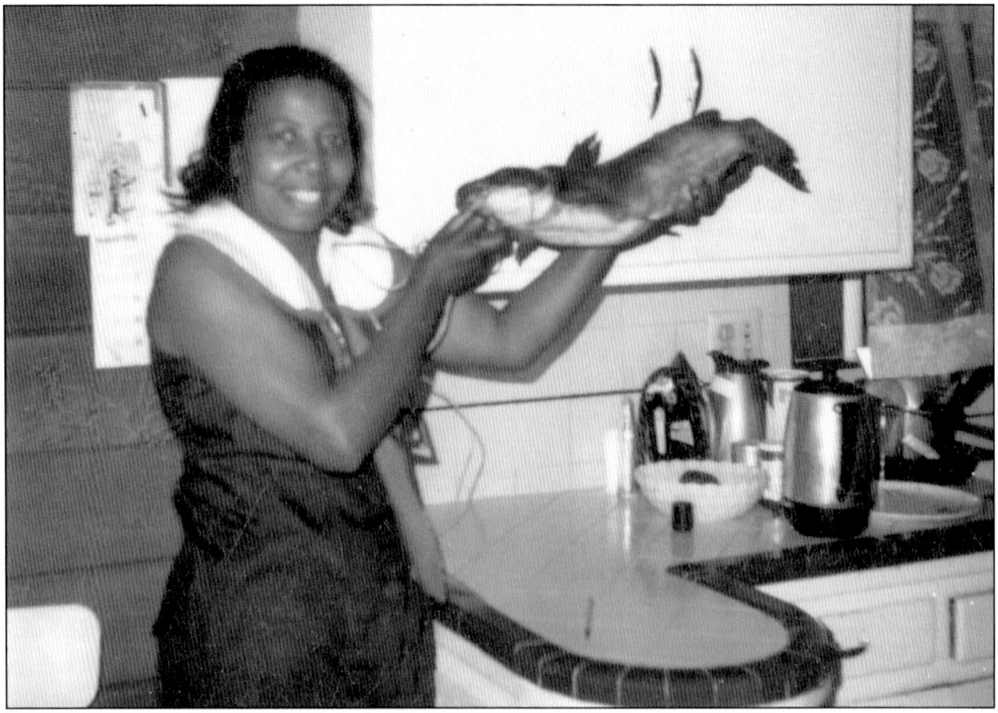

Noveline Simmons proudly poses for the camera with a trophy-worthy catfish. (Simmons Collection.)

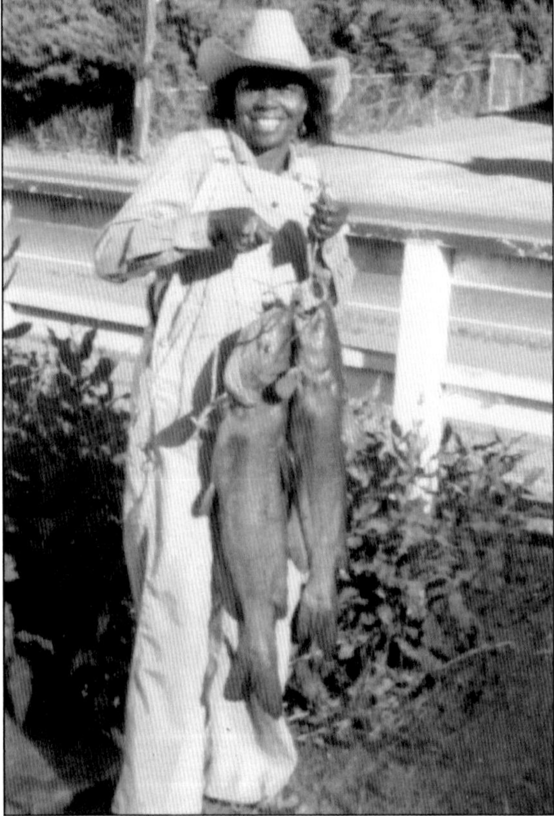

Noveline Simmons, dressed for casting from a riverbank, holds a string of catfish. (Simmons Collection.)

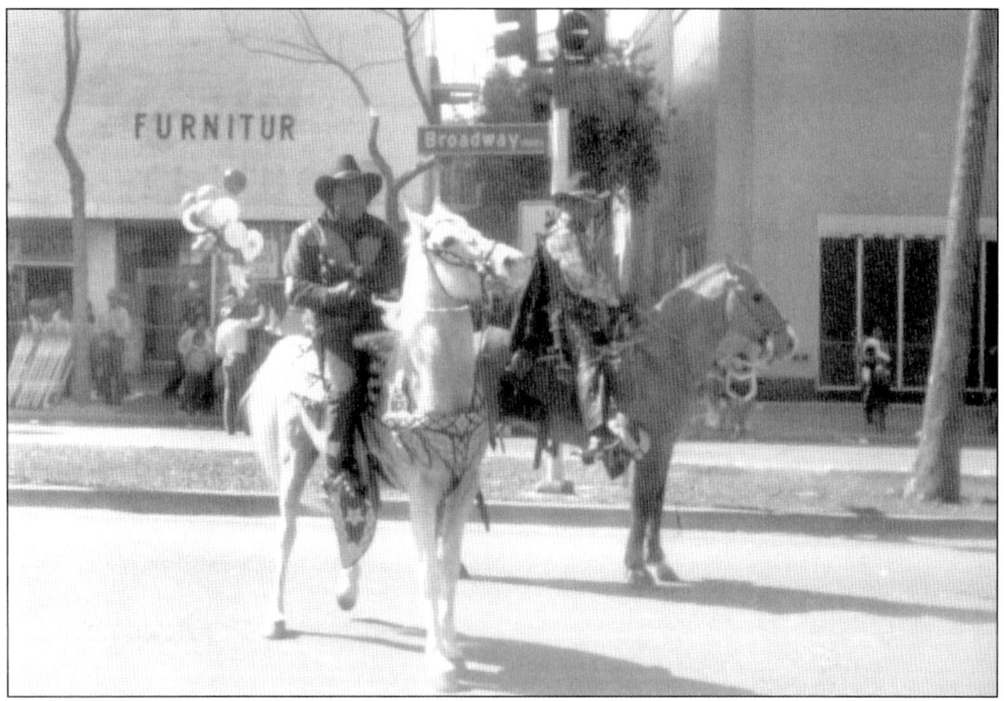


Two unidentified members of the Black Cowboys Organization ride in a downtown Oakland parade. (Simmons Collection.)

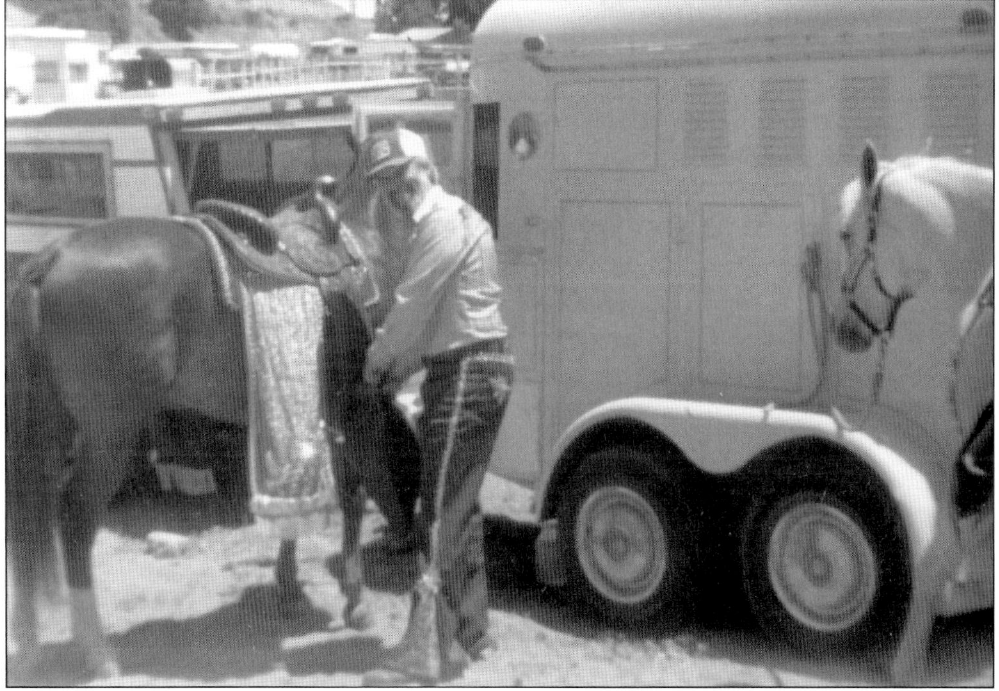

All the necessities for owning and exhibiting a horse—the horse, a handler, and a trailer—are visible here. Blacks who lived in Oakland used their American dream values to acquire and develop interests otherwise not affordable without their middle-class economic standing. (Simmons Collection.)

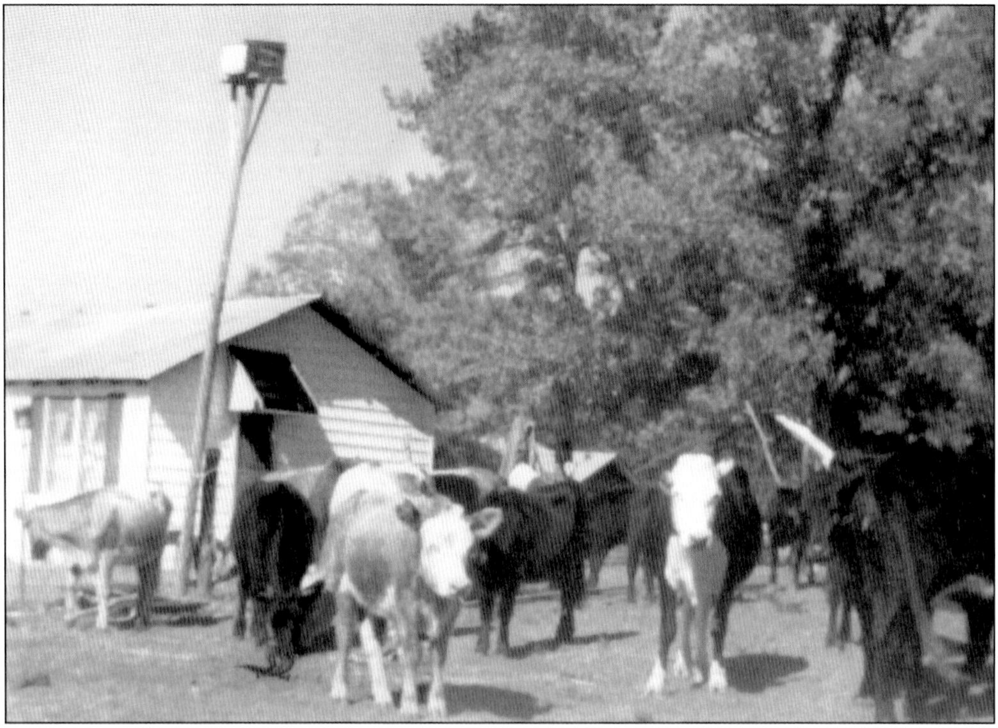

The Herman Simmons family vacation automobile trips included learning about other parts of the country. This farm photograph demonstrates how they valued learning during these vacation travels. (Simmons Collection.)

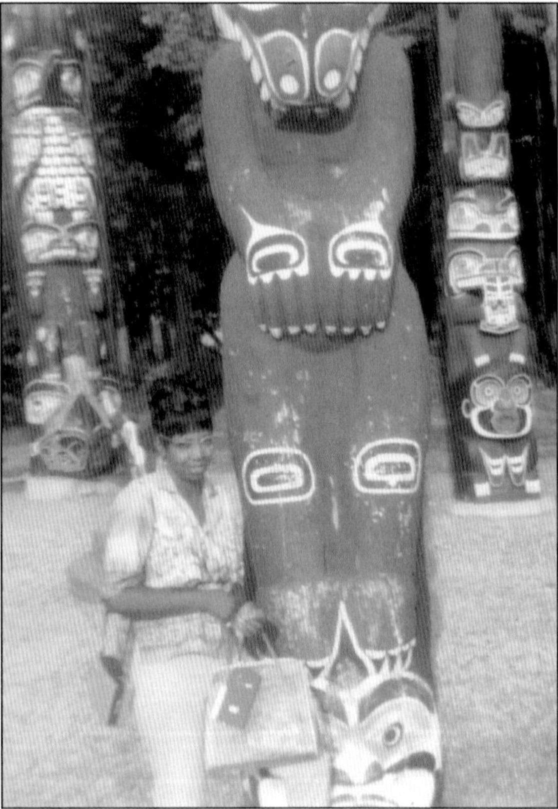

The Herman Simmons family collection included photographs taken at attractive stops during vacation automobile trips. The family photographer made sure to get a photograph of this Native American totem pole. (Simmons Collection.)

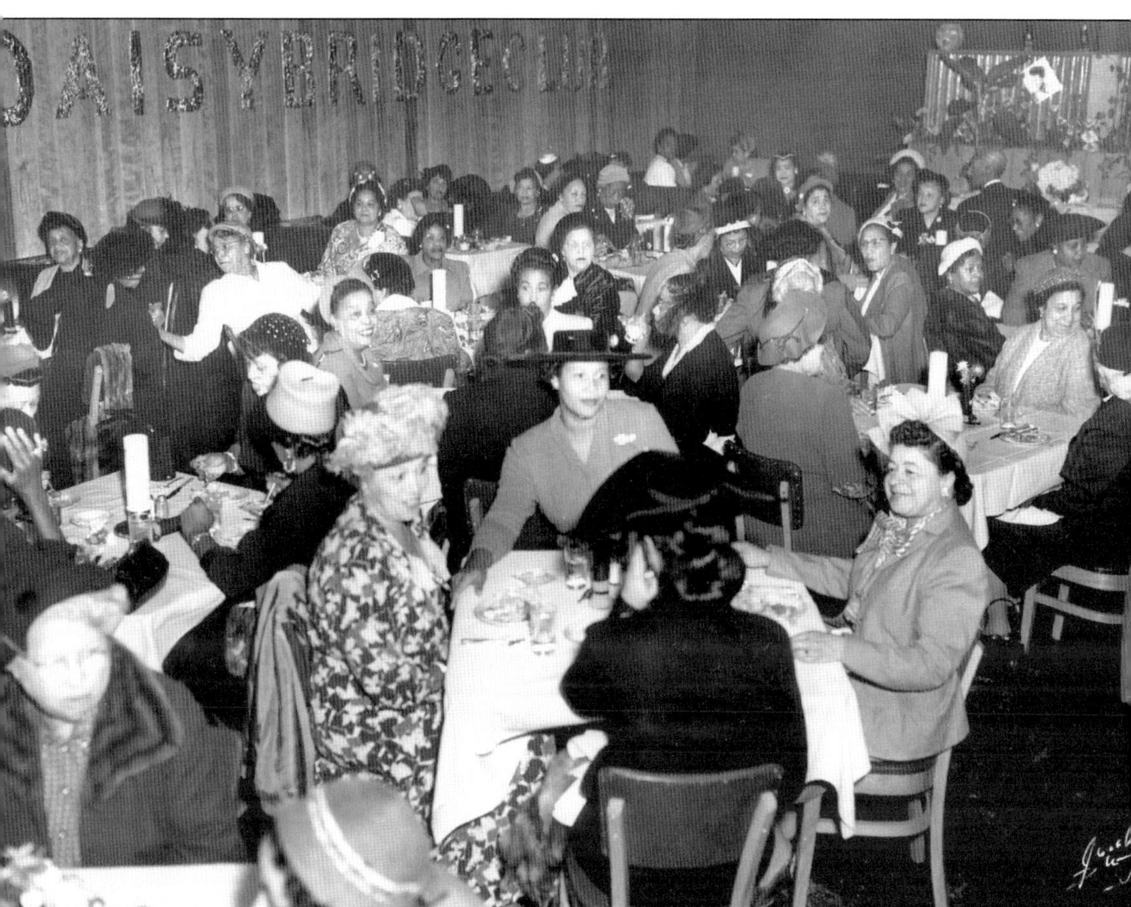

Pictured here is the Daisy Bridge Club showing that style was just as important as cards.

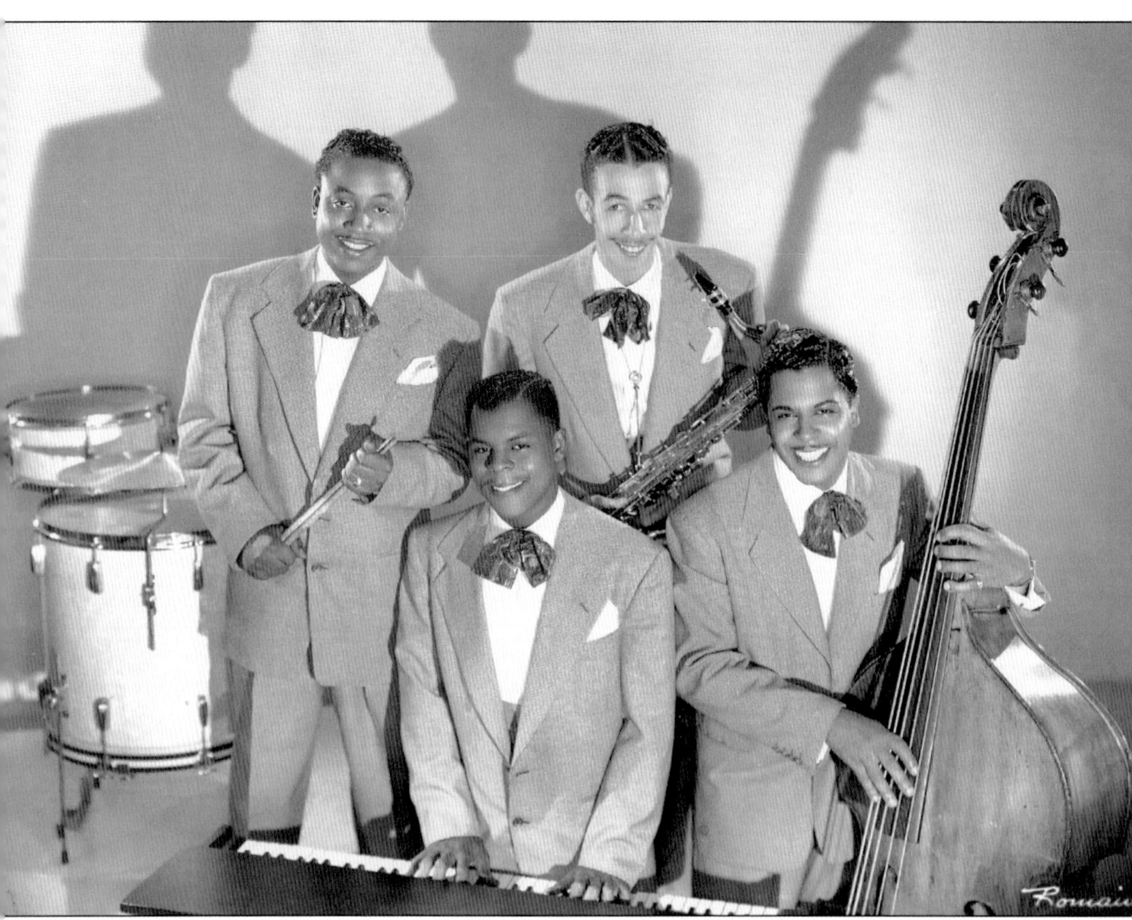

The Four Naturals—Tommy Smith, drums; Sammy Simpson, saxophone; Ed Hammond, bass; and Tyrone Parsons, piano—gave performances throughout Oakland.

# *Nine*

# LEADERSHIP FROM CLUBS AND ORGANIZATIONS

The West Oakland community received leadership from a variety of sources. The Brotherhood of Sleeping Car Porters Union directed African Americans in the legal fight for bargaining rights with America's business owners. Church pastors and congregations maintained the decorum for morality in the community. Mothers and fathers taught children their roles in society as they increased in age. Clubs and organizations addressed social inequities and cultural needs within the West Oakland community. West Oakland's black women were the foundation in establishing church congregations, voluntary organizations, and social support groups, and became more employed outside the home.

Oakland's clubs and organizations began forming as early as 1870 and continued throughout the 20th century. In 1884, the House of Ruth (an auxiliary of the Odd Fellows Lodge), the Ladies Beneficial Society, and the Daughters of Samaria began benevolent activities. In 1970, the Colored Citizen's Literary Association and the Literary and Aid Society addressed educational needs.

In 1897, Home for Aged and Infirm Colored People provided services for the elderly. Emma Scott headed five years of fund-raising to acquire a custom-built, two-story, 16-room Victorian building in which the motto, "Lifting as we climb," was emphasized. In 1899, the Fanny Jackson Coppin Club, considered the "mother" of the black women's club movement in California, took the early reigns, seeking ways to provide community support.

Newspapers published by blacks carried positive news relating to African Americans often missing from white-owned publications. The *Oakland Sunshine* (1897–1923), *Oakland Independent*, the *Oakland Times*, the *Pacific Times*, the *Western American*, the *Western Outlook*, the *California Voice* (1919), and the *Oakland Illustrated Guide* (1892–1896) were all newspapers that filled an important element of community communication. The *Oakland Tribune*, a newspaper at one time owned and edited by Robert Maynard, published Delilah Beasley's column covering Oakland's African American activities.

George Pullman began a company in 1869, which had a completely unanticipated positive outcome for African Americans. The company, run by true robber barons who were totally exploitative and denigrating to their black employees, provided the landscape for African American men and women to paint the gorgeous mural of an African American dreamscape centered in West Oakland.

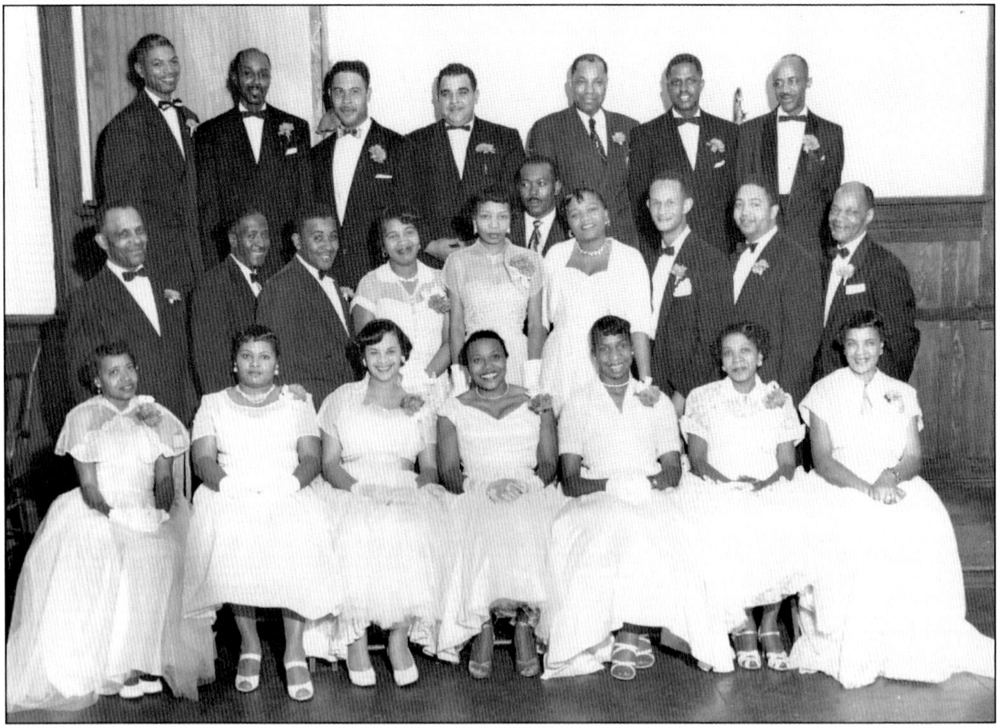

The elegance of those posing is easy to spot, as the Eli Baker Lodge and Rebecca Chapter pause for a picture in formal attire.

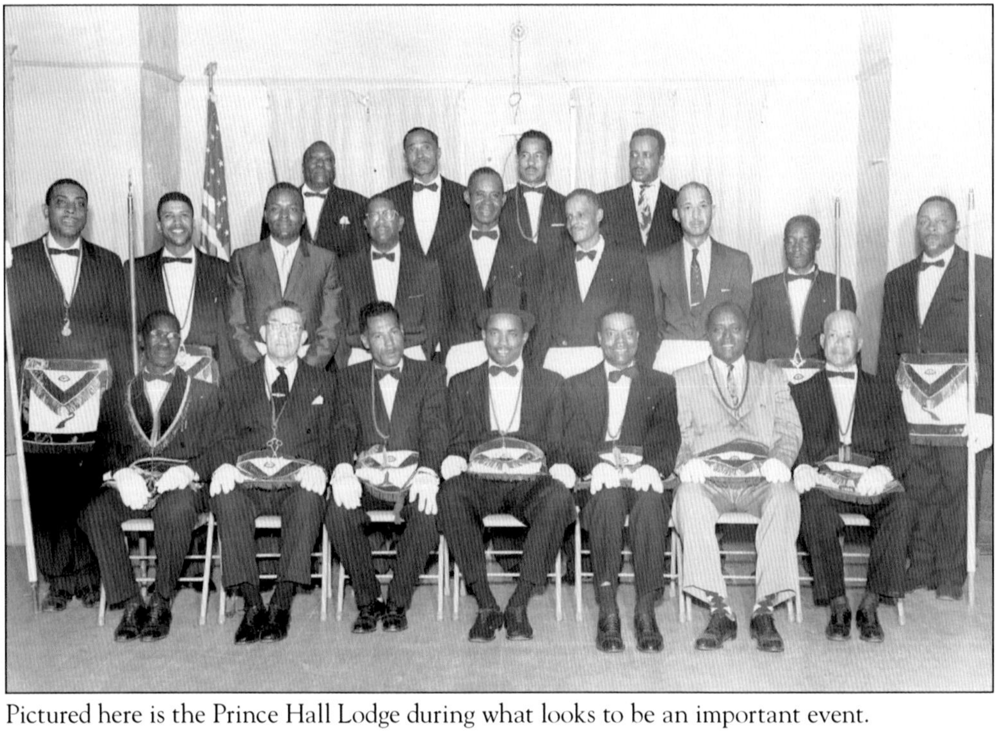

Pictured here is the Prince Hall Lodge during what looks to be an important event.

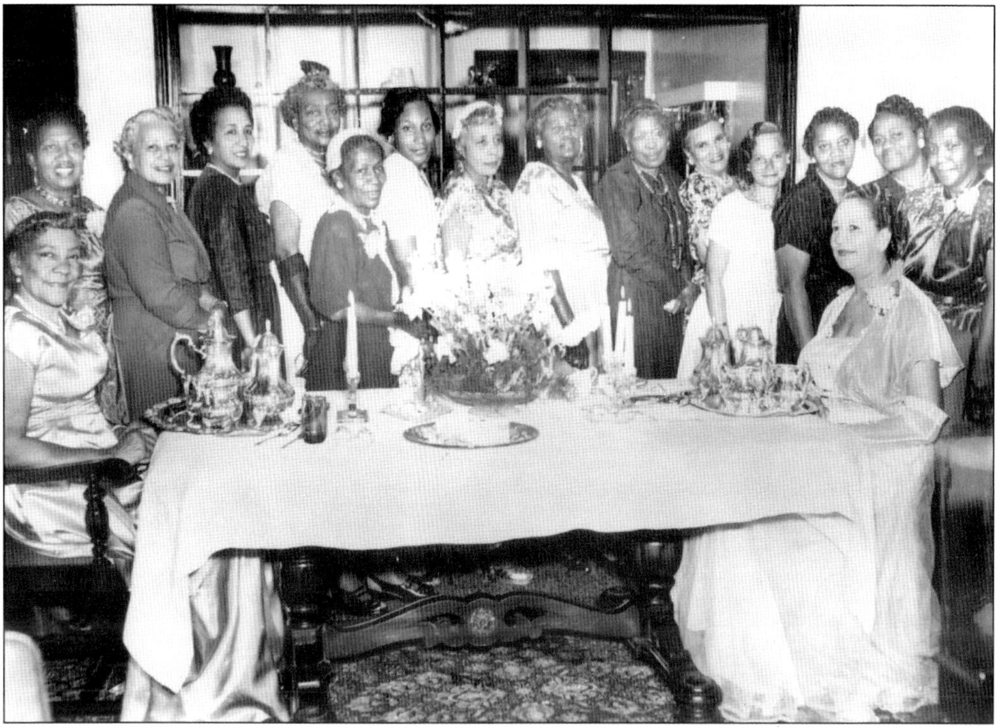

Pictured here is the Mary Church Terrell Club.

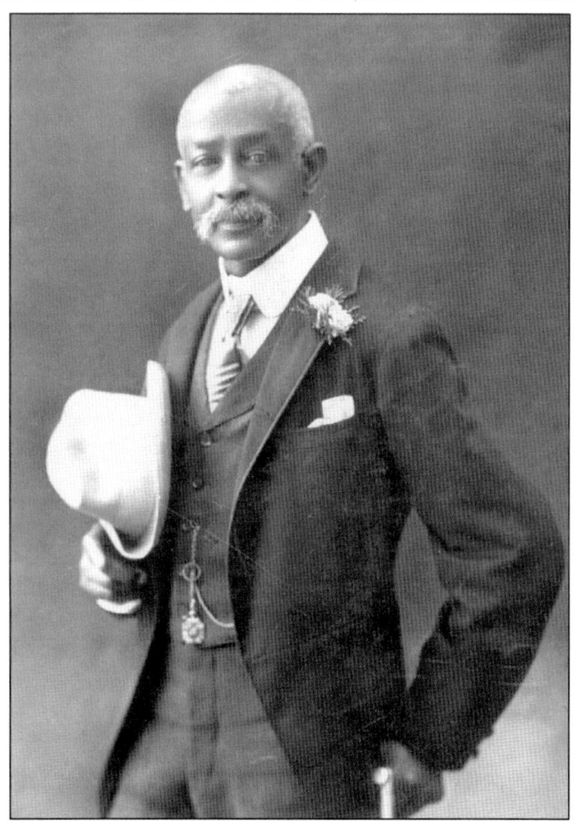

Joseph Hatton was the Past Grand Master of the Prince Hall Masons in 1902.

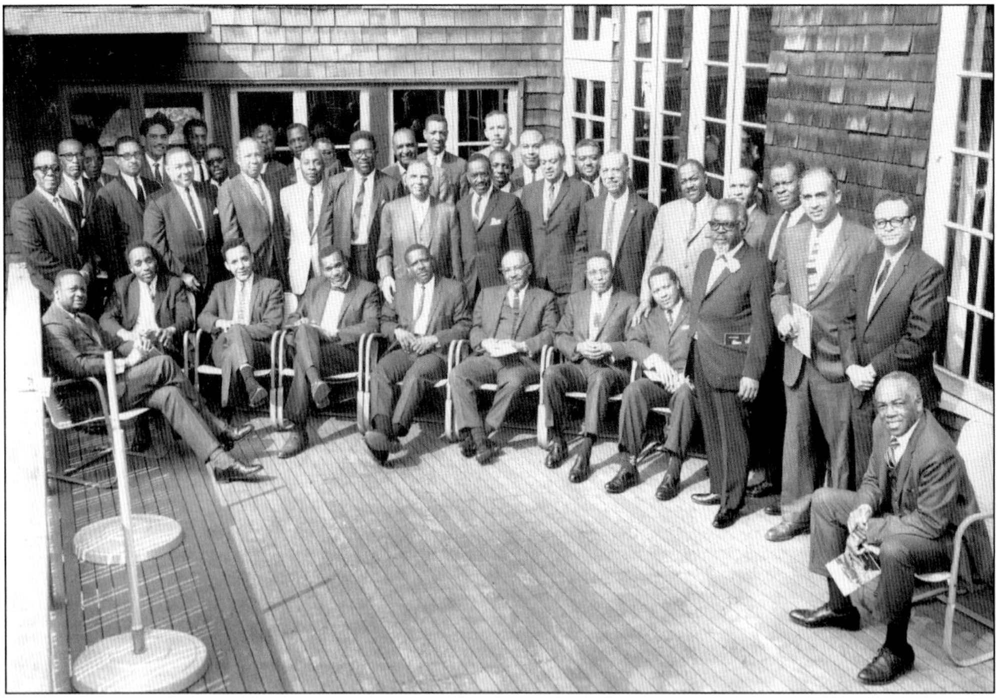

This shows a Men of Tomorrow community-relations luncheon of the Men's Faculty Club on the University of California, Berkeley campus.

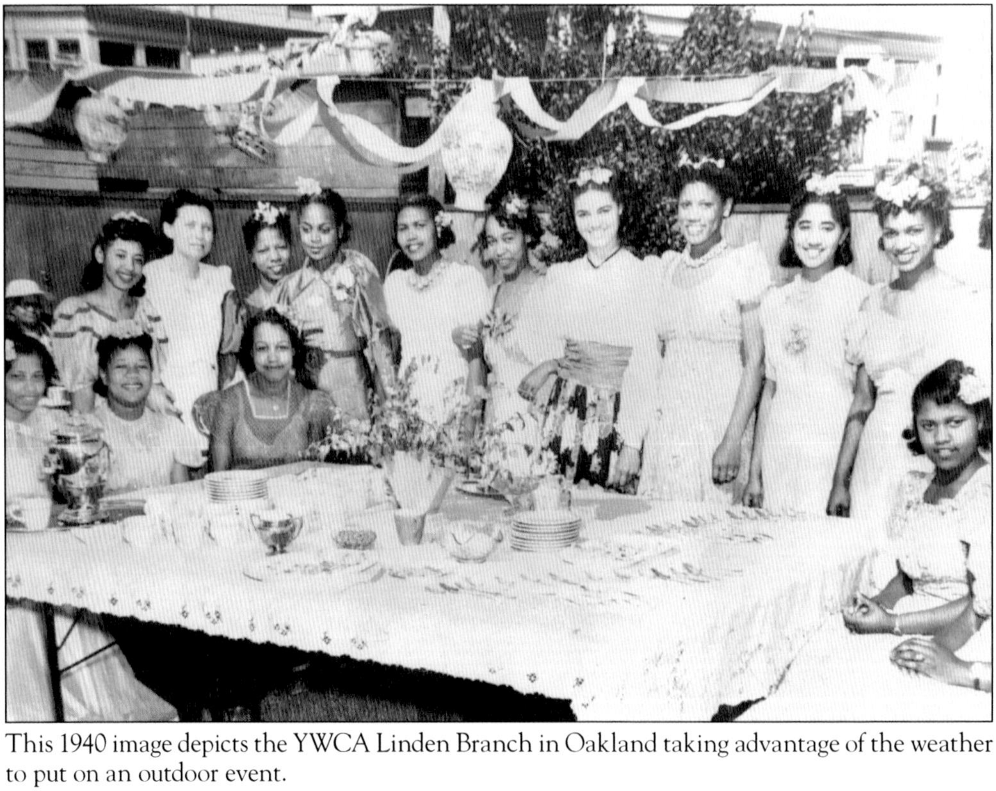

This 1940 image depicts the YWCA Linden Branch in Oakland taking advantage of the weather to put on an outdoor event.

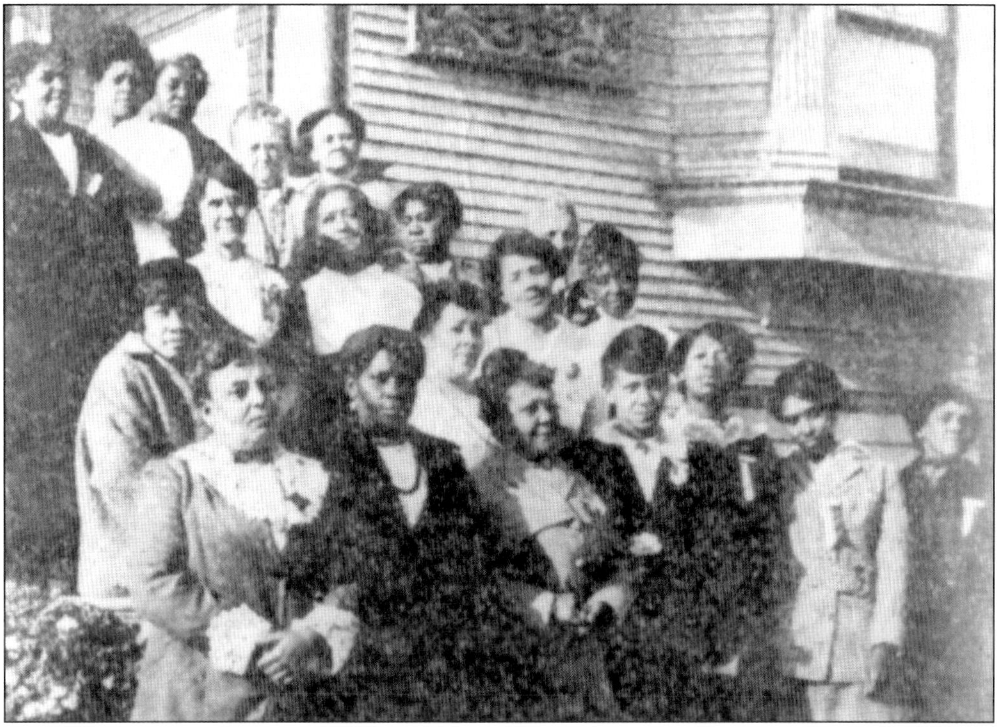

This is the Fanny Jackson Copper Club in March 1914.

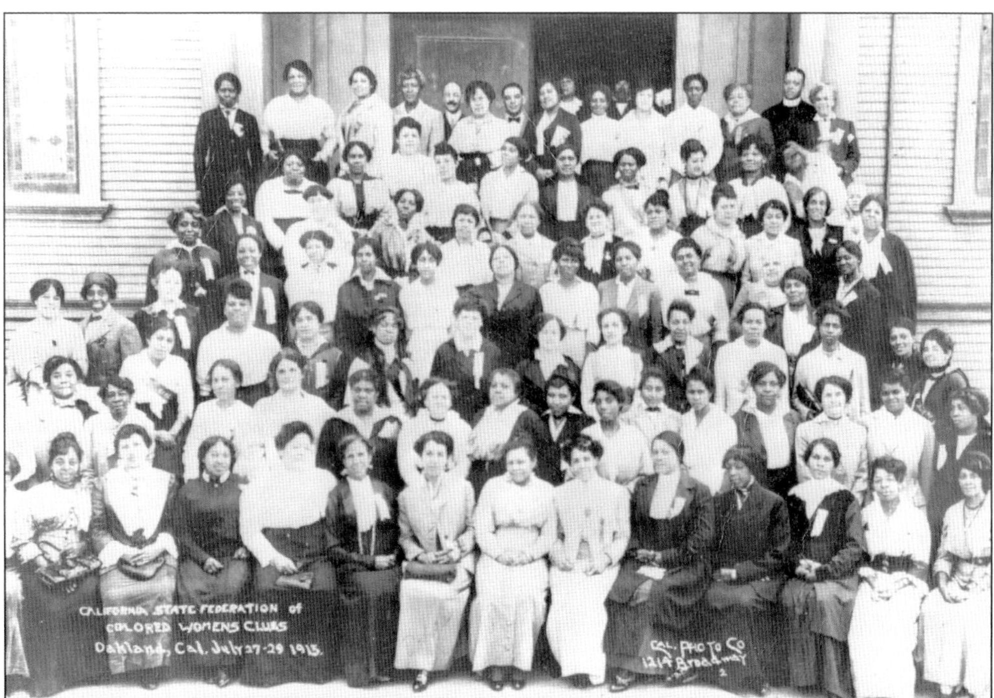


The California State Federation of Colored Women's Club met in Oakland from July 27 to July 29, 1915.

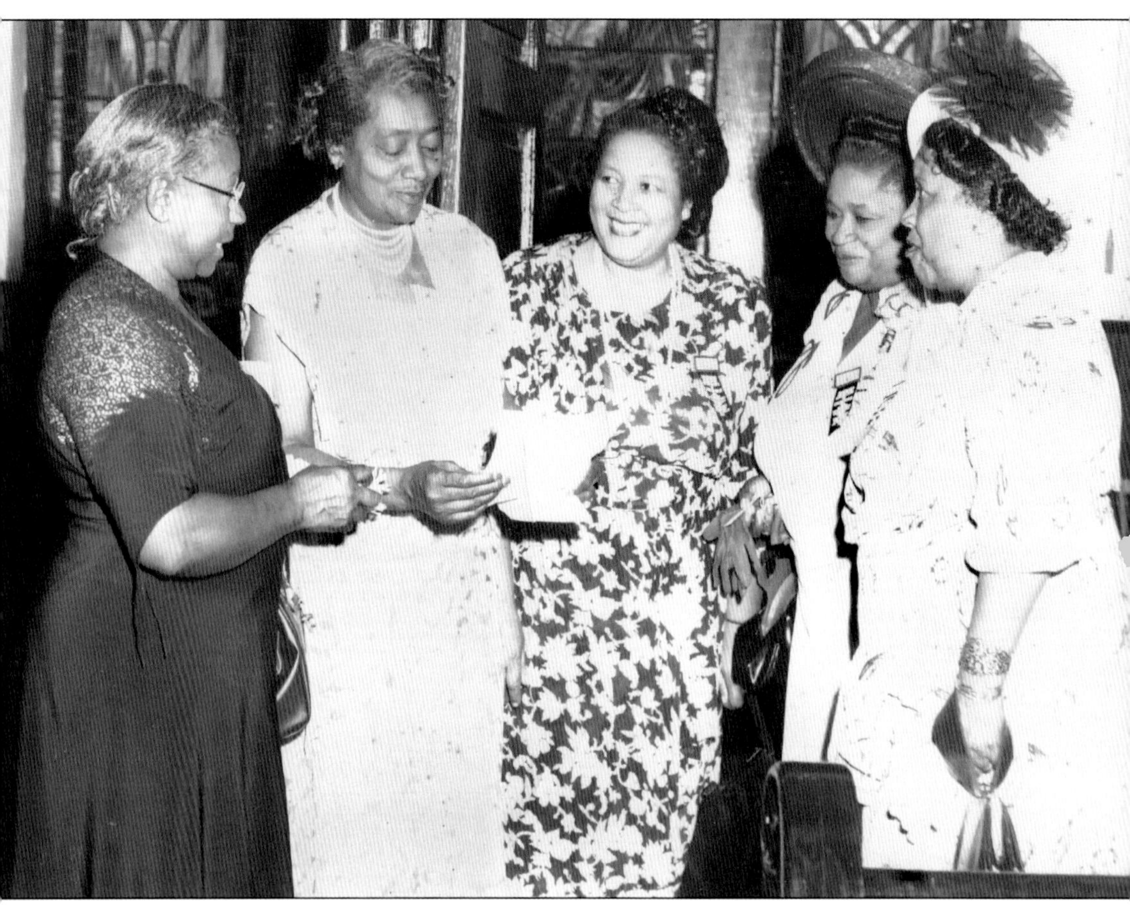

Pictured here on "reading night," a group of women read a letter from Earl Warren, the governor of California, inviting the NACW Convention to California in 1952. Lillian M. Dixon was the state president.

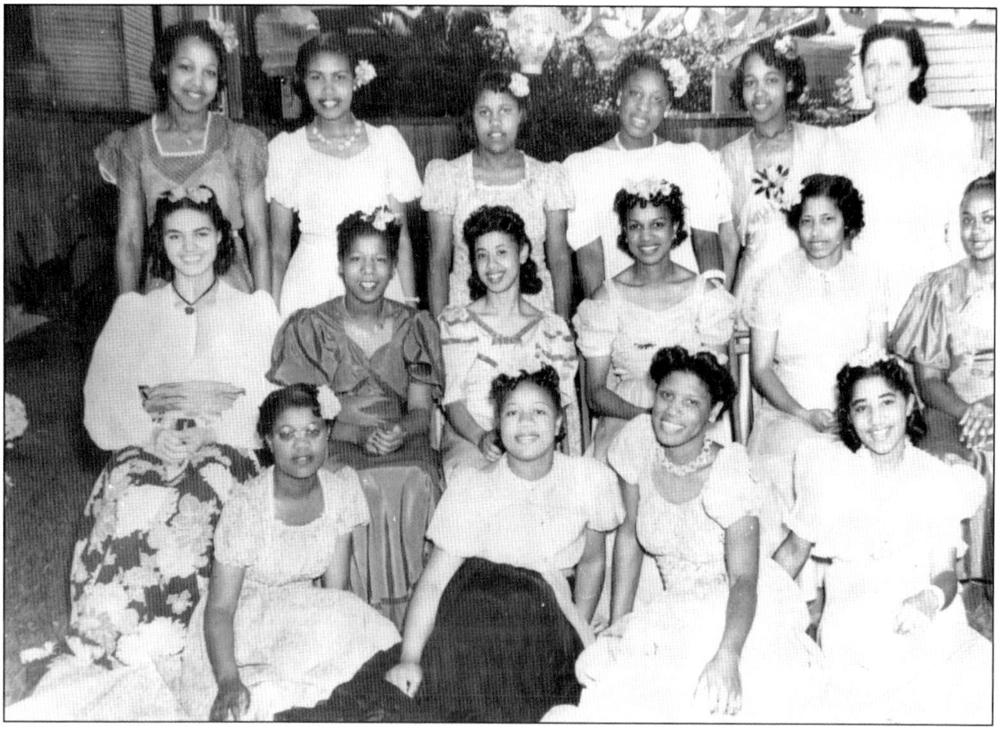

The YWCA Linden Branch moved to 815 Linden Street in 1928. The Fannie Wall Home, now the Fannie Wall Child Care Center, was located at 647 Fifty-fifth Street.

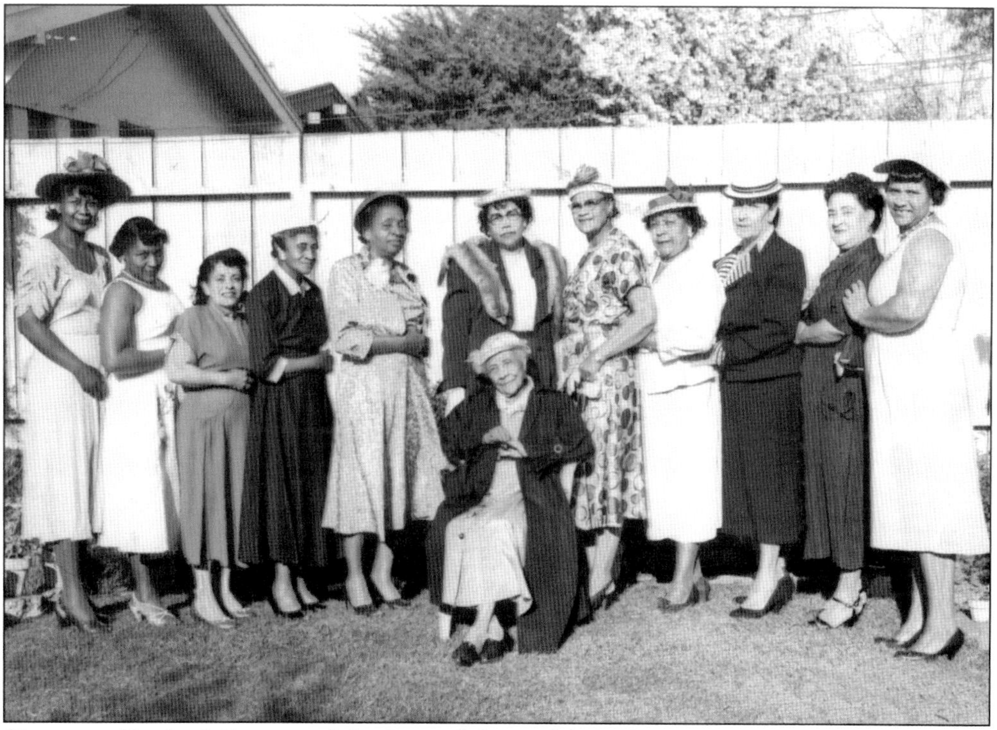

Shown are Elizabeth Brown and the Six and Over Club (Federated).

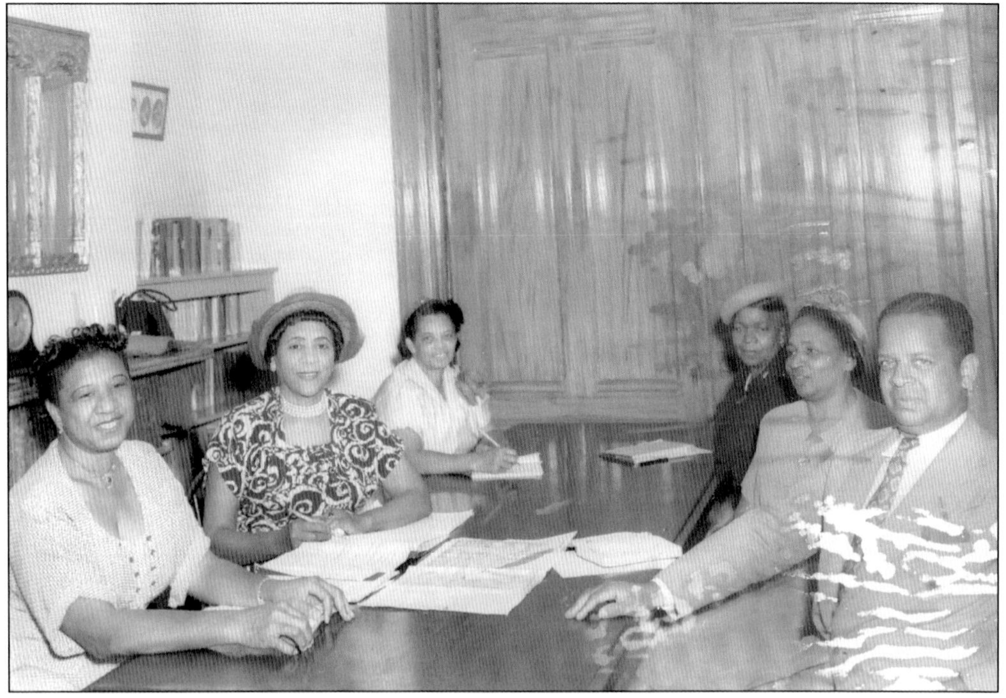

Fannie Wall Children's Home officials are, from left to right, Ida Pleasants, Chlora Hayes Sledge, Bessie Scholes, unidentified, Iantha Villa, and Kenneth Freeman.

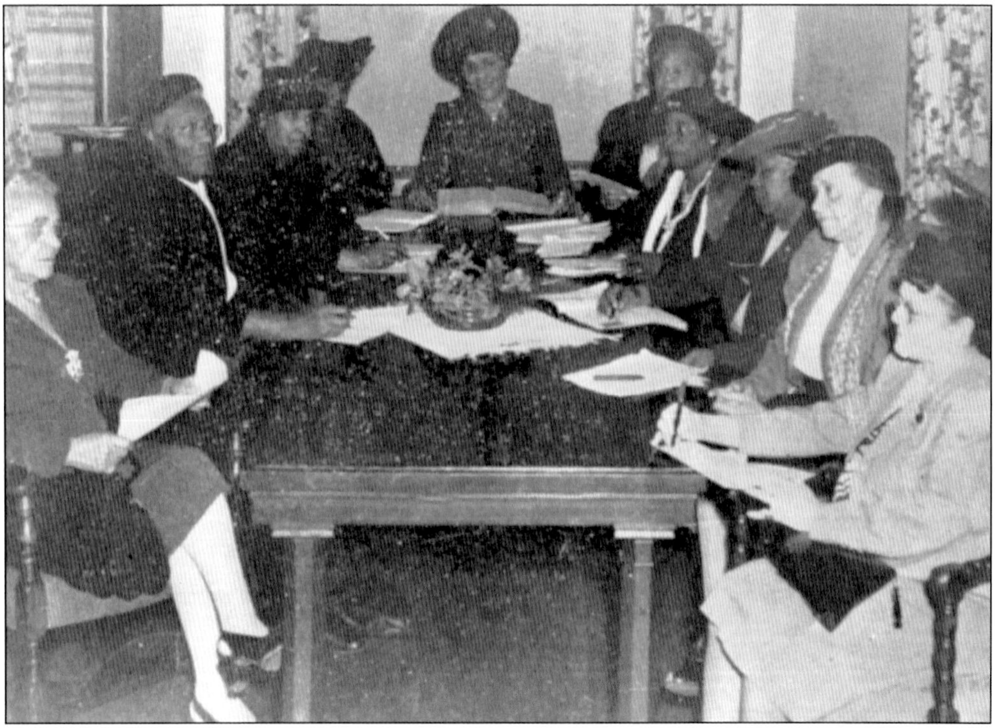

The Fannie Wall Children's Home officials and its board of directors are seen here in 1948.

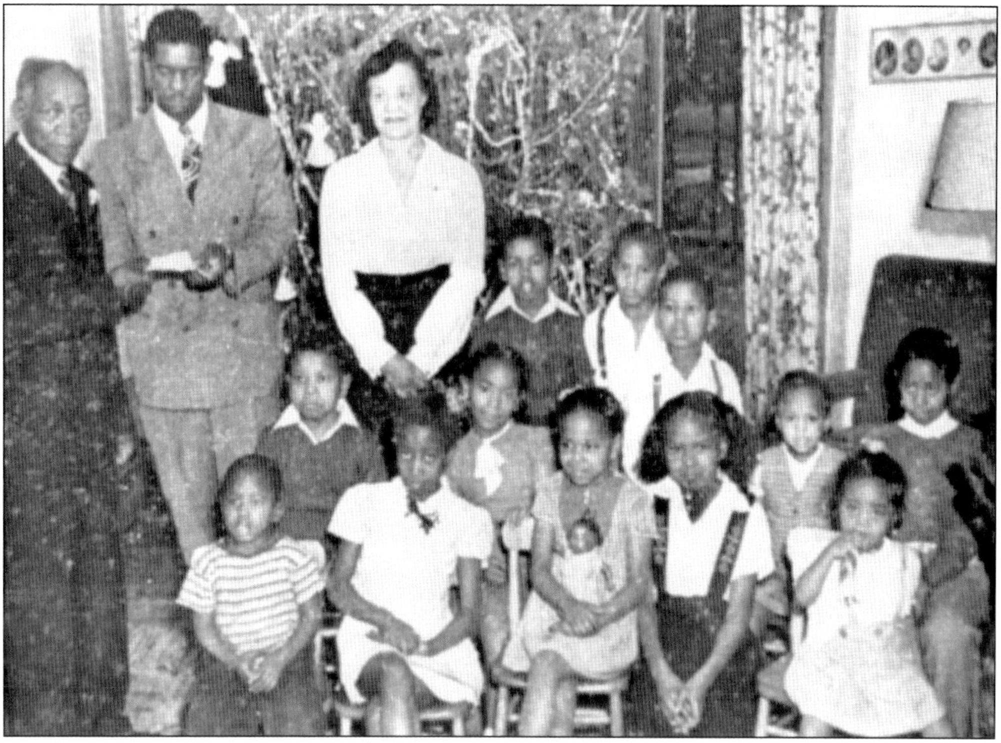

Henderson Davis, Dining Car Cooks and Waiters Union, presents check to Ira B. Ross, executive director of Fannie Wall Children's Home and Day Nursery in Oakland. Ruth Waits was the housemother in 1948.

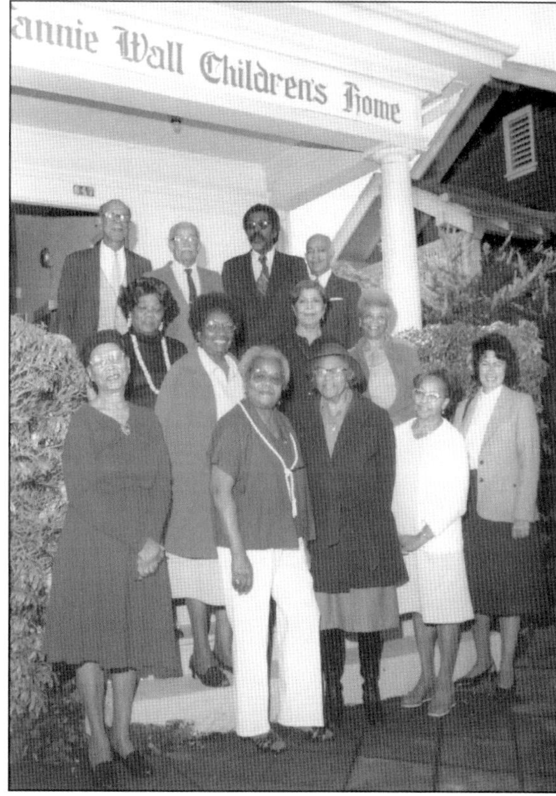


Seen here is the Fannie Wall mortgage-burning ceremony in 1948, at 647 Fifty-fifth Street.